Response to

"My father famously wrote that Go~~c~~
Your job is to see where He is worki..., ... Susan ..ccsc is
someone who has experienced that firsthand! When she told my father
the amazing things God was doing in her life, he urged her to put it into
print so many others could be blessed by her journey. What you hold
in your hand is the result. I know it will encourage you. God is at work
around your life as well. If you will join Him, He'll take you on the journey
of a lifetime!"

> **Dr. Richard Blackaby**, president of Blackaby Ministries International,
> co-author, *Experiencing God.*

"Serious, thoughtful, logical, and appropriate—these words describe
Susan Freese's approach to preparing new followers of Christ for the life
that honors God. Other words of praise should also be added: practical,
informative, and well-studied. As a result, *Your True Story* will gently
lead all believers to engage in Christian living and equip them for that
endeavor. I believe that this manual will help those who believe in Christ,
both new and seasoned, to fulfill the fivefold mandate of Deuteronomy
10:12: to fear, walk, love, serve, and keep (obey) . . . the Lord your God.
Absolutely, then, every disciple of Jesus should 'get this book' (pun
intended)!"

> **Dr. Archie England**, chair of Biblical Studies at New Orleans Baptist
> Theological Seminary

"As a women's minister, I am always on the lookout for a comprehensive,
easy-to-understand, theologically sound discipleship tool for new
or young believers. This is that tool. I've had the privilege of serving
alongside Susan Freese for several years. Through her strong grasp
of Scripture, obedience to the Holy Spirit's guidance, and passion for
discipling women, lives have been transformed. She firmly believes we can
change the world by equipping people to be disciples who make disciples.
This is what her book so clearly accomplishes."

> **Kelley Hastings**, minister to women at Chets Creek Church

"*Your True Story* is a timeless book for the ages as well as for all ages.
Dr. Susan Freese's unique ability to demonstrate synergy between
the practical and the inspirational is unique. *Your True Story* will help
generations of Christians regardless of where they are in their spiritual
journey. Those of us who learn by doing will especially appreciate this
carefully crafted 'road map' to help us write our own true story. It is a
'must read' for new Christians and yet challenging for the most mature
Christians."

> **Mac D. Heavener Jr.**, president, Trinity Baptist College

"One of the best discipleship tools I have read. Easy to read, yet thought-provoking and straight to the point. This practical, daily guide will be an asset for spiritual growth for any person, whether it be someone who is questioning what faith in Jesus looks like or for a seasoned Christ-follower. It is adaptable for people in any culture or geographical region on the planet. It will be an essential discipleship tool in my ministry toolbox moving forward. This is the type of book that will impact the world for generations!"

> **Chris Price**, pastor of Chets Creek Church at Nocatee, former missions pastor

"*Your True Story* is an excellent resource for those who want to discover their divine design. It's a deep study that will answer many of your questions about your spiritual journey. As a women's ministry leader, I am frequently asked, 'Where can I start if I want to have a personal relationship with Jesus?' 'How can I understand the message that the Bible has for me?' *Your True Story* will answer these questions and guide you into a deep understanding of your new life with Jesus."

> **Betzaida Vargas**, founder and executive director of Samaritana del Pozo

"The beauty and strength of *Your True Story* lie in Susan's commitment to weave together a meaningful theology of gospel discipleship and a transferable field manual of disciple-making. At one level this book is both compelling and easy to read; at another level its clarity stirs a vision for a global movement of disciple-making."

> **Bob Bumgarner**, lead missional strategist for Jacksonville Baptist Association

"I have had the opportunity to see Susan teach and model the principles on the mission field. She has the heart to see God glorified, new believers grow, and the church expand. These passions come out in *Your True Story*, which packs the essentials of the faith in a life-changing journey. You will know God's love in a deeper way and help others discover it too."

> **Scott Ray**, director of assessment and deployment for International Missions Board

"Susan Freese has long had a relentless desire for all people to know and love God deeply. *Your True Story* is Susan's heart work to produce a resource that can move all people to a deeper faith in God. Her writing is simple and straightforward enough to be universally well received, but complex enough to challenge each reader with self-examination and honest reflection. With the focus squarely on the truths of Scripture, this resource examines and explains how God initiated a relationship with us and our right response of relationship back to Him. *Your True Story* serves as an effective and extremely palatable and foundational resource for people who are new to Christian faith or longtime followers of God—and everyone in between."

Christy Price, pastor's wife & women's ministry leader at Chets Creek Church at Nocatee

"This book will guide you to know who you are as true worshipers and followers of Christ. When you find your true identity, one thing is for sure—everything changes! You will find your own true story coming to life through this intimate and inspired writing. I would encourage every new and mature follower of Christ to commit 50 days to read and meditate on the words of this book. One thing I can promise: the power of God will be revealed and experienced in ways that will impact not only you but also the sphere of influence God has placed around you until there is No Place Left."

Dr. Jeffery L. Crick, DO, catalytic leader for No Place Left Disciple-Making Movements

"Susan Freese is a faithful servant of Christ. I am certain the truth contained in this study will be used by the Holy Spirit to lead many people to KNOW Jesus as Savior, LOVE Jesus as Lord, and SERVE Jesus in obedience to the Bible. All to the Glory of God."

Ginger Soud, state committeewoman of Florida

"Susan and her team have developed a wonderful guide for new followers of Jesus Christ that prepares them to walk out their Ephesians 2:10 life. *Your True Story* will equip all believers with the information, resources, and tools to lead lives that fulfill the Great Commission by making disciples who make disciples."

Bob Shallow, managing chair of C12

"As Christians, we often become comfortable in our faith walk and assume others automatically know how to grow their faith and maneuver the Christian life once introduced to Jesus. Susan Freese does not make that assumption and wisely offers *Your True Story* as a faith-building, Christ-following journey. A must for every believer and can be used at any point in their own story."

Lauren Crews, MDiv, author of award-winning *Strength of a Woman: Why You Are Proverbs 31*

"It is my honor to be Susan and Brett Freese's pastor and to whole-heartedly recommend her book, *Your True Story*, to you. I have had the privilege of seeing Susan grow in her relationship with Christ and being there when God called her to full-time ministry. From taking that step of faith, leaving a prestigious corporate position, to going to seminary and equipping women around the world, she has chosen to do everything with excellence. God has used her in a powerful way, and this book is the next step in her journey of making a difference in people's lives. I am looking forward to utilizing this great resource in our church and hope you will as well."

Spike Hogan, senior pastor of Chets Creek Church

"*Your True Story* is an enlightening road map for any individual, whether they are starting their spiritual journey or starting over. If the reader truly embraces this Scripture-saturated 50-day journey, they will be 'transformed by the renewing of their mind . . . to test and approve what God's will is' (Romans 12:2)."

Tammie McClafferty, EdD, MAR, MAT, executive director of Lifework First Coast

"Having pastored for 35 years and leading pastor training in Russia and India for 22 years, I've found that one universal need stands out all over the world—the need to reproduce authentic disciples. Authentic disciples who are grounded deeply in their relationship with Christ and His Word, and yearn to complete His commission in their geographical, family, and social circles of responsibility. My friend and practical visionary Susan Freese has felt this need deeply, and she has done something about it. Her manual, *Your True Story*, leads the participant on a journey into a consistent daily relationship with Christ through His Word and prayer in the power of the Holy Spirit. Her underlying goal is to engage every believer to understand who God is and who they are in Christ, and to grow in God's purpose for their lives. A tool of this importance will be transformative in churches all over the world. May God give it a wide hearing in many nations."

Wes Slough, pastor-trainer for Saturation Church Planting

"*Your True Story* is an invaluable resource. Much is covered, yet in my opinion, not a single word is wasted. You'll appreciate the clear and logical way content is organized, including big-picture explanations, impactful analogies, and practical next steps. Each day is saturated in Scripture, and the four daily apply sections will help you not only grow but be transformed. I believe the 50-day faith journey will be something to experience again and again as a reference for yourself and a tool to disciple others. I've never found a more thorough guide to lead all believers, and I give it my highest recommendation. Get the book, invite some friends, and commit to the 50 days. It will be so WORTH it!"

Riann Boyd, disciple-maker and ministry leader

YOUR TRUE STORY

This book is dedicated to Jesus—
the Hero of our story.

YOUR

TRUE

STORY

THE 50-DAY ESSENTIAL GUIDE
TO YOUR NEW LIFE WITH JESUS

SUSAN FREESE

100% of the net proceeds from this book
will support ministries helping marginalized
women and children around the world.

Published in Jacksonville, Florida, by All In Ministries Books.

Titles by All In Ministries Books may be purchased in bulk for educational, business, fundraising, or sales promotional use. For information, please email contact@allinmin.org.

Any Internet address, ministry, company, or product information printed in this book is offered as a resource and not intended in any way to be or to imply an endorsement by All In Ministries International, nor does All In Ministries International vouch for the existence, content, or services of those sites, companies, or products beyond the life of this book.

Cover design by Danita Brooks

Library of Congress Control Number: 2021900138

ISBNs:
978-1-7358780-0-3 (trade paperback)
978-1-7358780-1-0 (ebook)
978-1-7358780-2-7 (hardback)

Contents

Welcome

This book is for those who desire a closer relationship with Jesus. It's for those who want to apply a lifetime of sacred truths to their lives—without taking a lifetime to learn them all. It's for those who do *not* want an ordinary, one-day-a-week, stale religious faith.

The pages within this book hold life-giving treasures wrapped in words waiting to be opened. It has taken me nearly 50 years to collect these treasures, live these lessons, and now share them with you. Whether you are starting your relationship with Jesus or starting over, I invite you to take this 50-day faith journey to guide you on your next steps with Him. You will *not* hear personal stories (except true stories from God's Word) because this is not about someone else's faith journey. It's *your* faith journey.

Each week you'll learn more of the narrative woven through the Bible. Part 1 starts with a wide scope of the overarching story of God. Then, we'll narrow our focus to your place and purpose in God's Story. This life-changing foundation will stabilize the faith essentials covered in the second part of the journey. At this point, Part 2 also becomes a resource guide you can return to as life's unexpected circumstances come your way. You'll discover secrets of the Christian life, like how to abide in Christ, work through doubts, resist temptation, and worship God during seasons of suffering. You'll also learn practical ways to study the Bible, share your faith with people, and pray. If you have not started a relationship with Jesus, you'll have an opportunity to take that step. My prayer in sharing these life lessons is that you will encounter God's love, embrace your part in God's Story, and *learn from my mistakes.*

Growing up, I trusted Jesus as the forgiver of my sins but did not know to follow Him as the leader of my life. That ignorance cost me—in worldly pursuits, unhealthy thinking, and selfish living. Although I loved Jesus, my incomplete understanding of His role in my life left me restless and joyless. My career kept me distracted, and my shallow faith left me spiritually starving.

But through that wilderness season, God sustained me and revealed what I had been missing all my life: a daily relationship with Him . . . but more than that, an intimate friendship with Him.

I wish I could tell you I surrendered everything to Him then and began trusting Jesus not only for my salvation but also in every part of my life—but I hesitated. I feared what would happen to my children if I gave God leadership over my life. Would my children suffer for my surrender? Would they be taken away from me if I offered everything to God? Then, a woman at church gently shared with me how God loved my sons more than I ever could. I realized that my greatest responsibility as a mother (or in any other role in my life) was to love God with all my heart, all my soul, all my mind, and all my strength (Mark 12:30)—to give Him my all because *He has given me His all.*

Everything changed when I invited God to take over my life. I saw life no longer through a dark lens of worry or selfish ambition but through eyes of faith. Those steps of obedience and trust drew me closer to God. I wanted more of Him, and I wanted *Him* to have more of *me.* Through this journey, I discovered who God is, why I was created, and how to live well. I found *my* story in God's True Story.

As my story unfolded, God led me into full-time ministry and seminary. He gave me opportunities to share what I was learning in various settings and countries. No matter where I would serve, the need was the same—an authentic relationship with Jesus. By God's grace, the results were the same as well—beautifully transformed lives. With my husband and pastors' encouragement, All In Ministries International was born, and it grew. Local churches and missionaries asked for the material in written form. But I hesitated again. God used a conversation with Dr. Henry Blackaby[1] to encourage me to take this step to write—to place into one book everything I wish I had known when I started out with Jesus. My prayers for help were answered in each step to create *Your True Story.* This book is not meant to be comprehensive, but it contains life-giving truths that changed my life and the lives of countless others.

---

1 Dr. Blackaby is an international pastor, author, and founder of Blackaby Ministries International. He is most known for his Bible study, *Experiencing God.*

Now, it's your turn. I invite you to come with me on this journey through *Your True Story* in 50 daily readings—a carefully chosen chapter in God's Story and soon to be in yours, I pray. It won't always be easy or painless, but unfolding your true story is worth the work. Change is uncomfortable, and you get to choose how you will respond to it. Trust God in these next steps or stay the same.

As you choose to trust God through these brief chapters, you will experience passionate love, incredible joy, and supernatural peace. This transformation will help you live each day in oneness with God and prepare you for eternity. At last, you will know *your* true story as a part of God's True Story.

Then, I pray you will be like that woman at church who gently shared the truth with me. I pray you will gently invite another and then another and then another on a journey to discover God's great love and plan for His creation. That is how God designed our lives: to *be* changed and to *bring* change to others.

God's glory is our reward,
Susan Freese
John 3:30

Global Audience

This discipleship resource is for all people within all Christian faith communities worldwide. While our worship styles are diverse, we are united in our beliefs: Jesus Christ is Lord, the whole Bible is wholly true, and every believer has an important part in God's Story. This study complements the disciple-making workshops offered by All In Ministries International. For more information and free tools, visit www.allinmin.org.

Navigating the Bible

This study will feature a tour of the Bible and how to study it in Week 5. We use several reliable Bible translations to help you clearly see God's truth. It will be helpful for you to have a Bible ready for each day's study.

When referring to Bible passages, the book of the Bible is listed first, followed by the chapter number and then the verse(s) within the chapter. For example, John 3:16 refers to the Gospel of John in the New Testament (not to be confused with 1 John), chapter 3, verse 16.

John (Book) 3 (Chapter): 16 (Verse)

Old Testament books and abbreviations:*

Genesis (Gen.)
Exodus (Exod.)
Leviticus (Lev.)
Numbers (Num.)
Deuteronomy (Deut.)
Joshua (Josh.)
Judges (Judg.)
Ruth
1 Samuel (1 Sam.)
2 Samuel (2 Sam.)
1 Kings
2 Kings
1 Chronicles (1 Chron.)
2 Chronicles (2 Chron.)
Ezra
Nehemiah (Neh.)
Esther
Job
Psalms (Ps./Pss.)
Proverbs (Prov.)
Ecclesiastes (Eccles.)
Song of Solomon (Song of Sol.)
Isaiah (Isa.)
Jeremiah (Jer.)
Lamentations (Lam.)
Ezekiel (Ezek.)
Daniel (Dan.)
Hosea
Joel
Amos
Obadiah (Obad.)
Jonah (Jon.)
Micah (Mic.)
Nahum (Nah.)
Habakkuk (Hab.)
Zephaniah (Zeph.)
Haggai (Hag.)
Zechariah (Zech.)
Malachi (Mal.)

New Testament books and abbreviations:*

Matthew (Matt.)
Mark
Luke
John
Acts
Romans (Rom.)
1 Corinthians (1 Cor.)
2 Corinthians (2 Cor.)
Galatians (Gal.)
Ephesians (Eph.)
Philippians (Phil.)
Colossians (Col.)
1 Thessalonians (1 Thess.)
2 Thessalonians (2 Thess.)
1 Timothy (1 Tim.)
2 Timothy (2 Tim.)
Titus
Philemon (Philem.)
Hebrews (Heb.)
James
1 Peter (1 Pet.)
2 Peter (2 Pet.)
1 John
2 John
3 John
Jude
Revelation (Rev.)

Bible book abbreviations in parentheses are based on Chicago Manual of Style standards.

Commitment

Your life can change in 50 days, especially when you're committed to the journey. Before we begin, I'd like to challenge you not to miss a single day's reading. You set yourself up well when you schedule an appointment on your calendar. By signing your name and designating your time, you show the seriousness of your commitment, and your results dramatically improve.

With God's help, I commit the next 50 days of my life to discover my story in God's True Story.

_____
Your name

Set a daily time (30 minutes recommended) and place to read and respond to one chapter each day:

_____

Invite Your Friends

Journeys are better when we're together with friends. You will gain the most benefit from this faith journey and strengthen friendships if others join you. The fact is we follow God best with others. God gives us a family of faith—the church—to walk with us as we walk with Him. He never meant for us to be alone (Gen. 2:18). A wise man once said, "Two people are better off than one, for they can help each other succeed. If one person falls, the other can reach out and help. But someone who falls alone is in real trouble" (Eccles. 4:9–10). Let's not fall alone.

Pray and ask God to lead you to those who can join you through this study and beyond. I suggest you meet once a week to discuss what you learn. You can use the group discussion questions found at the end of each week as a guide for your gathering. List the names of the people God has led you to invite on your journey below:

_____   _____

_____   _____

Set a day, a time, and a location to meet weekly in person or online:

_____

PART I:

DISCOVERING YOUR STORY WITH GOD

You saw me before I was born.
Every day of my life was recorded in your book.
Every moment was laid out before a single day had passed.
How precious are your thoughts about me, O God.
Psalm 139:16–17

What if I said, "You are the reason this book was written"? What if I told you that you have an appointment with God right now? You may question if that's true or wonder why God has you on His calendar. But look around—is anyone else reading this book? Maybe not; so why you? Because God wants you to know He wrote you into His story. Perhaps you have an extraordinary journey to take to experience Him. Or, perhaps there is another person looking to you for answers. Either way, God planned this moment—at this time, in this place—for you to discover your true story as part of God's True Story.

No matter who you are or where you live, **the one true God is loving you right now. He has an important purpose for your life.** You might ask: How is He loving me? Why is my life important? How should I respond? These are all good questions. We invite you to take this 50-day faith journey to start answering them. Why 50 days? God set apart 50 days in the Bible for a special purpose. Once the Hebrew people began celebrating Passover (we'll study that in Week 7), God gave them another festival called the Feast of Weeks, later called Pentecost.[1] The one-day celebration took place seven

---

1   Pentecost comes from a Greek word meaning "fiftieth." The festival holiday is called *Shavuot* in Hebrew, meaning "weeks," and is also known as the Festival of Harvest.

weeks and one day (50 days) after Passover. Pentecost was a day of celebration and revelation. It commemorates the giving of the Torah (the first five books of the Bible) to Moses on Mount Sinai. After Jesus's time on earth, He gave the gift of the Holy Spirit to the disciples in Jerusalem on Pentecost. There is something significant about the fact that God chose the same fiftieth day, both in the Old Testament and New Testament, to give the gifts of Word and Spirit. Word and Spirit combine to bring us greater revelation.

God can use these 50 days in your life in a special way, too. Why put in the effort? Because **your life matters, and your life story makes a difference**. Our Creator made you on purpose, for a purpose. He has written a story for you—a story full of meaning that impacts eternity. But to understand your purpose—your true story—you need to know the Author. You need to encounter the one true God.

What is God like? Why did God create me? How can I know God?

Many of us have asked these questions. Do not ignore them because you fear you won't find the answers, or you are afraid you will not like the answers you find. God planted these questions in your heart to bring you on a faith journey closer to His heart. So, ask them.

You'll find answers in the Bible—also known as God's Word or Scripture (2 Tim. 3:16).[1] But more than answers, you will find God Himself. One of my prayers is that over the next 50 days you will experience how **God is real and the Bible is true**. Together, we'll answer some of your questions with truth from God's Word. Whether you are reading it for the first time or have studied it for years, God's Word is always perfect and fresh.

This study heavily quotes Scripture and refers you to Bible verses (including more than 1,400 references) so God's Word can speak for itself. I suggest you set aside thirty minutes each day with an open Bible to meet with God as you go through these brief chapters. Pray before you read to invite God to reveal Himself to you. Interact with what you discover. Mark up the pages as you wish and write your

---

1   You can find the Bible online at many different websites, including Bible Gateway (biblegateway.com), Bible Study Tools (biblestudytools.com), Bible Hub (biblehub.com), Blue Letter Bible (blueletterbible.org), and YouVersion (youversion.com).

thoughts in the margins. **Read one chapter a day so you can think and act on what you read.**

As we learn to love God with all our hearts, minds, souls, and strength (Mark 12:30), we'll approach this faith journey with Jesus's command in mind. You'll find four steps to complete at the end of each day:

1. Read Scripture related to the day's topic in "Let the Bible Speak."
2. Answer questions to process what you read in "Let Your Mind Think."
3. Start your conversation with God in "Let Your Soul Pray."
4. Record what steps God may be leading you to take in "Let Your Heart Obey."[1]

Please work through these four steps to absorb and apply each day's lesson. This is important. **Knowing new information will not transform our lives, but the application of biblical truth with God's help will.**

Let's preview the journey for Part 1:

First, in Week 1, you will learn about God and His overarching true story. God's Story affects every other story. We cannot cover all you might want to know about God in one week. Still, this summary will help you understand the context for your existence, your eternity, and your story within God's Story. Even if you've been a believer for some time, you may discover aspects of God's Story not widely taught. You will come away with a better understanding of God's whole story.

Then, in Weeks 2–3, you will learn about your part in God's Story. In the second week, you'll discover your identity in Christ (who you are), and in the third week, you'll find your purpose in Christ (what you do).

Are you ready to begin? First, pause to examine your heart. Are you sincerely seeking God? In Jeremiah 29:13, God says, "If you look

---

1   The Bible sometimes refers to obedience or a decision as an expression of the heart (Josh. 24:23; Joel 2:13; Rom. 10:9–10).

for me wholeheartedly, you will find me." Take a few prayerful moments and

- decide now to seek God with all your heart and soul (Deut. 4:29);
- decide to accept what you discover about Him, His Story, and how you fit into it, even if some things you find surprise or bother you in some way;
- pray and ask God to prepare your heart for the journey ahead and to give you friends to walk with you.[1]

Together, seek truth—seek God—with an open heart. And as you pursue Him, you will discover that He has always, always pursued you.

---

1   See the Commitment on page xv.

WEEK ONE

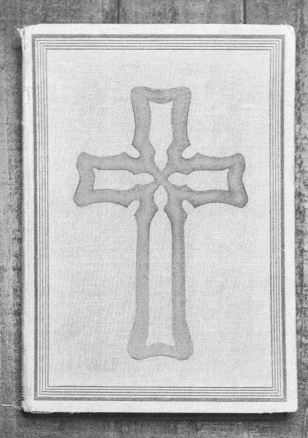

GOD'S STORY

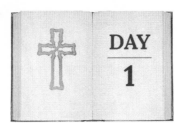

You Are Invited

For this is how God loved the world: He gave his
one and only Son, so that everyone who believes
in him will not perish but have eternal life.

John 3:16

How does it make you feel when you receive a special invitation? Something profound happens inside you. Knowing someone had you in mind changes the way you see yourself. Someone thought of you, and your presence is wanted. The reality is God is thinking of you, and the Bible is His written invitation. Through the pages of Scripture, God invites you to trust Him with your whole life. His invitation crosses every continent, every culture, every era. And our ability to listen and respond is its only limitation.[1]

Though written long ago, this story in the Bible is relevant *now*. It defines and explores our world. It explains why we suffer pain and injustice and promises that one day God will make everything right again. The Bible describes the people of Israel throughout the Old Testament and their relationship with God. But this story is not only for them. This story of redemption and relationship is for the whole world—including you. **You will want to listen carefully to what God is saying because He is saying it to *you*.**

When you read carefully, you will discover your true story. Yes, **your story is written into the Bible**. God created you to know Him and be changed by Him as part of His grand plan (Jer. 9:23–24). He

---

1   Cheryl Hauer, "God's Invitations," Bridges for Peace, November 21, 2017, https://www
.bridgesforpeace.com/letter/gods-invitations/.

has a divine purpose for your life. But you will only discover God's unique calling for you by studying His Word and living it out in your life—with His help. In God's Story, you will find the meaning of *your* story and every story in the world—past, present, and future.

Even though the Bible is complete, God's Story is still unfolding all around us. The last book of the Bible, Revelation, shows us what will happen at the end of time. But it also reveals that God's Story has no end. God invites us to eternal life through Jesus—now and forever (John 3:16). Eternal life is unending friendship with God and trusting Him to write our story as part of His True Story (John 17:3; Heb. 12:2).

For the next few moments write down what your story has been so far. How do you know God?

Just as a book is made up of many chapters that tell one story, the Bible is a collection of books revealing God's Story for us. Each book—and the chapters and verses within it—works together with all the others to reveal God and His relationship with us. God's Story leads us to the One who created us, the One who came to us in the person of Jesus Christ. The whole story rests on Him. The whole Bible points to Him.

As we begin our journey together, you and I need to have a greater vision of God's Story as a whole. It can be divided into four basic parts: (1) creation, (2) sin, (3) Jesus, and (4) re-creation—God's creation restored. The Old Testament (the first thirty-nine books of the Bible) tells us about creation and sin (and the Rescuer to come). The New Testament (the last twenty-seven books of the Bible) tells us about Jesus (the Rescuer) and re-creation. These four parts provide a framework to understand all the stories of the Bible—and the significance of our lives.

PART ONE: CREATION
God created us and wants to have a close relationship with us.

The Old Testament begins with the story of creation. God made everything from nothing and called it all "good," with one exception (Gen. 1). When God made people, He made us in His image and then called everything "very good." He took special care in creating us because He wanted to have a close relationship with us. The reality is God did not need to create us. He already lived in perfect community. The Bible reveals **there is only one God who exists in three persons: Father, Son (Jesus), and Holy Spirit.** God took pleasure in creating us. Best of all, we have the pleasure of knowing Him (Col. 1:10). Our first ancestors, Adam and Eve, lived, worked, and walked with God in the perfect garden of Eden. Joy and peace filled their lives as children of God.

PART TWO: SIN
Because sin separates us from God, we need a Rescuer.

Everything changed when the serpent (Satan, the enemy) entered the story. He twisted God's words to deceive Adam and Eve. Deception led to discontentment, which led to disobedience. Rather than trust God, they believed Satan's lie and turned against God. They ate the fruit that God had forbidden. That is what **sin** is—turning away from God's will in our attitudes or actions. Sin spoiled God's good creation, and everything broke. Adam and Eve's rebellion separated them from God. It introduced the consequences of sin: death, greed, sickness, violence, and pain in the world. Darkness now filled their lives as enemies of God (Rom. 5:10). The rest of the Old Testament tells the story of people struggling because of sin, disobedience to God's commands, and

Sin: Turning away from God's will in our attitudes or actions.

neglect of His presence—despite the call of the prophets to repent and return to Him. More importantly, it foretells the story of God's rescue plan. The world needed a Savior, a Rescuer.

PART THREE: JESUS
Jesus rescues us from our sin and restores our relationship with God.

The New Testament reveals to us our Rescuer: Jesus Christ, the Son of God. He came to free us from the grip of the enemy and restore our relationship with our heavenly Father. His mission: to seek and to save the lost (Luke 19:10). The beginning of the New Testament teaches us about Jesus's life and tells us how He rescued us. God is just, and our sin deserves His judgment and the penalty of death. Out of God's great love, Jesus took our punishment by taking our place—dying on a cross for us. That was not the end but the beginning of new life. Jesus defeated death and rose from the grave to ensure sin could never again separate us from Him. He conquered sin and death once and for all!

PART FOUR: RE-CREATION—GOD'S CREATION RESTORED
God will make all things new, starting with us.

A new chapter of God's Story began with Jesus's empty tomb. We find ourselves in this chapter today: Jesus is preparing a place in heaven for those who trust Him. He has given believers a new purpose on earth and promised to return for us. The rest of the New Testament teaches about the rescue plan spreading into all nations and changing people's hearts and lives for all eternity. Even now, creation prepares for Jesus to return. When He does, He will make all things new. There will be no more brokenness. Jesus will create a new heaven and a new earth, perfect and untouched by sin. Then believers will worship God and enjoy Him forever in His new creation.

God extends His invitation to trust Him in each part of His Story. For the rest of this week, we'll look at each part in more detail. We'll discover how God demonstrates His love for every nation and every person (John 3:16). **You and I and everyone else—we were all created by His love, for His love, and to share His love.** God's invitation awaits.

DAY 1

Let the Bible Speak:
Read Genesis 1 (Optional: Romans 5:12–21)

Let Your Mind Think:
1. What does Genesis 1 tell you about God?

2. How does it make you feel to know your story is part of God's Story?

3. How does knowing God loves everyone change the way you see God, yourself, and others?

Let Your Soul Pray:
Lord, thank You for revealing Your Story through the Bible and inviting me to trust You. Help me as I seek You. Soften my heart and open my eyes to Your truth as I begin this faith journey. I want to know You and my place in Your Story . . . In Jesus's name I pray, amen.

Let Your Heart Obey:
(What is God leading you to know, value, or do?)

DAY
2

God's Perfect Creation Displays His Glory

In the beginning God created the heavens and the earth. . . .
Then God looked over all he had made,
and he saw that it was very good!
Genesis 1:1, 31

Between the Bible's large size and its ancient languages and cultures, reading it can seem intimidating to a lot of people. Some people think the Bible is too massive to read in one's lifetime. But actually, if we read it for one hour a day, we could read it all in roughly eighty days. Others think the Bible is too complicated and requires advanced training to understand it. But the revelation of God is just that—His revelation. He wants to be known. We may not understand everything, but God helps us learn many of His timeless truths. Sometimes people assume God's Word is a rule book, giving us a list of dos and don'ts. But when we read it, we discover the most magnificent narrative of deliverance and freedom in the history of the world. It's God's Story.

As we learned yesterday, the Bible starts with the creation of all things and ends with re-creation. It's for the whole world, but it's also personal. God's Story celebrates the wonder of every person's formation, including yours (Psalm 139). You did not choose your background, but the Bible reveals that God did. It is the starting point on God's path to your destiny (Acts 17:26–27). But to understand God's Story and your place in it, you need to first understand that

God's Story does not center around us. God's Story centers around God and His glory. All things exist to praise His greatness. You will soon discover why that is, but for now, let's start at the beginning of time.

God created everything—every single thing—for His glory, including you and me. He powerfully spoke all of creation into existence: light, land, sea, plants, and animals. All of creation glorifies God by displaying "his eternal power and divine nature" (Rom. 1:20 ESV). Even the "heavens declare the glory of God; the skies proclaim the work of his hands" (Ps. 19:1 NIV). From the stars in the sky to the most hidden parts of our bodies, all of creation speaks of God's brilliance and goodness. Men, women, and children declare the glory of God, too. Like the moon reflecting light from the sun, we reflect God to the world. Our reason for existence—for His glory (Isa. 43:7).

> **Glory:**
>
> One of the Hebrew words for *glory (kabod)* literally translates as "heavy" and "weighty," indicating worthiness. Our response to someone whose presence is heavily felt is honor and respect.
>
> *Glorifying* God means to think, act, speak, and serve in ways that reflect God's greatness. It's our life purpose.
>
> Source: Ludwig Koehler et al., *The Hebrew and Aramaic Lexicon of the Old Testament* (Leiden: E.J. Brill, 1994–2000), 456.

God displays His glory most beautifully in His great love for us. God desired a close relationship with humankind, so He created us with special care—in His image and with His breath. "God said, 'Let us make human beings in our image, to be like us.' . . . Then the LORD God formed the man from the dust of the ground. He breathed the breath of life into the man's nostrils, and the man became a living person" (Gen. 1:26; 2:7). The God of the universe formed human beings from the dust of the earth. As a potter molds clay, God took personal and intimate care in our design. He did not keep His distance when He created Adam and Eve in the beginning, and He does not keep His distance from you now. **He wants to be close to you.**

God also created us to enjoy relationships with one another. Right from the start, God said, "It is not good for the man to be alone" (Gen. 2:18). So, God created Eve to be Adam's partner.[1] In this role, God designed Eve as Adam's essential and equal counterpart to fulfill God's purposes for humanity. This first marriage provides an example of the closest of human relationships. More importantly, it serves as a picture of our relationship with God. What should marriage be like? Selfless love. Intimate friendship. Shared work. Divine purpose. Faithful presence. That is how we should approach our relationship with God because He delights in us. "As a bridegroom rejoices over his bride, so will your God rejoice over you" (Isa. 62:5 NIV). Regardless of your marital status, remember that your deep connection with your Creator is far more valuable than any human marriage. "Your Creator will be your husband" (Isa. 54:5). **God knows you intimately, and He is faithful.** He calls His people the "bride" of Christ, fully known and fully loved (Rev. 19:7–9; see also Eph. 5:25–27). Even the best earthly marriage is a shadow of the depth of love God pours into your relationship with Him.

We may better understand God's extravagant, selfless love if we have children of our own. That may be why **God created us to have close relationships with our children.** He commanded Adam and Eve to "be fruitful and multiply" (Gen. 1:28 ESV) so they could share God's blessings and His teachings with their offspring (Deut. 6:5–7). Parenting can help us better understand how we, as children of God, can relate to Him as our Father in heaven. Consider how a young child crawls up onto the lap of her mother and rests in her arms. Secure. Loved. Connected. Let's approach our relationship with God that way. Resting in faith. Sharing our day. Listening for His voice. Trusting Him. Obeying Him. Whether or not you have biological children, God created you to reproduce. When you pass on your

---

1 According to *The Hebrew Aramaic Lexicon of the Old Testament* by L. Koehler and W. Baumgartner, there are more examples in the Old Testament of the word meaning a counterpart (partner) who helps us than the other meaning it sometimes has of "strength." In light of this, Dr. Archie England, professor of Old Testament and Hebrew at New Orleans Baptist Theological Seminary, suggested that the original Hebrew word for "partner," *ezer kenegdo*, is better translated in this context as "his counterpart," meaning "the one beside him helping." Dr England also suggested that Eve's role as a counterpart does not mean that there is a hierarchy. Eve's role is not a servant but a partner. Beside her husband, Eve helps him succeed.

faith to the next generation, you have spiritual children—blessed relationships that will last forever. God made us to parent and to be parented by Him.

Our relationships extend to the rest of creation. Starting from the beginning of Genesis, we see God at work, fashioning the earth. He then entrusts the earth to us "to work it and keep it" (Gen. 2:15 ESV). God worked to create it, and we work to maintain it. Right at the beginning of time, we discover the biblical concepts of calling, vocation, and work. We learn that God wants us to enjoy the natural world and allows us to manage it for Him through our work. There are many vocations, and we all have different passions and skills. We might not like the work that we do all the time, but we can choose to be grateful. No matter what we do, we can give God glory in our work because God designed us for it (1 Cor. 10:31).

The first two chapters of the Bible reveal much about God's Story. Today, we've learned that (1) God's Story centers on God and His glory, and (2) He created all things, including work, to display His glory. God loves us and wants us to have a close relationship with Him. He also blesses us with creation, helps us to create, and invites us to manage His creation. We are created to reflect our creative God.

Let the Bible Speak:
Read Genesis 2 (Optional: Psalm 148)

Let Your Mind Think:
1. What can creation teach you about your Creator?

2. The one true God created us to know Him. No other religion views their god(s) that way. Why is it important for us to know God personally?

3. How does thinking about God as your spouse and your parent change the way you see Him?

Let Your Soul Pray:
Lord, You are worthy "to receive glory and honor and power, for you created all things, and by your will they were created and have their being" (Rev. 4:11 NIV). Thank You for Your perfect creation. As I enjoy Your glory displayed in the beautiful world around me, remind me that Your glory is even more beautifully displayed in Your love for me. Please grow my relationship with You . . . In Jesus's name I pray, amen.

Let Your Heart Obey:
(What is God leading you to know, value, or do?)

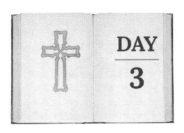

Sin Ruins Everything

All have sinned and fall short of the glory of God.
Romans 3:23 NIV

As the wind blew, a familiar sound in the garden of Eden caused an unfamiliar feeling. Adam and Eve's hearts pounded with a strange grip of fear. God was there to spend time with His precious image-bearers. But rather than walk with God, they hid from Him in the trees. This was the day sin ruined everything.

Only three chapters into Genesis, and we see how this story unfolds. God looked over all of creation, both seen and unseen, and it was "very good" (Gen. 1:31). People and angels had a perfect relationship with God. He abundantly met all their needs and wants. They also had a choice—a choice to love and trust God or to rebel. They chose to rebel.

But they weren't the first rebels. No, there was one "anointed . . . guardian cherub" who was "blameless" *until* wickedness was found in him (Ezek. 28:14–15 NIV). Satan, known then as Lucifer, was beautiful and brilliant, and he knew it. So much pride filled his heart that he wanted to become equal to God (Isa. 14:12–14). He even convinced one-third of the angels to join him in his rebellion (Rev. 12:4–9).

In response to this evil, God—who is both loving *and just*—punished Satan by sending him away from heaven in disgrace (Ezek. 28:14–18). Satan hated God, so he aimed to destroy what God loved most: His precious **image-bearers**. That's you and me.

What started as rebellion in the unseen world led to deception in our visible world. Satan came into the garden as a serpent, tempting

Adam and Eve to rebel against God. He deceived them by questioning God's words to them. Satan asked, "Did God really say . . . ?" (Gen. 3:1). Then he suggested that God's command not to eat of the fruit of one tree in the middle of the garden deprived Adam and Eve of something good: "You surely will not die! . . . You will be like God" (Gen. 3:4–5 NASB). Instead of believing in God's love, goodness, and abundant provision for them, Adam and Eve started questioning God's commands and promises to them.

> **Image-bearers:**
> Unlike angels or animals, people—both male and female—are made in God's image (Gen. 1:27). We think, invent, plan, feel, create, know right from wrong, have memories and ideas, and birth new life. Most importantly, we can worship, know, and love God.

Satan had created doubt, and this doubt led to disobedience. Satan still deceives us today, just like he deceived Adam and Eve. He tricks us into questioning God's Word and God's goodness. He stirs up discontentment in our hearts and tempts us to disobey God, just as he did by planting seeds of doubt in the hearts of Adam and Eve. As a result, they *both* disobeyed God, and sin entered our world (Gen. 3:6).

Sin ruined everything. Because of sin all of creation groans (Rom. 8:22). Along with sin came death, pain, shame, sickness, violence, fear, depression, and every kind of evil. The presence of sin even corrupted how our bodies functioned. Childbirth became more painful. Work became hard. The earth suffered from destructive natural disasters, poisonous animals, and thorns that made it difficult to farm the land. Sin affected even the smallest details of creation, just as sin affects the smallest details of our lives. **The perfect relationships God had formed–through marriage, parenting, and work–all shattered.** Worst of all, sin destroyed our most important relationship: our relationship with God.

We create a harmful separation from God when we do things our way instead of His way. As you may recall, that is what **sin is: turning away from God's will in our attitudes and actions**. Adam and Eve's sin caused them to suffer spiritual death immediately and face physical death eventually.

After eating the forbidden fruit, Adam and Eve realized they were naked because **shame follows sin**. When we sin, we feel filthy and exposed because we have betrayed our Creator. In our sin, we rebel against the One whose image we bear. We become confused about our identity. Disoriented and ashamed, we often do the same thing Adam and Eve did: we hide from God (John 3:20).

Adam and Eve sewed fig leaves together to cover their shame (Gen. 3:7). We try to cover up our sin and shame too, but we don't use fig leaves. Instead, we might lie to cover up our mistakes, or we do extra good deeds to make up for our failures. None of those efforts last for long because **our attempts to cover our sins are as flimsy as fig-leaf clothing**. Adam and Eve knew their fig leaves did not cover their sin, yet they still hid from God when they heard Him calling for them in the garden.

Before we find out how God responded to Adam and Eve's sin, let's remember that we cannot blame Adam and Eve for *our* sin. We *all* break God's rules. "No one is righteous—not even one" (Rom. 3:10). The Ten Commandments (Exod. 20:2–17) teach us to love and serve God alone, respect God's name, honor our parents, and rest in God. They also teach us not to kill, commit adultery, steal, lie, or want what other people have. Jesus made these rules even harder to follow. He taught that persistent anger is as evil as murder and that intentional lust is as evil as adultery (Matt. 5:21–22, 28). **God cares about our hearts just as much as our actions.** That means that even when we do good things for the wrong reasons, we sin. God commands us, "Be holy, for I am holy" (Lev. 11:44–45 ESV). *Impossible*, we think. And so, we sin, feel shame, and hide from God, just like Adam and Eve did.

But God did not abandon Adam and Eve, and He does not abandon us. God came looking for them, just as He comes looking for us. "Where are you?" He asked (Gen. 3:9). This question was asking about not their physical location but their location in relationship to God.[1] We all need to ask ourselves the same question. Adam and Eve admitted their disobedience but used excuses and blame to rationalize their behavior. When we sin, we sometimes make excuses and blame others. But there are no excuses for sin. Deception does not excuse sin. **Our wounds do not give us the right to wound**

---

1 Ian Jones, *The Counsel of Heaven on Earth: Foundations for Biblical Christian Counseling* (Nashville: Broadman & Holman Publishers, 2006), 31–32.

others. Adam and Eve could have returned to God with their questions, and we can seek Him with ours as well. Since God's standards are perfect and He looks at the heart, He did not accept Adam and Eve's blame-shifting confessions. Sin is always a serious offense. The damage had been done. In God's perfect justice, a death penalty for that sin needed to be paid. Life is in the blood (Lev. 17:11), and their blood was now spiritually polluted with sin.

God never intended for His beloved image-bearers to pay the penalty for their sin. So, He immediately revealed His rescue plan, a plan that would take the weight of sin from us and place it on God's only Son, Jesus Christ. God turned from Adam and Eve and spoke to the real enemy, Satan: "I will put enmity between you and the woman, and between your offspring and hers; he will crush your head, and you will strike his heel" (Gen. 3:15 NIV). Satan would be allowed to strike the Rescuer and cause Him pain. But in the end, the Rescuer would succeed in *crushing* the enemy that seeks "to steal and kill and destroy" so that we might "have life, and have it to the full" (John 10:10 NIV).

Before God banished Adam and Eve from the garden, He killed an animal and replaced their withering fig leaves with durable leather clothing. This foreshadowed the many sacrifices that would be made to cover the sin of humanity until the complete and final sacrifice of Jesus (Lev. 1–7).[1]

Yes, Jesus would die to pay our debt instead of us. Inconceivable, but true. God provides a way to cover—*atone for*—our sin and restore our spiritual life. Through the sacrifices of blood—first from certain animals and ultimately from Jesus, the Lamb of God—our relationship with Him could be restored (Heb. 9:26; 10:4). Clean blood to cover unclean blood. Jesus's death in our place was a complete and final sacrifice never to be repeated.[2]

Even in this dark time when sin entered the world, God's tender love shone even more brightly. **He came looking for us. He covered us and promised to rescue us**. Oh, how He passionately loves us!

---

1 Wayne Grudem, *Systematic Theology: An Introduction to Biblical Doctrine* (Grand Rapids, MI: Zondervan, 1994), 626–627.

2 Norman L. Geisler, *Systematic Theology: In One Volume* (Bloomington, MN: Bethany House Publishers, 2002), 801.

DAY 3

Let the Bible Speak:

Read Genesis 3 (Optional: Psalm 51)

Let Your Mind Think:

1. If God asked, "Where are you?" what would you say?

2. Are you hiding from God in any way? If yes, explain.

3. How does knowing that God is looking for you make you feel (Ezek. 34:11–16; Luke 19:10)?

Let Your Soul Pray:

Lord, *"You are my hiding place; you will protect me from trouble"* (Ps. 32:7, NIV). *May I never hide from You, but instead hide in You, knowing that You will forgive me and protect me . . . In Jesus's name, amen.*

Let Your Heart Obey:

(What is God leading you to know, value, or do?)

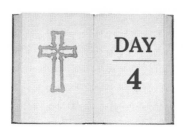

DAY 4

Jesus Rescues Us, Forgives Us, and Leads Us

Christ suffered for our sins once for all time. He never sinned,
but he died for sinners to bring you safely home to God.
1 Peter 3:18

Of all the literary genres included in God's Story—history, poetry, prophecy, letters—mystery is not one of them. But for thousands of years, God's people may have felt like there were too many unknowns. God promised to send a Rescuer—the "seed" that would crush the enemy (Gen. 3:15 NASB). And Scripture provided hundreds of prophecies so that the Rescuer could be recognized and believed. There were wars and wilderness wanderings to protect God's seed. But the details of God's rescue plan remained hidden, which raised many questions: Who could save us from our brokenness and this sin-infected world? How could God's wrath against sin be satisfied? How could we ever escape the punishment we deserve?

The Bible warns that the consequence for our sins—our attitudes or actions that violate God's commands—is total separation from God. Forever. But God never intended for our story to end this way. **Separation from God would mean separation from everything good, lovely, wise, pure, beautiful, heroic, and true**. Every good thing that reflects God would be gone from our existence.

For a long time, it seemed like God's words were gone too. The Old Testament told of the coming Rescuer—the Messiah, God's promised Deliverer. For hundreds of years, prophets told God's people to prepare for the Rescuer by **repenting** (turning away from their sin and turning back to God). But then, it seemed, God stopped speaking. The Old Testament ended.

> **Repentance:** Turning away from sin and turning back to God.

Silence . . . and waiting.

Until one day, at the perfect time, and in the perfect way, *a perfect Rescuer came* (Gal. 4:4). God broke the silence, revealed the mystery of His will (Eph. 1:9), and spoke directly to us through His Son, Jesus (Heb. 1:2). The One who spoke creation into existence showed up *in creation* to speak to us. He was fully human and fully God. Jesus was called Immanuel, meaning "God is with us" (Isa. 7:14; Matt. 1:23). The Word of God came, not in written form, but in human form (John 1:14). What would the Word of God say?

Nothing at first, because He was born as a baby—a fragile infant whose birth we celebrate on the day now called Christmas. Instead of choosing a midwife and carefully preparing baby supplies, Jesus's mother, Mary, spent the last, grueling stages of her pregnancy traveling hard, dusty roads. When she and her husband, Joseph, finally arrived in Bethlehem to be counted for a Roman census, the small city was so crowded that they could not find a place to stay. So Mary birthed her son in an animal stable and placed Him in a feeding trough to sleep (Luke 2).

Unimaginable. But Jesus, King of the universe, was born poor for a reason.

Jesus's great love for creation caused Him to willingly set aside the royal privileges that were rightfully His. "Though he was God . . . he gave up his divine privileges . . . and was born as a human being" (Phil. 2:6–7). **He became poor so we might become rich in God's mercy and grace** (2 Cor. 8:9).

Instead of a royal birth announcement and wealthy attendants, angels announced Jesus's arrival as a baby to shepherds—the poorest of the poor. Even creation proclaimed the glory of God as a new star revealed the King of kings to the magi—the wisest of the wise. The supernatural and the natural shouted His arrival to the whole world, great and small, rich and poor. **The Word of God came for all**.

Christe:
God's "anointed one." It is the Greek translation for the Hebrew word *Messiah*.

Why did the Rescuer come in this way? Jesus humbled Himself and became one of us so He could do for us what we could never do for ourselves. **"For God made Christ, who never sinned, to be the offering for our sin, so that we could be made right with God through Christ"** (2 Cor. 5:21). This is the **gospel**—good news—message in one verse. Take a moment to read it again.

In the ultimate expression of love, God sent His one and only Son, Jesus, to live a perfect life and suffer the punishment for our sins. He was falsely accused, brutally beaten, and nailed to a cross. In reality, **we should have been on that cross**, but "he was pierced for our rebellion, crushed for our sins. He was beaten so we could be whole. He was whipped so we could be healed. . . . Yet the LORD laid on him the sins of us all" (Isa. 53:5–6). Jesus suffered all the punishment for all our sins, "and not for ours only but also for the sins of the whole world" (1 John 2:2 ESV). **He took *our* place on that cross.**

Gospel:
"Good news." This refers to the good news that the death of Jesus provided the full payment for the penalty of sin and anyone who turns to the living Jesus and trusts Him alone for salvation is forgiven, is made new, and has eternal life.

We remember Jesus's ultimate sacrifice on Good Friday every year. We're still talking about that event—and people are still martyred for talking about it—more than two thousand years later. But, thank God, His Story did not end there.

Three days later, everything changed. Tragedy turned into victory! Death was defeated, and Jesus Christ rose from the dead! He appeared to more than five hundred people, instructed and empowered His followers, and ascended into heaven. He not only reconciled His relationships on earth, but He also made a way for us to be with Him in heaven forever. We may lose our physical bodies to death and decay as the result of living in a fallen world. But our spirit/soul will live forever because Jesus conquered death and gives us eternal life through faith in Him.

Jesus's victory over death gives us victory over sin. His victory is what we celebrate on Easter–Resurrection Sunday. God celebrates too! Our **reconciliation** brings Him great joy because of His great love for us. "This is real love–not that we loved God, but that he loved us and sent his Son as a sacrifice to take away our sins" (1 John 4:10).

> **Reconciliation:** Repaired or restored relationship.

God offers us a priceless gift in Jesus Christ. "The wages of sin is death, but the gift of God is eternal life in Christ Jesus our Lord" (Rom. 6:23 NIV). Just as any gift can only be enjoyed if it is received and opened, **we need to *receive* the free gift of a restored relationship with God**. How? By turning toward Jesus and turning from our sins. We ask God for forgiveness and follow Jesus as our Leader.

Devastatingly, many people refuse this gift. Some do not believe their sins deserve punishment. Some work to become **righteous** on their own. But the Bible is clear: "No one is righteous–not even one" (Rom. 3:10). No one is good enough because "everyone has sinned; we all fall short of God's glorious standard" (Rom. 3:23). Others reject Jesus because they believe there are many ways to heaven. Still, the Bible is clear: "There is salvation in no one else! God has given no other name under heaven by which we must be saved" (Acts 4:12). Jesus Himself said, "I am the way, and the truth, and the life. No one comes to the Father except through me" (John 14:6 ESV). Even Jesus asked the Father if there was any other way to rescue us than by His death on a cross (Matt. 26:39–42). **But there was no other way**. Jesus had to die. Only through Jesus can we find forgiveness and reconciliation with God.

> **Righteous:** Just, upright, innocent, faultless, guiltless.

When we ask Jesus for forgiveness, the sin that separates us from God disappears. We now have God's Spirit living in us, helping us to live for Jesus each day. We begin to change! Sin no longer controls us. God adopts us into His family, and we are His. No more separation, and no more condemnation (Rom. 8). We are loved. Forever.

And this is only the *beginning* of our true story with God. Tomorrow, we'll discover what happens when we are made new.

Let the Bible Speak:
Isaiah 53 (Optional: John 19–20)

Let Your Mind Think:

1. Isaiah 53 was written centuries before Jesus. Do you know of anyone else in history who fulfills these prophecies?

2. Have you ever received Jesus's gift of forgiveness and eternal life? If so, who can you share this gift with today? If not, will you receive His gift now? **To learn more about this important decision, read "Receive Jesus Today" at the end of Day 7.**

Let Your Soul Pray:
Lord, Your Word says that You came to seek and rescue all who are lost, including me (Luke 19:10). Thank You for this priceless gift, and help me share this gift with others . . . In Jesus's name I pray, amen.

Let Your Heart Obey:
(What is God leading you to know, value, or do?)

God Makes All Things New: Re-Creation

Therefore, if anyone is in Christ, he is a new creation. The old has passed
away; behold, the new has come. All this is from God, who through
Christ reconciled us to himself and gave us the ministry of reconciliation.
2 Corinthians 5:17–18 ESV

If we stop and think about it, most of us have a few moments in our
lives we wish we could do over again. (Some of us have more than a
few.) Maybe it was something we said that embarrassed ourselves or
another person. Perhaps it was something we did or didn't do that
we regret. If we could go back in time and live it over, we'd gladly
make different choices. We'd want a new start.

Only a few chapters into the Bible we see a "new start" theme
emerge. God's epic story opens with creation. But when sin breaks
everything, God extends infinite mercy and grace, offering re-
creation—His creation restored. Yes, in the *re-creation*, God fixes
everything broken by sin. He starts with His image-bearers—you
and me. He changes us and restores the most significant casualty
of sin—our relationship with Him.

No more hiding from God like Adam and Eve.
Now we run to God.

No more living in darkness imprisoned by sin.
Now we live in the light, free from the bondage of sin.

No more reflecting the wickedness of the world.
Now we reflect God's goodness to the world.

This change is only possible through Jesus. God restores us as His image-bearers by making us like His Son, who is "the visible image of the invisible God" (Col. 1:15), "the radiance of God's glory and the exact representation of his being" (Heb. 1:3 NIV). Through the process of re-creation, "we shall also bear the image of the man of heaven" (1 Cor. 15:49 ESV).

Re-creation mirrors creation. Just as creation came through Jesus as creator God, re-creation comes through Jesus (John 1:3; Col. 1:16). God "has created us anew in Christ Jesus" (Eph. 2:10). In creation, God spoke light into existence first. God will start re-creation the same way, with light–spiritual light. "God, who said, 'Let there be light in the darkness,' has made this light shine in our hearts so we could know the glory of God that is seen in the face of Jesus Christ" (2 Cor. 4:6). We, then, reflect His light in a dark world.

God is a consistent God. He told Adam and Eve to "be fruitful and multiply" (Gen. 1:28), and in re-creation, we, too, bear fruit and multiply–spiritually. We grow in the spiritual fruit of "love, joy, peace, patience, kindness, goodness, faithfulness, gentleness, self-control" (Gal. 5:22–23 ESV). Our fruit draws others to Jesus, and we multiply spiritually as we obey Christ's command to "go and make disciples" (Matt. 28:19).

However, re-creation differs from creation in some ways. **We did not have to cooperate in our creation, but we get to cooperate in our re-creation**. We choose to trust God and believe what He says in His Word. But people have a long history of resisting God. The idea of letting go of the things of this world and trusting God evokes fear and anxiety. That may be why God encourages us repeatedly in the Bible not to be afraid. When life does not turn out the way we expect and others hurt our hearts, we may draw back from God. We may resist Him because of the fear of being hurt again. Yet, it is the love of God that heals us, changes us, and gives us the courage to trust Him. Choosing to cooperate with God leads to our re-creation and a life far better than we can ever imagine (John 10:10).

You may find these concepts difficult, or you may question how life could exceed your imagination. That is what this faith journey will help you understand. We'll learn more about being made new next week. Now, know that cooperating in re-creation means trusting Jesus as our Savior, then following Jesus as our Lord—the Leader of our lives. We ask Him what He wants to do in and through our lives because we "live for Christ," not for ourselves (2 Cor. 5:15).

Trusting Jesus is the key to re-creation. To trust, we need to believe He knows what is best. But this decision to trust is not a one-time, easy choice. **Following Jesus is a daily, sometimes minute-by-minute, choice**. We receive Jesus as our Rescuer at a specific moment in time, but we need to choose to follow Jesus as Lord from that point on—*every day*. Jesus tells us, "If any of you wants to be my follower, you must give up your own way, take up your cross daily, and follow me" (Luke 9:23).

But as you may know, following Jesus *daily* is difficult. Why?

When Jesus rescues us, God gives us a new start with a new heart. "I will give you a new heart, and I will put a new spirit in you. I will take out your stony, stubborn heart and give you a tender, responsive heart" (Ezek. 36:26). But our new hearts are inside of our old bodies. Our new hearts and our old sin natures oppose each other. The apostle Paul describes this inner conflict: "Although I want to do good, evil is right there with me. For in my inner being I delight in God's law; but I see another law at work in me, waging war against the law of my mind and making me a prisoner of the law of sin at work within me" (Rom. 7:21–23 NIV). This conflict is why we feel so torn between following our sin nature and following Jesus.

Thankfully, there is a way to overcoming our sin nature and following Christ: love. Yes, your true story begins with God's love for you (John 3:16). But your life, your purpose, your story is transformed by *Jesus's love* for you and *your love* for Jesus. When you experience the depth and magnitude of God's love (Eph. 3:17-19), it changes you and motivates you to follow Jesus. "*Christ's love compels us*, because we are convinced that one died for all . . . [so] that those who live should no longer live for themselves but for him who died for them and was raised again" (2 Cor. 5:14–15 NIV, emphasis added). Because Jesus loved us first, we love Him (1 John 4:19) and want to demonstrate it by obeying Him (John 14:21). But God's love is not based on what we do—it's who He is. And becoming like Christ is what re-creation is all about. Jesus knew the power of His love. That is why He commanded us: "Love . . . as I have loved you" (John 13:34). But how can we love like God?

This supernatural love comes from a supernatural source: the Holy Spirit (Week 7). At the moment of salvation, we are re-created—born again—by the power of the Spirit (John 3:5–8). The Holy Spirit comes to live in and through us. Love is *His* fruit. Love is the greatest gift He gives (1 Cor. 13). Love does not just *come from* God; it *is* God (1 John 4:7–8). When we surrender to Jesus's leadership, love flows in us and guides us into truth.

To grow in love with God, we get to know Him in His Word (Week 5). And loving God leads to loving everything about Him—including His will and His ways. As we obey God, we learn we can trust Him, knowing His commands are for our good and His glory. But remember, **re-creation is not about following rules; it's about our restored relationship with God**. Through that intimate relationship, we become like the One whose image we bear. Simply put, to reflect God clearly, we do what God does. We love (John 15:12). We forgive (Col. 3:13). We are compassionate (Luke 6:36). We are holy (Lev. 20:26).

Are you just now beginning the process of re-creation? Do not be discouraged. **God offers new starts and delights in every small step of obedience**. "Do not despise these small beginnings, for the LORD rejoices to see the work begin" (Zech. 4:10). Read what the apostle Paul wrote about his own re-creation experience:

> I don't mean to say that I have already . . . reached perfection. But I press on to possess that perfection for which Christ Jesus first possessed me. No, dear brothers and sisters, I have not achieved it, but I focus on this one thing: Forgetting the past and looking forward to what lies ahead, I press on to reach the end of the race and receive the heavenly prize for which God, through Christ Jesus, is calling us. (Phil. 3:12–14).

You may be at the starting line, but keep running your race. Tomorrow, we'll learn about the heavenly prize God promises us.

DAY 5

Let the Bible Speak:
Romans 12 (Optional: 1 John 4:7–21)

Let Your Mind Think:
1. Why do our old sin habits not immediately disappear after we've been made new?

2. How can you reflect Jesus to others? What small steps of obedience have you taken already?

3. Why is your *relationship* with God a more effective motivation than *rule-following* when cooperating with your re-creation?

Let Your Soul Pray:
Father, remake me in Christ. In Your perfect time, fix all that sin has broken in me. Your Word says You have started a good work in me and will complete it when I meet You in heaven (Phil. 1:6). Thank You for promising to fully restore me as Your image-bearer. Help me trust and obey You as You make me like Jesus, Your perfect Image-Bearer . . . In Jesus's name I pray, amen.

Let Your Heart Obey:
(What is God leading you to know, value, or do?)

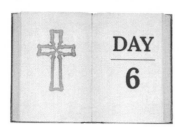

DAY 6

Life After Death

I saw a new heaven and a new earth, for the old heaven and the old earth had disappeared. . . . I heard a loud shout from the throne, saying, "Look, God's home is now among his people! He will live with them, and they will be his people. God himself will be with them. He will wipe every tear from their eyes, and there will be no more death or sorrow or crying or pain. All these things are gone forever." And the one sitting on the throne said, "Look, I am making everything new! . . . It is finished!"
Revelation 21:1, 3–6

There is something Jesus said that I want you to think about. Jesus said, "I am the resurrection and the life. Anyone who believes in me will live, even after dying. Everyone who lives in me and believes in me will never ever die" (John 11:25–26). What does this mean to you?

Be encouraged, friend: the grave is not the end. Jesus spoke about heaven as a physical place, a *real* kingdom. One day, all of us who trust Jesus as Lord and Savior will be there together. But what about the meantime?

Even though heaven is in our future, God tells us to **focus our thoughts on heaven** *now* (Col. 3:1–2). Here's why:

- When we feel a deep longing inside, we will remember that we were created for more. We are not of this world, so we will never truly be satisfied here (John 17:16).
- When sickness and loss of life break our hearts, we will remember that we were not designed to die. Living for

eternity is set in our hearts (Eccles. 3:11), and death is a precious matter to God (Ps. 116:15).

- When evil and injustice infuriate us, we will remember that Jesus is on the throne. He is not worried about the future. He is in control, and justice will prevail. He is preparing a place for those who trust Him, and He promises to come back for us (John 14:1–2).

Yes, Jesus is preparing a literal place for you–a place called heaven. It is sometimes poorly portrayed as a dreamy world of puffy clouds, harp-playing angels, and boring religious services. Nothing could be further from the truth.

To understand heaven, we need to again look in God's Word, where it is mentioned more than 200 times in the New Testament alone. This heavenly country is described as an enormous place with beautiful gardens and a life-giving river, a massive city with jeweled gates and streets of gold (Heb. 11:16; Rev. 21). There will be homes, feasts, friendships, and laughter. Jesus describes heaven as a physical place where we will have perfect physical bodies and the ability to recognize one another (Luke 24:39–40). We will not turn into angels (as people sometimes say), but we will live with them. We will never be bored because we will be filled with joy and eternal pleasures (Ps. 16:11). Our sin and mortal bodies will no longer hinder our relationship with God. His presence will be our light: "And there will be no night there–no need for lamps or sun–for the Lord God will shine on them" (Rev. 22:5).

To experience a little of what heaven will be like, look around and imagine our world without sin.[1] The earth is a shadow of heaven (Heb. 8:5). God created us to live on earth and wants to dwell with us here. Yes, sin has temporarily made the world imperfect, but God will never abandon His plan for the world or for us. One day, God's kingdom will come to earth and be restored to its original sinless condition. Then God will physically dwell with us forever.[2] His original plan will be fulfilled. God will say, "Look! I am creating new heavens and a new earth, and no one will even think about the old ones anymore" (Isa. 65:17).

---

1 Randy Alcorn, *Heaven Study Guide* (Nashville: LifeWay Press, 2006), 36–37.
2 Isa. 65:17–25; Matt. 19:28; Rev. 21.

There will be no more crying, no more pain, no more death, no more sorrow (Rev. 21:4), *but also* no more opportunities to tell others about Jesus.

Only Jesus can take away our sin and lead us safely home to heaven. God is perfect and just. He cannot allow sin to reside where He does. That is why we need to share the good news of Jesus's rescue now before it is too late. Everyone we know will die and face judgment (Heb. 9:27), but we can share Jesus with them before they do.[1]

Most people are unaware of judgment day—the most important day in our future. Every person will have a review of their life, but not everyone will go to the same judgment.

The Bible speaks of two judgments—one for believers and one for unbelievers. The judgment of believers is called the judgment seat of Christ (Rom. 14:10–12; 2 Cor. 5:10). This is *not* a place where salvation is questioned; believers already belong to Jesus because of their faith in what He accomplished on their behalf (Eph. 2:8–10). Rather, this judgment is a time where good works are revealed. Believers will receive rewards ("crowns") for things they have done on earth that reveal their faithful perseverance in following Jesus (1 Cor. 3:11–15; 2 Tim. 4:8; James 1:12; 1 Pet. 5:4).

In this judgment, God will examine the lives of believers, rewarding where we served . . .

. . . **with love** (1 Cor. 13; Phil. 1:9–11),

. . . **in His strength** (Zech. 4:6; John 15:5), and

. . . **for His glory alone** (1 Cor. 3:11–15; 4:4–5).[2]

Most believers are unaware this judgment day will determine our possessions and standing for eternity.[3] The rewards and heavenly work assignments we receive then will be based on our loving-kindness and faithfulness *now*. Shocking, right? What we do now affects forever. Again, understand that this judgment is *not* to earn salvation. We cannot add anything to the finished work of Jesus on the cross.[4] Also, this judgment is not a time where sin is condemned

---

1 Learn how to share Jesus with others in Weeks 3 and 7.

2 Woodrow Kroll, *Facing Your Final Job Review: The Judgment Seat of Christ, Salvation, and Eternal Rewards* (Wheaton, IL: Crossway Books, 2008), 136–137.

3 Matt. 6:19–21; Luke 19:12–27; 1 Cor. 3:11–15; Rev. 2:26; 22:12.

4 2 Cor. 5:21; Heb. 10:12; 1 Pet. 2:24; 1 John 2:1–2.

(Rom. 8:1). Our sins are already gone, removed "as far as the east is from the west" (Ps. 103:12 NIV). The judgment seat of Christ does not punish sin but rewards faithful service and endured suffering. But the greatest reward will be "the morning star," Jesus Christ Himself (Rev. 2:28). We will experience the presence of our God *forever*.

Enjoying God and seeing Jesus face-to-face will change everything. Because of our encounter with Him, "we shall be like him, because we shall see him as he is" (1 John 3:2 ESV). God will complete our re-creation and fully restore us as His image-bearers. "He will take our weak mortal bodies and change them into glorious bodies like his own" (Phil. 3:21). "Then, when our dying bodies have been transformed into bodies that will never die, this Scripture will be fulfilled: 'Death is swallowed up in victory'" (1 Cor. 15:54).

The painful reality is not everyone will trust Jesus. Not everyone will go to heaven and live on a new earth. It is very difficult to accept, but it is true: those who do not trust in Jesus alone for salvation will die in their sins. If we hold on to our sin—by either refusing to acknowledge it or believing the lie that we can atone for it on our own—we hold on to the consequences of that sin as well and remain separated from God forever. **We either let Jesus take our punishment, or we remain condemned** (John 3:17–18).

You may be asking, "How is this decision even possible?"

The possibility of genuine, voluntary love requires the possibility of rebellion. **God created us with the ability to choose between loving Him and rejecting Him.** Everyone who rejects Jesus rejects God's only provision for sin and a restored relationship with Him. As we've said before, those who reject God will ultimately separate themselves from everything good, lovely, wise, pure, beautiful, heroic, and true.

Unbelievers will face the judgment called the great white throne judgment. This judgment is not like the judgment of believers, where sinful deeds are atoned for by Jesus and only good deeds are rewarded. Instead, this great white throne judgment is for every deed done by all those who choose to hold on to their sin:

> And I saw a great white throne and the one sitting on it. The earth and sky fled from his presence, but they found no place to hide. I saw

the dead, both great and small, standing before God's throne. And the books were opened, including the Book of Life. And the dead were judged according to what they had done, as recorded in the books. The sea gave up its dead, and death and the grave gave up their dead. And all were judged according to their deeds. Then death and the grave were thrown into the lake of fire. This lake of fire is the second death. And anyone whose name was not found recorded in the Book of Life was thrown into the lake of fire. (Rev. 20:11–15)

Hell is not meant for people. It is an "eternal fire prepared for the devil and his demons" (Matt. 25:41). **Hell is not Satan's kingdom; it is his place of torment. He has no authority there**. Those who reject Jesus Christ will forever be separated from God—separated from all things good—in that terrible place. "They will be punished with eternal destruction, forever separated from the Lord and from his glorious power" (2 Thess. 1:9).

We do not like to think or talk about hell, yet most teachings about hell in the Bible are from Jesus. He spoke clearly about the danger of hell because He did not want anyone to go there. Hell is a terrible place of torment and suffering, a place of raging fire and darkness, "where the maggots never die and the fire never goes out" (Mark 9:48). Jesus pleads with us to avoid hell: "If your hand causes you to sin, cut it off. It's better to enter eternal life with only one hand than to go into the unquenchable fires of hell with two hands" (Mark 9:43). Jesus is not telling us to literally cut off our hands; He is telling us to do everything to trust Him as our Savior and Lord.

If you turned from your sin and trusted Jesus alone for salvation, you will go immediately into His presence when your physical body dies (Luke 23:43; 2 Cor. 5:6–8).[1] Together, with all our sisters and brothers in Christ, we will declare: "Hallelujah! For our Lord God Almighty reigns. Let us rejoice and be glad and give him glory!" (Rev. 19:6–7 NIV).

In the meantime, let's get ready. Let's love well in God's strength for His glory alone! Let's share Jesus with others, so they will be with Him in heaven too.

---

1 If you want to know more about making this important decision, go to "Receive Jesus Today" at the end of Day 7.

Let the Bible Speak:
Revelation 21:1–22:5 (Optional: Luke 16:19–31)

Let Your Mind Think:

1. How does your knowledge of heaven and hell change the way you see the present?

2. How does knowing God will reward faithful service change how you use your time on earth?

3. Why must all of our works be done in love, in God's strength, and for God's glory alone?

Let Your Soul Pray:
Lord, You are coming soon. Your Word says to keep my heart and mind focused on heaven, not on worldly things (Col. 3:2). Please help me see everything and everyone from an eternal perspective. Help me make the best use of my life on earth. Help me serve with Jesus and share Him with others . . . In Jesus's name I pray, amen.

Let Your Heart Obey:
(What is God leading you to know, value, or do?)

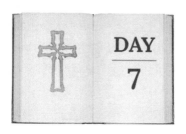

God's Story–
Focus on Jesus

*Fixing our eyes on Jesus, the author and perfecter of faith, who
for the joy set before Him endured the cross, despising the
shame, and has sat down at the right hand of the throne of God.*
Hebrews 12:2 NASB

You discovered God's triumphant true story in our journey this
week–and its four parts. It's the only story that explains how everything started (creation), how everything broke (sin), how everything
could be rescued (Jesus), and how everything will end (re-creation).[1]
Now, we have a better understanding of where we started and where
we'll end up. These four parts give us an eternal perspective that
shapes how we set our priorities and how we face life's problems.

But inside the story, did you notice Jesus on every page? God's
Story centers on Jesus, "the author and perfecter of faith" (Heb. 12:2
NASB). Read this next passage of Scripture–slowly. Watch how God's
Story unfolds in Christ:

> The Son is the image of the invisible God, the firstborn over all creation.
> For in him all things were created: things in heaven and on earth, vis-
> ible and invisible, whether thrones or powers or rulers or authorities;
> all things have been created through him and for him. He is before all

---

1 Hugh Whelchel, "The Four-Chapter Gospel: The Grand Metanarrative Told by the Bible,"
Institute for Faith, Work & Economics, February 14, 2012, https://tifwe.org/the-four-chapter
-gospel-the-grand-metanarrative-told-by-the-bible/.

things, and in him all things hold together. And he is the head of the body, the church; he is the beginning and the firstborn from among the dead, so that in everything he might have the supremacy. For God was pleased to have all his fullness dwell in him, and through him to reconcile to himself all things, whether things on earth or things in heaven, by making peace through his blood, shed on the cross. (Col. 1:15–20 NIV)

God's Story is all about Jesus. Think about how each part of God's Story points to **Jesus, the Beginning and the End** (Rev. 22:13):

1. Creation came into existence through **Jesus, our Creator and the Author of life** (Gen. 1:26; John 1:3; Acts 3:15).

2. Sin enslaved us, but God promised to send **Jesus, our Rescuer, to set us free** (Gen. 3:15; 12:3; Gal. 1:4).

3. Jesus came and died for us. The punishment for our sins fell on **Jesus, our Savior** (Luke 23:33–34; Acts 4:12).

4. Re-creation fully restores our relationship with God through **Jesus, our Healer and our King** (1 Pet. 2:24; Rev. 19:16). Jesus will also fully restore all that is wrong in nature by creating a new heaven and a new earth.

God's Story centers on Jesus. Yours does too. Your story depends on your response to what Jesus did for you on the cross.
No matter what _you have done_, God will forgive you.[1]
No matter what has been _done to you_, God will heal you.[2]
You are worth rescuing! And when Jesus rescues you, He does not just rescue you _from_ sin. Jesus rescues you _for_ a good purpose with a new identity (Eph. 2:10). **God has written your story. You are His masterpiece, and you are created for a specific good purpose.** This is just the beginning. Stay with us. We'll explore your story next week.

---

1 Ps. 103:12; Mark 3:28; Rom. 5:20; Eph. 3:20; 2 Pet. 3:9.
2 Pss. 72:12–14; 22:24; 23:3; 34:18; Luke 4:18–19; 2 Cor. 5:17.

Receive Jesus Today

Now that you know God's Story, you probably realize you have a choice to make. It's time to decide how you will fit into His Story. How will you respond to God's invitation? At this moment, you can receive forgiveness, freedom from sin, and adoption into God's forever family through Jesus. Will you receive Him (John 1:12)? "We speak for Christ when we plead, 'Come back to God!'" (2 Cor. 5:20). You do not need to struggle with feelings of emptiness or guilt, or with a constant fear of death and judgment. You can be reconciled with God now.

You may be tempted to push this decision away because of fear or doubt. But in doing that, you risk suffering a life of brokenness here on earth and an eternity separated from God. Instead, seek God with all your heart, and ask Him to open your eyes to the truth. He will. God gives more evidence than what is needed to know He is real. But He will not force His love. You must decide to receive Jesus.

You may try to make things right on your own or fill the emptiness inside some other way. But no matter what you achieve or acquire, it is never enough. No matter how you numb the pain, it is still there after the pleasure is gone. Thankfully, Jesus is greater than any mistake or sin you may have committed. Because "the wages of sin is death" (Rom. 6:23), Jesus took your punishment Himself. His death paid the penalty for your sin. His resurrection from the grave gives you new life (Rom. 6:4).

> **Faith:**
> Believing God's Word and acting on it, regardless of feelings, because we trust God is good.
>
> "Now faith is confidence in what we hope for and assurance about what we do not see" (Heb. 11:1 NIV).

But you will not have endless chances (Matt. 24:44; Luke 12:20). If you are ready to receive Jesus as your Forgiver and life Leader, pray to Him. Ask for forgiveness from your sins. Place your faith and trust in Jesus alone for salvation. Thank Him for rescuing you. Ask Him to help you turn from your old way of life to God's way of life (2 Cor. 5:15). The Bible teaches, "If you confess with your mouth that Jesus is Lord and believe in your heart that God raised him from the dead, you will be saved" (Rom. 10:9 ESV). Belief involves action.

If you received Jesus now, welcome to the family! You've made the greatest decision of your life. You are now ready to move forward in this faith journey.

DAY 7

Let the Bible Speak:
Ephesians 1 (Optional: Revelation 19:11–16)

Let Your Mind Think:
Answer Week 1 Discussion Questions.

Let Your Soul Pray:
Lord, thank You for revealing Your Story in the Bible. You will accomplish all Your purposes, and You will be glorified in all creation. Father, show me my place in Your Story. Help me fulfill Your purposes for my life and glorify Your name . . . In Jesus's name, amen.

Let Your Heart Obey:
(*What is God leading you to know, value, or do?*)

WEEK 1 DISCUSSION QUESTIONS:
**Review this week's lessons and answer the questions below.
Share your answers with your friends when you gather this week.**

1. How does each part of God's Story (creation, sin, Jesus, re-creation) show God's love for us and His desire for a close relationship with us? How does God's love for you change the way you feel about Him?

2. Has learning about God's Story shown you your next step with God?

    • Do you need to place your faith in Jesus as your Rescuer?
    • Do you need to obey Jesus as the Leader of your life?
    • Do you need to remember eternity as you live your daily life?

3. Does the reality of life after death affect your willingness to share the good news about Jesus? Who in your life is far from God? Pray for opportunities to introduce them to Jesus.

4. Have you found two or three friends to walk with you on this journey? If not, who can you ask to do these daily lessons with you? If so, how have you and your friends encouraged one another this week?

5. Knowing God's Story from beginning to end will help us to understand our role in God's Story—our focus for next week. What do you hope to learn about your story?

WEEK TWO

YOUR STORY,
YOUR IDENTITY

You Are Chosen

Even before he made the world, God loved us and chose
us in Christ to be holy and without fault in his eyes. God
decided in advance to adopt us into his own family by
bringing us to himself through Jesus Christ. This is what
he wanted to do, and it gave him great pleasure.

Ephesians 1:4–5

Last week we learned about God's Story. Now, it is time to learn about your story. Or, perhaps relearn your story. From the day you were born, the world's culture has tried to tell you who you are. Spoken or unspoken, the message we're told is that our value is found in family status, possessions, appearance, or accomplishments. The enemy of our souls twists our story to create insecurities, doubt, isolation, and despair. When others disappoint us or we don't meet their expectations (let's face it—both are inevitable because no one is perfect but Jesus), the enemy tells us we have no worth. We feel unloved, unwanted, helpless, and alone. Our story seems like a failed tragedy.

To discover your true story you need to look to your Creator. You need to come to know the One who created you. Only He can show you why you were made. Only He can show you how your story is filled with hope, love, purpose, and everlasting life.

God is the Author of life and the Author of your story. He does not give you an assignment and just send you on your way. Instead, He gives you a relationship and walks *with you* every step of the way. All you are and all you do flows from your relationship with Him.

Your story unfolds as you walk *with Him*. "I am the Lᴏʀᴅ your God who takes hold of your right hand and says to you, Do not fear; I will help you" (Isa. 41:13 ɴɪᴠ).

God planned you on purpose for His pleasure (Rev. 4:11). He has always loved you. You exist for His delight. There is nothing you can do to earn God's love and nothing you can do to lose God's love.[1] Read that last sentence again. Remind yourself of this fact every morning before you start your day. The choice you have is whether to receive His love.

God chose you even before He created you (Eph. 1:4). When He created you, He carefully chose your every detail: "You made all the delicate, inner parts of my body and knit me together in my mother's womb. . . . You saw me before I was born. Every day of my life was recorded in your book. Every moment was laid out before a single day had passed" (Ps. 139:13, 16). God carefully designed you and carefully planned your days.

You are so important to God that He wants to live with you for eternity.

Read the letter below from your heavenly Father. Each line comes from His Word. Listen attentively, and you will begin to discover your story in Him.

My precious child,

I know everything about you. I am familiar with all your ways.[2] I have even numbered all the hairs on your head.[3] **You are My child**. I created you in My own image[4]—you are so fearfully and wonderfully made![5] I knew you before you were conceived,[6] and I chose you before I created the world.[7] You are not a mistake. All your days are already written in My book, carefully planned.[8] I even chose your birthday and decided exactly where you would live.[9]

People who do not know Me have misrepresented Me. I am not distant and angry but compassionate and slow to anger.[10] I am the

---

1 John 15:9–11; Rom. 5:6–8; 8:38; Eph. 1:4–5; 1 John 3:16a; 4:8–10.
2 Ps. 139:3.
3 Luke 12:7.
4 Gen. 1:26.
5 Ps. 139:14 (ᴇsᴠ).
6 Jer. 1:5.
7 Eph. 1:4.
8 Ps. 139:16.
9 Acts 17:26.
10 Exod. 34:6.

complete expression of love.[1] I lavish My love on you simply because you are My child,[2] and I am your Father—your perfect Father.[3] I offer you more than your earthly father ever could.[4] I am your provider.[5] I am also the compassionate Father who comforts you in all your troubles.[6] **When you are brokenhearted, I come even closer to you**.[7] One day, I will wipe away all your tears and take away all your pain.[8]

My plan for your future overflows with hope[9] because I love you with an extravagant, everlasting love.[10] You cannot escape My love.[11] My loving thoughts toward you are as countless as the grains of sand on the seashore.[12] I think about you all the time, and I rejoice over you with singing.[13] **You are My treasured possession;[14] make Me yours**. Seek Me like treasure.[15] If you seek Me with all your heart, you will find Me.[16] I promise. Delight in Me, and I will give you the desires of your heart[17]— after all, I gave you these desires, and I alone can fully satisfy them. I can do more for you than you can possibly imagine.[18] Trust Me.[19]

Do you know that I love you as much as I love My Son, Jesus? I do. I sent Him to prove that I am for you, not against you.[20] I am not counting your sins.[21] I am not waiting to point out your mistakes. I am not like that. That is why I sent Jesus to take your punishment and erase your sins.[22] They are gone! They do not have to separate you from Me anymore. Jesus's death was the ultimate expression of My love for you.[23] If you receive the gift of My Son, Jesus, you receive Me, and nothing will ever separate you from My love again.[24]

Come home, and all of heaven will celebrate your arrival![25] I have always been your Father. I will always be your Father. My question is, will you be My child?[26]

Love,
Your Dad, Almighty God

---

1 1 John 4:8.
2 Rom. 8:15.
3 Matt. 5:48.
4 Matt. 6:9–15.
5 Phil. 4:19.
6 2 Cor. 1:3–4.
7 Ps. 34:18.
8 Rev. 21:4.

9 1 Pet. 1:3.
10 Jer. 31:3.
11 Rom. 8:38–39.
12 Ps. 139:17–18.
13 Zeph. 3:17.
14 Deut. 7:6.
15 Matt. 6:33; 13:44.
16 Jer. 29:13.

17 Ps. 37:4.
18 Eph. 3:20.
19 Prov. 3:5–6.
20 Rom. 8:31–32.
21 2 Cor. 5:19.
22 2 Cor. 5:21.
23 1 John 4:10.
24 Matt. 10:40; Rom.

6:23; 8:39.
25 Luke 15:7, 24.
26 Adapted from *Father's Love Letter* by Father Heart Communications, 1999. Edited and used by permission.

Let the Bible Speak:
Psalm 139 (Optional: 1 John 3:1–3)

Let Your Mind Think:
1. How does the world or the enemy try to write your story?

2. What was it like to read God's letter to you? What two or three things stood out to you about how God feels about you?

3. Which ideas were most encouraging? If any of the ideas were difficult to accept or unfamiliar, look up the scriptural references.

Let Your Soul Pray:
Father, thank You for choosing me. Thank You for creating me. Thank You for including me in Your Story. Help me grow closer to You as we walk through this unfolding story together . . . In Jesus's name, amen.

Let Your Heart Obey:
(What is God leading you to know, value, or do?)

You Are a Worshiper

Let everything that has breath praise the LORD.
Psalm 150:6 NIV

The moment all heaven and earth waited for was drawing near—the time for a new order of worship for all people, for all eternity. God's promised Messiah, the Anointed One, was finally here. Jesus's family urged Him to reveal Himself, but His hour had not yet come (John 2:4). Until this unusual time, in this unusual place, Jesus would turn sinners into true worshipers of God.

It started as a typical day of travel, but Jesus knew He was walking into an eternity-changing conversation. He sent His disciples ahead for food and waited at a well. The Samaritan woman approached to draw water, not knowing she had an appointment with Jesus. She was going about her ordinary day feeling less than ordinary. Her life had been poisoned with hurts and hardships. Jesus knew this, and that is why He walked miles out of His way and waited for her.

He asked her hard questions at the well.[1] His words dropped deep into her soul to draw out her heart. With each question, she pointed out problems, but Jesus pointed to the truth. Finally, she revealed the question on her heart: a question of worship. Where should we worship? Here or there? But Jesus knew worship was not about an external location, or a religious system, but about an internal position and priority.

---

1   The story of the Samaritan woman is found in John 4:1–42.

Jesus said to her, "Woman, believe me, the hour is coming when neither on this mountain nor in Jerusalem will you worship the Father. You worship what you do not know; we worship what we know, for salvation is from the Jews. But the hour is coming, and is now here, when the true worshipers will worship the Father in spirit and truth, for the Father is seeking such people to worship him. God is spirit, and those who worship him must worship in spirit and truth." (John 4:21–24 ESV)

She responds to Jesus, "I know that Messiah is coming (he who is called Christ). When he comes, he will tell us all things" (John 4:25 ESV).

Then in an indescribably glorious, shocking statement, Jesus plainly responds: "I who speak to you am he" (John 4:26 ESV).

The moment of true worship had come! But why would Jesus reveal His deity to *this woman* in this *way*?

The Father was seeking true worshipers to worship Him in spirit and truth. It was about relationship, not rules. Starting with Jesus, He began breaking the man-made rules.

Speaking to a Samaritan.
Jews hated Samaritans.

Speaking to a woman.
Women were not spoken to in public.

Speaking to a divorced woman who lived with a man who was not her husband.[1]
Jesus broke every cultural rule speaking to a rejected, diminished woman.

---

1 The exact historical circumstances of this Samaritan woman's domestic situation are unknown. However, at that time men were allowed to divorce women for any trivial reason. A woman did not have this same right. The fact that this woman had multiple husbands leads the author to believe the woman experienced multiple divorces and/or much untimely death as a widow. If she had committed adultery, she would not be considered a suitable prospect for remarriage, or even remain alive (John 8:4–5). Concubines were not recognized as married by Jews ("The man you now have is not your husband" [John 4:18 NIV]). Considering first-century culture, the teaching that this woman is a harlot is not definitive. Regardless of how her marriages ended, this woman experienced significant hardship and pain.

But God's ways are not the world's ways (Isa. 55:8–9). With compassion and respect, Jesus taught the woman—and us—that no person is invisible or unheard. No matter our status, position, gender, ethnicity, or location, we are all designed as worshipers. **Yet, how and what we worship says the most about us**. That's why Jesus came to reveal the Father (Matt. 11:27)—to turn us into true worshipers. Only "the blood of Christ will purify our consciences from sinful deeds so that we can worship the living God" (Heb. 9:14).

In the coming weeks, we'll learn about what worship looks like in practice and what worshiping in spirit and truth means. For now, let's understand our identity as true worshipers.

Worship is a heart issue. We all worship, all the time. We worship whatever rules our hearts. Even if we say we worship God, our hearts may be more loyal to a false god or to an idol, which is often ourselves. The very first sin came from our desire to "be like God" (Gen. 3:5). When we want the control to live life our way instead of God's way, we worship ourselves. When we fret about what others think of us, we worship our reputation. When we worry, we worship fear. Even Satan worships, and when he rebelled against God, he began worshiping himself.

> **Worship:**
> Giving worth to something. Jesus said true worshipers "will worship the Father in spirit and in truth" (John 4:24). This means worship takes place on the inside of a person—offered with a humble, pure heart.

Examine yourself to find out who or what you worship:

- *What do I value most?*

- *What influences my decisions most?*

- *Who do I depend on for help during a crisis?*

- *Who/what do I make sacrifices for?*

Good things often become false gods. These things can even include family, a job, beauty, health, or volunteer work. If you struggle with wanting these good things more than you want God, you will be restless. Nothing else satisfies our purpose than to please and worship God. When we let anything rule our hearts in place of God, we struggle to enjoy God. We even find it difficult to enjoy the good things He gives us. But when Jesus is the center of your life—when **Christ becomes your life** (Col. 3:4)—everything flows through your close relationship with Him. You can enjoy Him and the good things He gives you. That's why it is no surprise the Ten Commandments start out with a focus on worship:

> I am the LORD your God, who rescued you from the land of Egypt, the place of your slavery. You must not have any other god but me. You must not make for yourself an idol of any kind or an image of anything in the heavens or on the earth or in the sea. You must not bow down to them or worship them, for I, the LORD your God, am a jealous God who will not tolerate your affection for any other gods. (Exod. 20:2–5)

God does not want a piece of your life, even if that piece is at the top of your priority list. **He wants to be your life**. Together, God and you live through everything that happens to you. As you go through your day, God works in you and through you. Through this close relationship, worship flows naturally as an expression of love, reverence, and adoration. We surrender all—heart, soul, mind, and strength—to the One who is worthy of it all (Mark 12:29–30). Everything we do—except sin—can be done to please God in an act of worship.

The trouble is we all have wandering hearts. We need a plan to stay surrendered to God. The Bible tells us how: We renew our minds (Rom. 12:2)—exchanging lies for the truth—with God's Word. Our thought life is incredibly powerful. **What we focus on expands**. The more we focus on God, the more we will worship Him. But the enemy and the world distract us. We need to "take every thought captive to obey Christ" (2 Cor. 10:5 ESV).

As you know, captives do not like to stay captive. So, we need to choose to focus on "what is true, and honorable, and right, and pure, and lovely, and admirable . . . excellent and worthy of praise" (Phil. 4:8). Consider filtering all your thoughts *and words* through Philippians 4:8. When you do, you'll find godly thinking leads to godly actions, which is another form of worship. "Whatever you do, do it all for the glory of God" (1 Cor. 10:31 NIV). Even the most mundane tasks become holy when done to glorify God. Worship God with all you are *and* all you do.

We worship God because we love Him, not out of obligation or because we want something from Him. We do not worship God to earn favors or pressure Him into blessing us. God cannot be manipulated. He sees through religious masks and empty words: "The Lord says, 'These people say they are mine. They honor me with their lips, but their hearts are far from me. And their worship of me is nothing but man-made rules learned by rote'" (Isa. 29:13). God wants your heart, not your words. If your worship feels forced, ask God to reveal Himself. Ask Him to fill your heart with wonder. **Remind yourself of who God is and what He has done**.

When the Samaritan woman realized who was speaking to her, she responded with faith. She put everything down at the feet of Jesus and ran to tell everyone the Messiah had come (John 4:28–29). Worship poured out of her heart, and many in her town believed (John 4:39). She didn't have any special training or seminary degrees. But she did have an encounter with Jesus. And that is enough to change her life. And the lives of the people who heard her. She was a true worshiper. You can be, too. Look *through* creation to the Creator. Delight in the One who is good, lovely, wise, pure, beautiful, heroic, and true. "In him our hearts rejoice" (Ps. 33:21).

DAY 9

Let the Bible Speak:
Revelation 5 (Optional: Psalm 145)

Let Your Mind Think:
1. Today you learned that the more you focus on something, the more it influences every area of your life. How does focusing on God in worship affect your attitudes and actions?

2. What good things distract you from God?

3. What do you think it means to worship "in spirit and in truth"?

Let Your Soul Pray:
Lord, You are the only One worthy of my worship. As I seek You, fill me with joy and gladness that overflow into sincere praise (Ps. 40:16). Take over my whole life—my desires, emotions, thoughts, and actions. You lead; I will follow. Help me see everything I do as an opportunity to worship You . . . In Jesus's name I pray, amen.

Let Your Heart Obey:
(What is God leading you to know, value, or do?)

You Are Forgiven and Made New

If we confess our sins to him, he is faithful and just to forgive us our sins and to cleanse us from all wickedness.
1 John 1:9

Tears streamed down the woman's face and fell onto the feet of Jesus. She was overwhelmed as she realized her unworthiness next to Jesus's worthiness. Her sinful life was a stench to her soul and a foul presence in the room. Everyone looked at her with scorn. Everyone except Jesus. She broke open her alabaster jar full of costly perfume and poured it on Jesus's feet. As the room filled with the sweet aroma, Jesus saw what filled people's hearts toward her: disgust and disgrace. But Jesus responded with grace. He turned to Simon and said:

"A certain moneylender had two debtors. One owed five hundred denarii, and the other fifty. When they could not pay, he cancelled the debt of both. Now which of them will love him more?" Simon answered, "The one, I suppose, for whom he cancelled the larger debt." And he said to him, "You have judged rightly." Then turning toward the woman he said to Simon, "Do you see this woman? I entered your house; you gave me no water for my feet, but she has wet my feet with her tears and wiped them with her hair. You gave me no kiss, but from the time I came in she has not ceased to kiss my feet. You did not anoint my head with oil, but she has anointed my feet with ointment. Therefore I tell you, her sins, which are many, are forgiven—for she loved much. But he who is forgiven little, loves little." And he said to her, "Your sins are forgiven." Then those who were at table with him began to say among themselves, "Who is this, who even forgives sins?" And he said to the woman, "Your faith has saved you; go in peace." (Luke 7:41–50 ESV)

Forgiveness changes us completely.

When we move from separation from God to a relationship with Him, it's like being raised from death to life. "You were dead because of your sins . . . Then God made you alive with Christ, for he forgave all our sins" (Col. 2:13). We cannot buy or earn forgiveness; it is a priceless gift offered through Jesus Christ. In Christ, God makes you a completely new creation.

Our faith in Jesus Christ does not *improve* us. We are not better people. **We are made new** (Day 5). When God forgives you, He not only makes you new but also reconciles you to Himself (2 Cor. 5:18)— fully restoring His relationship with you and welcoming you into His presence.

You were his enemies, separated from him by your evil thoughts and actions. Yet now he has reconciled you to himself through the death of Christ in his physical body. As a result, he has brought you into his own presence, and you are holy and blameless as you stand before him without a single fault. (Col. 1:21–22)

Imagine being brought into God's presence. You stand before Him without a single fault. Even more, **when God sees you, He sees Jesus's righteousness**. God not only cancels your sin record, but He also credits you with Christ's perfect righteousness (2 Cor. 5:21). This is called **justification**, another amazing aspect of forgiveness. "God will credit righteousness . . . [to] us who believe" (Rom. 4:24 NIV). Friend, "since we have been justified through faith, we have peace with God through our Lord Jesus Christ" (Rom. 5:1 NIV). What un-deserved kindness! What amazing grace! "I am overwhelmed with joy in the LORD my God! For he has dressed me with the clothing of salvation and draped me in a robe of righteousness" (Isa. 61:10). You are justified and covered with Jesus's righteousness so you can be at peace with God.

Consider the beautiful word pictures the Bible uses to illustrate forgiveness:

- "Though your sins are like scarlet, I will make them as white as snow. Though they are red like crimson, I will make them as white as wool" (Isa. 1:18). When God forgives you, He cleanses you not only from sin but also from the stain of sin on your life.
- "As far as the east is from the west, so far has he removed our transgressions from us" (Ps. 103:12 NIV). When God forgives you, He separates you from the sin that once separated you from Him.
- "You will trample our sins under your feet and throw them into the depths of the ocean!" (Mic. 7:19). When God forgives you, He crushes and disposes of your sins forever.

Jesus also gives us a picture of forgiveness in the story of the **prodigal** son. This rebellious young man insulted his father by demanding his inheritance early. He took the money, went far away from home, and spent everything on sinful living. There was a famine, and the only job the son could find was working with filthy pigs. He was starving, dirty, and desperate. He thought his father would still be furious with him, but he decided to return home anyway and ask to work as a servant. The son started toward home.

Prodigal: Wasteful spending of money or resources.

But while he was still a long way off, his father saw him and was filled with compassion for him; he ran to his son, threw his arms around him and kissed him. The son said to him, "Father, I have sinned against heaven and against you. I am no longer worthy to be called your son." But the father said to his servants, "Quick! Bring the best robe and put it on him. Put a ring on his finger and sandals on his feet. Bring the fattened calf and kill it. Let's have a feast and celebrate. For this son of mine was dead and is alive again; he was lost and is found." So they began to celebrate. (Luke 15:20-24 NIV)

God offers us the same kind of forgiveness. When you turn toward Him, He meets you right where you are. You are pardoned, embraced, and celebrated. God's forgiveness is truly an amazing **grace** that never ends.

> **Grace:**
> Undeserved loving-kindness; unmerited favor.

Because even as followers of Jesus, we need to be forgiven often. And God is gracious to extend forgiveness often. "We are no longer slaves to sin," but we still sin (Rom. 6:6). "If we claim we have no sin, we are only fooling ourselves and not living in the truth. But if we confess our sins to him, he is faithful and just to forgive us our sins and to cleanse us from all wickedness" (1 John 1:8-9). **Ask God to show your sin to you**. Pray, "Search me, O God, and know my heart; test me and know my anxious thoughts. Point out anything in me that offends you, and lead me along the path of everlasting life" (Ps. 139:23-24).

Walking in the light—being honest about our sin—is how we grow closer to God and closer to others: "If we walk in the light, as he is in the light, we have fellowship with one another, and the blood of Jesus, his Son, purifies us from all sin" (1 John 1:7 NIV). We can live in the light—not because we are sinless, but because we are forgiven.

How do we respond to God's love and forgiveness?

We love and forgive others. **Love and forgiveness are not based on emotions; we need to choose to love and forgive**. Sometimes, it is a long and challenging process. That is why Jesus sees the faith of the woman pouring oil on His feet and reminds Simon—reminds us—that to love much, we need to remember that we have been forgiven much (Luke 7:47).

Take a moment to think about God's forgiveness in your own life. How often have you sinned and needed forgiveness? Forgiveness is the gift we all need to receive, but we struggle to give it away. Withholding forgiveness from others actually hurts us. Being easily offended and holding grudges ruin relationships. Seeds of resentment grow into bitter roots that entangle and corrupt many

(Heb. 12:15). When we are bitter, we want to hurt others, but we end up hurting ourselves; we become captives of sin (Acts 8:23). That is why God commands us to get rid of bitterness and "forgive as the Lord forgave" us (Col. 3:13 NIV).

The Lord forgives you quickly and generously.

Forgiveness does not mean that you forget or excuse the evil actions of others. You don't stay in a position where you are in danger. It simply means that **when you forgive others, you release the offense and trust God to deal with their sin, in His gracious way, just as He's dealt with your sins.** In the process, God will set you free from the bondage of unforgiveness as you give your hurt to Him. You may find it hard to forgive, but the Holy Spirit in you will help you. As the saying goes, you are the most like Jesus when you forgive.

Peter, one of Jesus's closest followers, denied being associated with Jesus three times. Jesus warned Peter that he would do this, and Peter insisted that would never happen. Then it did happen, and Peter wept bitterly (Matt. 26). With amazing grace, Jesus forgave Peter and restored Him to ministry (John 21:15–19). This same Jesus who forgave those who denied Him also forgives you, and He will help you forgive others. He knows your hurt because He experienced it too, but His command still stands: "Love your enemies and pray for those who persecute you" (Matt. 5:44 NASB).

If it is hard for you to release others when they have wronged you, allow God to work through you (Phil. 2:13). You may need to forgive the person several times a day, as they come to mind. Forgive and release them to God each time. The next day do the same . . . and the next day . . . and the next day until eventually you've completely forgiven them. "Even if that person wrongs you seven times a day and each time turns again and asks forgiveness, you must forgive" (Luke 17:4). **God places no limits on His forgiveness, and neither should we.**

As Jesus said to the woman, He says to you: "Your faith has saved you; go in peace" (Luke 7:50). You are forgiven and made new.

DAY 10

Let the Bible Speak:
Matthew 18:15–35 (Optional: Psalm 32; Luke 15:11–32)

Let Your Mind Think:
1. What feelings come to mind as you think about how God has forgiven you?

2. We must forgive others as we have been forgiven (Eph. 4:32). Who do you need to forgive? Forgive today. The longer you delay forgiveness, the longer you will delay your own healing. Release it to God. You can—in *God's* strength.

3. Focus on Matthew 18:21–35. After you forgive someone, if you feel your heart start to harden, forgive again, remembering that God forgives us again and again too.

Let Your Soul Pray:
Father, Your Word says that heaven rejoices over one sinner who returns to God's path (Luke 15:7). Help me remember this when my sin makes me want to hide from You. Help me come to You with confidence and walk in the light, knowing that You are quick to forgive. Embrace me as Your child. Help me forgive others as You have forgiven me . . . In Jesus's name, amen.

Let Your Heart Obey:
(What is God leading you to know, value, or do?)

You Are Adopted

God sent his Son . . . so that he could adopt us as his very
own children. And because we are his children, God has
sent the Spirit of his Son into our hearts, prompting us to
call out, "Abba, Father." Now you are . . . God's own child.
And since you are his child, God has made you his heir.

Galatians 4:4–7

Rahab was as unlikely a person as any to be part of God's Story,
much less His family. A prostitute in the Canaanite city of Jericho,
Rahab had heard about the Israelites' escape from Egypt. She knew
it was the one true God who had rescued them and fought for them
on their journey through Canaan. And now the Israelites were approaching her city. When God led the Israelite spies to *her* door, she
showed great courage. By faith, she protected them from her own
king, risking her life for God's people. "I know the LORD has given you
this land," she told the spies. "For the LORD your God is the supreme
God of the heavens above and the earth below" (Josh. 2:9, 11). Rahab
hid the Israelite spies, and they successfully escaped capture. Then
God led them in great victory over the city of Jericho, toppling its
walls. But not before He rescued Rahab and her family and made
them a part of His own.[1]

In God's True Story, we learn the city of Jericho was easily
defeated. God miraculously tore down the city walls *without any
human intervention*. So, were the spies needed? Why did God allow

---

1 Read the story of Rahab found in Joshua 2 and 6.

them to risk their lives? Could it be because Rahab was there? Rahab was worth rescuing. We learn later that not only was Rahab's life saved physically, but she also was saved spiritually. Rahab would be the great-great-grandmother of King David and, more importantly, part of the family line of Jesus (Matt. 1:5). Regardless of her sinful past or sinful people. Irrespective of her ethnic or religious background. She surrendered her ties to the Canaanites and surrendered her life to the Lord. Even today, Rahab continues to be an example of faith in action: "[Rahab] was shown to be right with God by her actions when she hid those messengers and sent them safely away by a different road" (James 2:25). God received her and gave her special honor (Heb. 11:31). She was forgiven, made new, and adopted into God's forever family. What extravagant grace!

Of all the wonders that come with salvation, one of the most comforting, nourishing, and uplifting truths is knowing we become children of God. Like Rahab, we can find love and acceptance by the Father and a new family here and in heaven—regardless of our backgrounds, our nationalities, or even our sinful pasts. Adoption is true intimacy, a genuine relationship with God, and the heart of the gospel.

God wants to adopt us into His family forever—we are born again as His very own children (John 3:7). And He chooses us *in advance* by bringing us to Himself through Jesus Christ (Eph. 1:5). What does this mean? **You are wanted and dearly loved**. "See what great love the Father has lavished on us, that we should be called children of God! And that is what we are!" (1 John 3:1 NIV).

In Christ, we have "the right to become children of God" (John 1:12). God wants to be your father, the one you know and trust intimately. "Now we call Him, 'Abba, Father,'" like Jesus did (Rom. 8:15). Your sinfulness does not keep God from wanting to adopt you. He is not embarrassed by you. No matter what mistakes you have made or what has been done to you, your **Abba** Father always welcomes you and accepts you where you are.

Think about your earthly father. Was he kind or cruel? Involved or absent? Even if you had a good relationship with your earthly father, your relationship with your heavenly Father is much better. Jesus wants us to experience the intimate connection we have with our Father in heaven. He tells us, "Don't address anyone here on earth as 'Father,' for only God in heaven is your Father" (Matt. 23:9). Jesus is not asking us to disown our human fathers, but He does want us to value our relationship with our heavenly Father much more. How do we do that? We start by learning all we can about this perfect Father of ours.

> **Abba:**
> In the Aramaic language spoken at the time of Jesus, the word *abba* meant father and was primarily used within a family and in prayer.
>
> Source: Robert H. Mounce, *Romans*, vol. 27, *The New American Commentary* (Nashville: Broadman & Holman Publishers, 1995).

First, we need to understand how deeply our Father cares for us. He adopts us as spiritual babies and helps us "grow up in every way . . . into Christ" (Eph. 4:15 ESV). "Like newborn babies, [we] long for the pure milk of the word, so that by it [we] may grow" (1 Pet. 2:2 NASB). As we grow up to be like Jesus, we hear and imitate our Father's voice. We imitate His actions (Eph. 5:1). Even Jesus did only what He saw the Father doing (John 5:19) and said only what He heard the Father saying (John 8:28). He did not obey out of obligation or an unhealthy need for approval. Jesus Christ's obedience flowed out of the loving relationship He shared with His Father. When you truly love someone, it is your greatest pleasure to *act* on it—with honor, respect, and obedience.

God loves us enough that He is willing to discipline us. As His adopted children, we need His loving discipline from time to time. None of us enjoy it, but we all need it. Because God loves us, He corrects us when we wander away from His will in our thoughts, attitudes, or actions: "The LORD corrects those he loves, just as a father corrects a child in whom he delights" (Prov. 3:12). God loves us, and "God's discipline is always good for us, so that we might share in his holiness" (Heb. 12:10). God corrects us to protect us from the devastating consequences of sin. Just like a parent delights in the growth of a child, God delights to see us thrive in what He has planned for us (Eph. 2:10).

Our Father is our perfect Provider. He "knows exactly what you need even before you ask him" (Matt. 6:8). So "don't be concerned about what to eat and what to drink. Don't worry about such things. These things dominate the thoughts of unbelievers all over the world, but your Father already knows your needs" (Luke 12:29–30). Rest in knowing that "God will supply every need of yours according to his riches" (Phil. 4:19 ESV). If good human parents know how to give their children good gifts, how much more will our heavenly Father provide for those who ask Him (Matt. 7:9–11)?

God also knows that we need community—a place to belong. God adopts everyone Jesus rescues, so we have many brothers and sisters in our family of faith (Rom. 8:29). It is a good thing our "Father's house has many rooms" (John 14:2 NIV). But there is no room for sibling rivalry because all God's children are considered equal (Matt. 23:8; Gal. 3:28). God has no favorites in His family (1 Pet. 1:17). We do not compete with our siblings or discriminate; we care for them. We recognize their part in God's Story (1 Cor. 12). "Sympathize with each other. Love each other as brothers and sisters. Be tender-hearted, and keep a humble attitude" (1 Pet. 3:8). We are encouraged to give up our lives for our brothers and sisters in Christ just as Jesus gave up His life for us (1 John 3:16). When we love our brothers and sisters, we give them the love of our Father. **Extravagant love runs in the family**.

Just as earthly families desire to care for their future genera-tions, **our Father gives His children, His "heirs," an inheritance** (Rom. 8:17). "Now we live with great expectation, and we have a priceless inheritance—an inheritance that is kept in heaven for [us], pure and undefiled, beyond the reach of change and decay" (1 Pet. 1:3–4). In heaven, we will enjoy God's glory forever, celebrate His goodness, and rest in His love. Best of all, we will enjoy His pres-ence with pleasure and joy beyond comprehension (Ps. 16:11). "What a wonderful inheritance!" (Ps. 16:6).

DAY 11

Let the Bible Speak:
John 14 (Optional: Romans 8:15–17)

Let Your Mind Think:
1. Friend, you are adopted and dearly loved. Forever. Your place in God's family is secure (John 10:29). Is there anything that keeps you from feeling fully secure and loved by God?

2. What does your adoption—being chosen like Rahab—tell you about God's love for you?

3. How does it impact your current and future relationships to see other believers as equally loved and valued family members (Gal. 3:28–29)? How can you encourage a sister or brother today?

Let Your Soul Pray:
Lord, thank You for adopting me. Your Word says, "As a father has compassion on his children, so the LORD *has compassion on those who fear him" (Psalm 103:13* NIV). *Help me see You as my compassionate Father. Help me grow up to be like Jesus, and help me rest in knowing that You will meet all my needs. Make me an encouraging member of my forever family . . . In Jesus's name, amen.*

Let Your Heart Obey:
(*What is God leading you to know, value, or do?*)

You Are Never Alone

You go before me and follow me.
You place your hand of blessing on my head.
Such knowledge is too wonderful for me,
too great for me to understand!
I can never escape from your Spirit!
I can never get away from your presence!
If I go up to heaven, you are there;
if I go down to the grave, you are there.
If I ride the wings of the morning, if I dwell by the farthest oceans,
even there your hand will guide me,
and your strength will support me.
Psalm 139:5–10

A bolt of fire had just fallen from heaven, defeating the prophet Elijah's enemies. The first rain cloud after years of drought was forming in the sky. The nation of Israel was changing physically with rain and spiritually with repentance (1 Kings 18). Elijah was a wanted man; men were searching to kill him. Although Elijah had witnessed God's provision, protection, and power through years of the nation's rebellion, he was weary. He was done—or so he told God:

"I have had enough, Lord," he said. "Take my life . . . I have been very zealous for the Lord God Almighty. The Israelites have rejected your covenant, torn down your altars, and put your prophets to death with the sword. I am the only one left, and now they are trying to kill me too." (1 Kings 19:4, 14 NIV)

But Elijah was not alone. God was with him. He was not the only true believer remaining because God had preserved seven thousand believers who had not bowed down to idols (1 Kings 19:18). What Elijah needed was to rest, to refresh, and to remember. God provided food for his body and rest for his soul. And when the time was right, God gave Elijah his next set of instructions.[1]

Sometimes as a believer you may be used by God in powerful ways, and then the enemy will try to retaliate. Doubt, discouragement, or despair can set in. You may feel alone, believing the lie that God has abandoned you or that your usefulness for God has expired. Like Elijah, you need to be refilled. You need an "Elijah rest." Here is what you need to know:

You are never alone. God—Father, Son, and Holy Spirit—is always with you. Every minute of every day He has always desired to be close to you. That is why He created you with such care. That is why He sent a Rescuer to destroy the sin that separated you from Him. That is why He sent His Spirit to live in you. He never leaves you alone to feel abandoned.

When we look to others for support and they aren't there for us, we may feel all alone. But this is not true. God is *always* present (Pss. 46:1; 139:7–10). *You are never alone.*

Jesus is God with you. He is also called *Immanuel*, "God with us" (Matt. 1:23 ESV), because He lived as a human being and dwelled among us. He grew hungry and tired. He was tempted to sin. He was mistreated and falsely accused. And ultimately, He was betrayed, tortured, and killed. Because of this, no matter what hardships we face, Jesus knows our suffering: "This High Priest of ours understands our weaknesses, for he faced all of the same testings we do" (Heb. 4:15). Jesus suffered the kinds of things we suffer—and more—so He knows how to pray for us, and He continually does pray for us (Heb. 7:25). As our perfect High Priest, Jesus stands in God's presence on our behalf (Heb. 9:24). We no longer need a temple in Jerusalem or a special priest to stand between us and God.[2] Jesus also promises to

---

1 Read the story of Elijah's mountaintop experiences found in 1 Kings 18 and 19.
2 Wayne Grudem, *Systematic Theology: An Introduction to Biblical Doctrine* (Grand Rapids, MI: Zondervan, 1994), 626–627.

be with us "always, to the very end of the age" (Matt. 28:20 NIV). *You are never alone.*

The Holy Spirit is God *in* you. Jesus says, "I will ask the Father, and he will give you another Helper, to be with you forever, even the Spirit of truth . . . You know him, for he dwells with you and will be in you" (John 14:16–17 ESV). He is *with* you and *in* you . . .

- **when you read and meditate on God's Word:** "The Holy Spirit . . . will teach you all things and will remind you of everything I have said to you" (John 14:26 NIV).
- **when you pray:** "The Holy Spirit helps us in our weakness. . . . We don't know what God wants us to pray for. But the Holy Spirit prays for us" (Rom. 8:26).
- **when you are tempted:** "When you are tempted, [the Holy Spirit] will show you a way out so that you can endure" (1 Cor. 10:13).
- **when you suffer:** God will never simply *send* comfort and strength in your time of need—instead, He will *show up* as *the source* of comfort and strength. His very presence provides a healing balm for your broken heart. "The LORD is close to the brokenhearted; he rescues those whose spirits are crushed" (Ps. 34:18). He will be our help and comforter forever (John 14:16–17).

You are never alone.

You are also never alone because God has given you a place to belong: the church. (See "How to Find a Good Church" on the following page.) We are all members of God's forever family, and He is building us into a community where His Spirit dwells (Eph. 2:19–22). Our "family of believers" (1 Pet. 2:17) is so closely connected that God calls us the body of Christ (1 Cor. 12:27). You may be the only believer in your family or town, but in Christ you are a part of a large family of believers across the world. Just as God preserved believers during the time of Elijah, He is preserving believers today. "The human body has many parts, but the many parts make up one whole body. So it is with the body of Christ. . . . All the members care for each other. If one part suffers, all the parts suffer with it, and if one part is honored, all the parts are glad" (1 Cor. 12:12, 25–26). You are never alone in your pain. Not only does Jesus know your pain, but also "your family of believers all over the world is going through the same kind of suffering you are" (1 Pet. 5:9). God weaves your story along with the story of every Jesus follower together into His own story. *You are never alone.*

Because you are never alone, you never need to fear—that's not God's will for us. "Be strong and courageous. Do not be afraid; do not be discouraged, for the LORD your God will be with you wherever you go" (Josh. 1:9 NIV). But when we are afraid, God comforts us, as He did with Elijah. No matter what troubles come, "God is our refuge and strength, a very present help in trouble. Therefore we will not fear" (Ps. 46:1–2 ESV). God was with us yesterday. He is with us now, and He will be with us in our future. *We are never alone.*

How to Find a Good Church

If you are a Christ-follower with access to a church, joining a faith family is one of your highest priorities for prayer, biblical teaching, fellowship, communion, and more. If you do not have access to a church, you can gather in your home (more on this later). God's Word commands us not to stop meeting together (Heb. 10:25). We need a church family, and here is what to look for in a good one:

1. **Servant-Leader Pastor:** Called by God, the pastor has a caring heart and both teaches and obeys the Bible. Not a dictator or a people-pleaser. The pastor exalts Jesus, not a person.

2. **Spiritual Growth:** The church challenges you to grow up spiritually, teaching you how to be an abiding disciple of Jesus who makes disciples for Jesus.

3. **Sharing Environment:** The people of the church love and care for one another. There is a feeling of family unity.

4. **Outward Service:** The church is not inwardly focused but reaches out to the community and to the world to spread God's love in word and action.

There is no such thing as a perfect church (only Jesus is perfect). If you find a good church, be faithful to your faith family. Be faithful with your time, attending worship gatherings regularly and fulfilling your commitments with excellence. Be faithful with your talents, getting involved and not looking for others to do it all. Be faithful in your giving, not being stingy. Take the initiative to meet people and get involved. You will be blessed.

Let the Bible Speak:
Isaiah 41:10–20 (Optional: Deuteronomy 31:6)

Let Your Mind Think:
1. How can you remind yourself that God is with you even when you feel lonely or afraid?

2. How might God's presence make you brave and give you joy (Deut. 31:6)?

3. Do you know anyone who feels lonely? Be a friend. Show them they are not alone. Share God's presence with them today.

Let Your Soul Pray:
God, I thank You that You are always with me, even when I feel lonely. You promise You will never leave me nor forget about me (Heb. 13:5). Give me a greater awareness of Your presence. May Your presence make me brave and fill me with joy. Show me lonely people who need to experience Your presence and kindness through me . . . In Jesus's name I pray, amen.

Let Your Heart Obey:
(What is God leading you to know, value, or do?)

DAY 13

You Are Holy

You must be holy because I, the LORD, am holy. I have set
you apart from all other people to be my very own.
Leviticus 20:26

Right now, even as you read the words on this page, incredible expressions of adoration are happening in the heavens. The prophet Isaiah got a peek of this very scene, and it is recorded for us in Isaiah 6. In his glimpse of God's throne room, he saw angelic beings loudly proclaiming, "Holy, holy, holy is the LORD Almighty; the whole earth is full of his glory" (Isa. 6:3 NIV).[1] More than eight hundred years later, the apostle John records a similar experience: "Day and night they never stop saying: "'Holy, holy, holy is the Lord God Almighty,' who was, and is, and is to come'" (Rev. 4:8 NIV). "Who will not fear you, Lord, and bring glory to your name? For you alone are holy" (Rev. 15:4 NIV). They could have described God as "Love, love, love" or "Grace, grace, grace," but instead, they repeat, "Holy, holy, holy." It is not enough to say that God is holy. It is not enough to say that God is holy, holy. No . . .

God is *holy, holy, holy.*

When something is repeated multiple times in the Bible, it usually means the statement is critical and significant. God is *holy, holy, holy.* So what does **holy** mean?

If you ever read an important word you do not know in the Bible, look up where that word first appears in Scripture.[2] You might

---

1 Read the story of Isaiah's commissioning in Isaiah 6.
2 A concordance lists all key words found in a text. Bibles occasionally include a concordance

discover its meaning in context. The word *holy* first appears in Genesis to describe the day that God set apart for rest. "God blessed the seventh day and made it holy, because on it he rested from all the work of creating that he had done" (Gen. 2:3 NIV). To be *holy* means to be set apart. Everything about God is holy and pure: His love, His mercy, His justice—even His anger. Nothing in all of creation compares to God's holiness, His infinite perfection. God is set apart from everything that is sinful (1 John 1:5).

> **Holy:**
> Set apart or dedicated to God in purity for honorable use.

Only a few people in the Bible saw visions of God's holiness, and all of them were terrified when they did. Moses hid his face (Exod. 3:6). Ezekiel fell on his face in fear (Ezek. 1:28). John fell down "as though dead" (Rev. 1:17 ESV). Isaiah cried out, "It's all over! I am doomed, for I am a sinful man. I have filthy lips, and I live among a people with filthy lips. Yet I have seen the King, the LORD of Heaven's Armies" (Isa. 6:5).

Because we are sinful, God's purity overwhelms us. God says, "No one may see me and live" (Exod. 33:20). God's holiness cannot tolerate any trace of sin (Hab. 1:13). "Who may climb the mountain of the LORD? Who may stand in his holy place? Only those whose hands and hearts are pure" (Ps. 24:3–4). Only the pure can see God's holiness and survive (Matt. 5:8). That is a problem for us because we all sin; none of us is righteous (Ps. 143:2; Rom. 3:23).

But Jesus rescues us from this death sentence by making us holy. For us to see the Lord, we need to be holy. God has "made you holy by means of Christ Jesus" (1 Cor. 1:2). By taking our punishment, "Christ made us right with God; he made us pure and holy, and he freed us from sin" (1 Cor. 1:30).

> Christ loved the church and gave himself up for her to make her holy, cleansing her by the washing with water through the word, and to present her to himself as a radiant church, without stain or wrinkle or

---

as a resource tool. If your Bible does not have a concordance, you can find Bible tools at many different websites, including Bible Gateway (biblegateway.com), Bible Study Tools (biblestudytools.com), Bible Hub (biblehub.com), and Blue Letter Bible (blueletterbible.org).

any other blemish, but holy and blameless. (Eph. 5:25–27 NIV)

Only Jesus could do this because He alone is "holy and blameless, unstained by sin" (Heb. 7:26). When you placed your faith in Christ, "you were cleansed; you were made holy; you were made right with God" (1 Cor. 6:11). "As a result, he has brought you into his own presence, and you are holy and blameless as you stand before him without a single fault" (Col. 1:22). Only in Christ can we obey God's command: "Be holy because I, the LORD, am holy" (Lev. 20:26). Only in Christ can we enter God's presence and live.

God is holy; therefore in Christ, you are holy. Holiness is God's very life *in* us. After the moment of salvation comes a lifetime of sanctification–the process of becoming holy. (We'll learn more about sanctification in Week 7.) As one Christian teacher explains it, "Our righteous position is gained in an instant of true belief, but our righteousness–our Christ-likeness–grows in depth over a lifetime of pursuing the things of God."[1] God commands us to "be holy" throughout the Bible to emphasize the importance of holiness.

But what does a holy life look like? We show our inner holiness outwardly with "holy lives, not impure lives" (1 Thess. 4:7). The Bible makes frequent references to clothing as an external sign of internal living. For example, brides wear special clothing, but their clothing does not *make* them brides; it simply *shows* that they *are* brides. In the same way, we wear our holiness. This outward holiness does not make us holy, but it shows others that we are living set apart in Christ. "Since God chose you to be the holy people he loves, you must clothe yourselves with tenderhearted mercy, kindness, humility, gentleness, and patience" (Col. 3:12). We are to put on these Christlike virtues every day, and "throw off your old sinful nature and your former way of life, which is corrupted by lust and deception. Instead, let the Spirit renew your thoughts and attitudes. Put on your new nature, created to be like God–truly righteous and holy" (Eph. 4:22–24).

When you think of holy living, does it seem intimidating? Maybe

---

1   Francis & Lisa Chan, *You and Me Forever: Marriage in Light of Eternity* (San Francisco: Claire Love Publishing, 2014), 34.

impossible or legalistic? When many people think of holiness, they picture pious behaviors and religious rituals. Holiness is not about rules and rituals. It's about honestly examining your heart and inviting God to purify your attitude and your actions. It's about living in freedom from sin. When God reveals sin, we can confess it immediately and repent, turning away from it and toward God's right, fulfilling way of living.

The Holy Spirit will weave holiness into your life day by day. After weeks, months, and years of trusting God and doing what He says, you will notice a growing pattern of holiness in your attitude and actions. For example, your choices in the books you read, the music you listen to, or the movies you watch may change as the Holy Spirit shows you how to guard your heart (Prov. 4:23). Your actions, words, and thoughts will transform as He teaches you how to honor God with your life (Col. 3:17). The Holy Spirit is shaping the details of your life. Sins that once entangled you become less powerful. Spiritual fruit—love, joy, peace, and more—becomes more plentiful (Gal. 5:22–23). These changes occur over time as we put on holiness daily.

Some days, we may struggle with temptations and frustrations that sometimes make our attempts at pursuing holiness feel like forever climbing a mountain, unable to reach the top. When those hard days come—and they will—we can still choose to put one foot in front of the other with Jesus as our guide. One day, we will not have to put on holiness because God Himself will clothe us in permanent, perfect holiness. In heaven, God will give us "'the finest of pure white linen to wear.' For the fine linen represents the good deeds of God's holy people" (Rev. 19:8).

Yes, friend, *in Christ* you are holy. You are not working to be holy in your own strength. God chose you before the creation of the world and set you apart for His purposes (Eph. 1:4). Put on holiness to become "a vessel for honorable use, set apart as holy, useful to the master of the house, ready for every good work" (2 Tim. 2:21 ESV). God desires holiness for you so you can be in relationship with Him, filled with more of Him, and set apart for all the good work He has planned for you. Next week, we'll learn more about what those plans are.

DAY 13

Let the Bible Speak:
1 Peter 1:13–25 (Optional: 1 Peter 2:1–11)

Let Your Mind Think:
1. How does thinking about God's holiness affect your attitude in worship?

2. What in your life may not be set apart to God?

3. How can you put on holiness each day?

Let Your Soul Pray:
God, You are holy. Thank You for making me holy through Christ. Your Word says that You saved us and called us to live holy lives—not because we deserved it, but because that was Your plan to show us Your grace through Jesus (2 Tim 1:9). I am so thankful that You called me. Please help me put on holiness each day . . . In Jesus's name I pray, amen.

Let Your Heart Obey:
(What is God leading you to know, value, or do?)

You Belong to God

We take captive every thought to make it obedient to Christ.
2 Corinthians 10:5 NIV

Who are you?

Before this week, you may have answered that question with something about your family, your occupation, your nationality, and more. Those descriptions may be accurate, but they are not your new identity. When you become a Jesus-follower, these become mere footnotes in your new story.

Your true story centers on who you are in Jesus Christ, so guard your identity carefully. Let's remember what defines you now:

- You are made to worship God.
- You are forgiven and made new.
- You are chosen and adopted into God's forever family.
- You are never, ever alone.
- You are holy and set apart for God's purposes.

Your new life has meaning and purpose—and makes you the enemy's target. Satan knows you belong to God, and he cannot snatch you out of God's hands (John 10:28–29). But he will do everything he can to keep you from enjoying your relationship with God and from sharing it with others. Satan (also called "the accuser" in Scripture) will attack your identity in Jesus by speaking negative thoughts into your mind or creating conflict with others to oppose who you are. Do any of these sound familiar?

- We are made to worship God, but the enemy tells us to worship ourselves or false idols.
- We are forgiven, but the enemy tells us we are guilty.
- We are chosen and adopted, but the enemy tells us we are unwanted.
- We are never alone, but the enemy tells us we are abandoned.
- We are holy, but the enemy tells us we are worthless.

If you have heard any of these lies that contradict God's Word, you need to choose to stop listening and remember who you are. Silence the enemy's attempts to keep you from God's best plans for you by reminding yourself of the truths in God's Word. Memorize the simple verse at the opening of today's lesson: "We take captive every thought to make it obedient to Christ" (2 Cor. 10:5 NIV). **The enemy wants to make us doubt God's love. Because if we do, our relationship with God will feel lifeless and obeying God will feel like a burden**. Let's not let the enemy deceive us! Nothing can separate us from God's love (Rom. 8:38–39). We will learn more about spiritual warfare later. For now, stay alert to the enemy's attacks on your identity as God's dearly loved child. "Resist the devil and he will flee from you" (James 4:7 NASB).

If you start to feel insecure, read Romans 8. In this chapter, you'll find there is *no condemnation* for those in Christ. **Consider feelings of insecurity as an invitation from God to find your peace *in who He is and what He has done for you***. Because what we think affects what we do. Let's carefully guard our thoughts. Remember, God not only saved us *from* sin; He also saved us for His purposes. "For we are God's handiwork, created in Christ Jesus to do good works, which God prepared in advance for us to do" (Eph. 2:10 NIV). **Yes, you are His handiwork, His masterpiece**. He chose you and has written a beautiful story for your life—one that no one else can live. Remember who you are in Christ.

Encourage your brothers and sisters in Christ, too. **We are *all* God's image-bearers**. In God's family, there is no room for prejudice or ranking. "There is no longer Jew or Gentile, slave or free, male and female. For you are all one in Christ Jesus" (Gal. 3:28). Do not let ethnicity, culture, age, education, gender, or social class affect how you see or treat other people. "God does not show favoritism," and neither should we (Rom. 2:11). **Love your brothers and sisters as God loves them. See them as God sees them—masterpieces one and all.**

There is still much to learn about our new identity in Jesus. More treasures left to discover. But all can be summed up and remembered in one phrase: *I am* **because of the** *great I* AM.

When God described Himself to Moses, He said, "I AM WHO I AM. Say this to the people of Israel: I AM has sent me to you" (Exod. 3:14). In John's Gospel, Jesus says: "I tell you the truth, before Abraham was even born, I AM!" (John 8:58).

"I AM" is the ultimate statement of God's all-sufficient, all-supreme, all-powerful presence. God is, was, and forever will be. He is the Uncaused Cause.[1] He is all-knowing, all-present, all-powerful. He is the great I AM! **We** *are* **because of** *who He is*!

- You are chosen because of God's great love to make you for His pleasure.
- You are a true worshiper because God is worthy to worship and He gave you His Spirit to reveal the truth.
- You are forgiven and made new because God forgave you and gave you new and eternal life.
- You are adopted because God is Father and chose you to be His child.
- You are never alone because God is always with you.
- You are holy because God is holy.

Think of what you learned this week about your value, worth, and identity. You are all of those things and more because of who God is. Remind yourself every day:

I am because of the great I AM!

This week, we have learned who we *are*. Next week, we will learn what we *do*.

---

1 Norman L. Geisler, *Systematic Theology: In One Volume* (Minneapolis, MN: Bethany House Publishers, 2011), 25.

DAY 14

Let the Bible Speak:
Romans 8 (Optional: Ephesians 2:1–10)

Let Your Mind Think:
1. What is the difference between "who I am" and "who I am in Christ"?

2. Answer Week 2 Discussion Questions.

Let Your Soul Pray:
Father, thank You for my new identity in Christ. Help me to guard it. When the accuser attacks my identity in You, remind me that I am a chosen, worshiping, forgiven, adopted, embraced, and holy child of God. Thank You for loving me now and forever . . . In Jesus's name, amen.

Let Your Heart Obey:
(What is God leading you to know, value, or do?)

WEEK 2 DISCUSSION QUESTIONS:

Review this week's lessons and answer the questions below.
Share your answers with your friends when you gather this week.

1. This week, we learned parts of your identity in Christ. You are
    (1) chosen, (2) made to worship, (3) forgiven and made new,
    (4) adopted, (5) never alone, and (6) holy. Which of these char-
    acteristics encourages you most? Why?

2. Which of these characteristics is hardest for you to accept?
    Why? How might God's Word or your friends help you embrace
    that part of your identity in Christ?

3. We are made to worship. How does our forgiveness, adoption,
    and holiness in Christ affect our worship?

4. Worshipers in heaven cry out that God is "holy, holy, holy." This
    is the only characteristic of God repeated this way in the Bible.
    Why do you think God's holiness is so important?

5. Satan, the accuser, attacks every part of our identity in Christ.
    How have the enemy's lies kept you from the freedom and
    peace Christ wants to give you? What truths from God's Word
    help you to silence the enemy's wrongful accusations?

WEEK THREE

YOUR STORY,
YOUR PURPOSE

Embrace Your New Purpose

For we are God's handiwork, created in Christ Jesus to do
good works, which God prepared in advance for us to do.
Ephesians 2:10 NIV

Long before you were born, God knew you (Jer. 1:5). He uniquely created you for a purpose to be fulfilled in *every* season of your life. You learned last week who God created you to be. This week, you'll learn what God created you to do. You have a divine purpose, and it is not to sit around and wait for heaven. God has work for you to do *with Him here*—your purpose affects heaven and brings true joy and real success.

Sometimes we are tempted to mistake the world's view of success for purpose.[1] We can be successful in a career or a hobby but not fulfill our purpose. Success is also not about fulfilling our potential. Jesus did not fulfill His potential on earth. After all, He was King of heaven and became a poor, humble man (Phil. 2:5–8). But He did achieve His purpose (John 17:4). That is our goal: to fulfill God's purpose for our lives. At the end of your life, let it be said of you what was spoken of King David: "When David had served God's purpose in his own generation, he fell asleep" (Acts 13:36 NIV).

You might be asking, *What is my purpose, and how do I fulfill it?* The rest of this faith journey is about helping you with that. For

---

1 Learn from King Solomon, the wisest man who ever lived. He documented his experiences and profound conclusions on success in an Old Testament book titled Ecclesiastes.

now, just know **our primary purpose is to glorify God and enjoy our relationship with Him forever.**[1] We live this purpose each day in three fulfilling ways:

1. **Love and obey God.**
2. **Love everyone.**
3. **Make disciples.**

We all share this purpose, but we each fulfill it uniquely. God has given each of us different relationships, skills, resources, and places, so fulfilling this purpose will look different in each of our lives, just as it did for each **patriarch** from Abraham to Moses.

In our first week together, we covered God's over-arching Story. Today, let's take a closer look at the very beginning of God's rescue plan to save humanity. The events of Genesis 1–11 happen over many years and throughout many generations of people, but in Genesis 12, the story slows suddenly and focuses on the fathers of our faith: Abraham, Isaac, and Jacob. This slower pace allows us to learn the importance of God's unique relationship with each person. As their stories unfold, we learn how God relates to His people:

> **Patriarch:**
> A spiritual father or male head of a family.

- God loves us and gives us a purpose.
- We show our love to God by fulfilling His purpose for us.
- When we fulfill our purpose, God blesses others through us.

Let's begin. We will start where we left off on Day 3 when God banished Adam and Eve from the garden of Eden . . .

After the exile from Eden, people multiplied. With them, sin also multiplied. As human wickedness became totally intolerable, God grieved and flooded the earth to blot out wicked humanity and make a new start. Only one family was spared: Noah's family. God placed Noah, his family, and sets of every kind of animal on an ark

---

1 Westminster Assembly (1643–1652). *The Assembly's Shorter Catechism, with the Scripture Proofs in Reference: with an Appendix on the Systematick Attention of the Young to Scriptural Knowledge* by Hervey Wilbur (Newburyport, MA: Wm. B. Allen & Co., 1816).

(like a giant houseboat) that He instructed Noah to build (Gen. 5–9). As Noah's descendants began to multiply on dry land, once again sin multiplied. God confused the people's language to keep them from uniting in rebellion against Him (Gen. 10–11).

God chose one man—Abraham[1]—to start the rescue plan (Gen. 12:1–3). We might assume Abraham was a righteous person to be entrusted with such an assignment. Surprisingly, he was not. He grew up worshiping idols (Josh. 24:2). He did not deserve to be chosen any more than we do. God told Abraham:

> "Leave your native country, your relatives, and your father's family, and go to the land that I will show you. I will make you into a great nation. I will bless you and . . . all the families on earth will be blessed through you." (Gen. 12:1–3)

Abraham knew he was to travel toward Canaan, but he was not told exactly where he and his family would settle. God invited him to trust Him one step at a time. Abraham did not have all the answers, but he bravely obeyed God. Through that relationship of trust, God blessed Abraham and all of us as well. Abraham's obedience led to our Rescuer's birth (Matt. 1:1).

God promised to send the Rescuer through Abraham's family line, but Abraham's elderly wife, Sarah, was barren. Despite the circumstances, Abraham chose to believe God would remain faithful to His promise. It wasn't always easy, and he struggled with obedience in this area. In the end, Abraham's best hope was to take God at His word. Sarah eventually became pregnant and gave birth to a baby boy named Isaac (Gen. 21).

Then Abraham's family began to multiply, just as God promised. Isaac grew up and had twin sons: Jacob and Esau (Gen. 25). These two brothers had a difficult relationship. In fact, every member of their family struggled with sinfulness and areas of weakness. The

---

1 At that time, Abraham (as we commonly refer to him) was still called Abram. Later, God changed his name to "Abraham," proclaiming God's calling on Abraham's life: "No longer shall your name be called Abram, but your name shall be Abraham, for I have made you the father of a multitude of nations" (Gen. 17:5 ESV).

Bible, however, makes no effort to hide their shortcomings. Remember, this is God's True Story of God's faithfulness for God's glory. He keeps His promises even when we do not.

Now we are a few generations closer to the Rescuer, but family problems arose again. Abraham's grandson Jacob, later named Israel, had twelve sons who became the founding fathers of the twelve tribes of Israel. Jacob's sinful favoritism toward one son, Joseph, created terrible jealousy in Jacob's other sons. Their hurt and anger led them to sell their brother Joseph into Egyptian slavery. Joseph experienced great suffering there and was imprisoned for a crime he did not commit (Gen. 37; 39–40). But God had not stopped working out His plan, and He gave Joseph great wisdom that saved all of Egypt from a great famine (Gen. 41). Pharaoh, the king of Egypt, recognized the relationship Joseph had with God and promoted him from prisoner to prime minister.

Through it all, **God changed Joseph's circumstances to change his heart**. Years later, Joseph's brothers came to Egypt looking for food. This provided Joseph an opportunity for revenge, but rather than use his power against them, Joseph *forgave* them. In one of the most faith-filled expressions of forgiveness, Joseph wisely told them: "You intended to harm me, but God intended it all for good. He brought me to this position so I could save the lives of many people" (Gen. 50:20). Joseph's faith not only blessed his whole family, now called the Israelites, but also blesses us. We can learn from his example. Friend, **God is always good**, and He works in all our circumstances—even the most difficult ones—for His glory and our good (Rom. 8:28-29).

Because of the famine and Joseph's invitation, the Israelites moved to Egypt. Abraham's family grew into a great nation there. They were so numerous that another pharaoh—who knew nothing of Joseph—felt threatened. Fearing an uprising, he enslaved the Israelites. The people of God were now in chains, and they cried out to God for help for four hundred years.

When the time was right, **God chose one man—Moses—to continue the rescue plan**. Moses resisted God's invitation at first because he felt insufficient. (Moses did not realize that no one is ever sufficient on their own to carry out God's plan. Only God can do that.) Moses was afraid, but he trusted God and confronted Pharaoh: "Let my people go" (Exod. 9:1). Just like God did with Abraham, Isaac, Jacob, and Joseph, God changed Moses's heart and tested him.

Repeatedly, Pharaoh would release the Israelites and then take them captive again. In response, God displayed His power and authority by sending terrible plagues to torment the Egyptian people and disgrace their false gods. In the end, Pharaoh finally let God's people go. Then when Pharaoh changed his mind and chased after them, God delivered them by miraculously making a dry path through the Red Sea for them to cross over to freedom (Exod. 1–15).

These men of faith—Abraham, Isaac, Jacob, Joseph, and Moses—each had an assignment from God. They fulfilled their purpose *with* God. Their obedience flowed from this relationship of trust, and blessings flowed from that obedience—blessings for them personally as well as countless others. Through Joseph, God rescued all of Egypt from starvation. Through Moses, God rescued all of His people from slavery. Through Abraham's offspring—Jesus Christ—God rescues all of us from sin.

The same God who called the patriarchs of our faith calls you. Will you respond to His invitation and His plan for your life?

God has chosen you and placed you exactly where you are for a good reason and to fulfill His good purpose for you. The patriarchs were weak, flawed people, just like us. The apostle Paul writes, "Remember, dear brothers and sisters, that few of you were wise in the world's eyes or powerful or wealthy when God called you. Instead, God chose things the world considers foolish in order to shame those who think they are wise" (1 Cor. 1:26–27). We do not need more money, education, free time, or popularity to answer His call. If we simply trust and obey, God will fulfill our purpose through us. You can start right now. **Love and obey God, love others, and make disciples (start by sharing God's Story) wherever you are, as only you can.**

Let the Bible Speak:
Isaiah 43:1–21 (Optional: Genesis 12:1–7)

Let Your Mind Think:
1. Where do you think God is leading you today? Are you willing to follow God as Abraham did? God may lead you across the world to do mission work, or He may lead you across the road to speak to a neighbor. Will you go?

2. How can you trust God to work everything—even evil—for good? Have you seen Him bring good from evil in your own life as Joseph did?

3. Are you willing to trust God with your weakness like Moses did? Why do you think God's power works best in weakness (2 Cor. 12:9)?

Let Your Soul Pray:
Father, help me fulfill Your purpose in my generation (Acts 13:36). Help me bring You glory by completing the work You have given me to do (John 17:4). Replace my fear with courage. Replace my doubt with faith. Replace my insecurity with confidence in You. May Your will be done and Your name be glorified in my life . . . In Jesus's name, amen.

Let Your Heart Obey:
(What is God leading you to know, value, or do?)

Represent Jesus Christ as His Ambassador

*So we are Christ's ambassadors; God is making
his appeal through us. We speak for Christ
when we plead, "Come back to God!"*
2 Corinthians 5:20

There is a trap to watch for on our faith journey—a dangerous pit of lies. The enemy may tell you what you do defines you or you need to earn God's love. Nothing could be further from the truth. When you put your faith in Christ, you become one with Christ, created to fulfill your purpose with Him. You work from a position of already being accepted rather than working to earn acceptance. Your identity in Jesus as a forgiven child of God is secure (John 10:28). And when you embrace the truth that God's grace is sufficient for you (2 Cor. 12:9), you want others to experience God's unconditional love too: **Your new identity in Jesus compels you to make known God's identity to the world**.

Before Jesus returned to heaven, He entrusted His mission to us—His **disciples**—to make more disciples. This mission, called the **Great Commission**, is so important that it is mentioned five times in five different books of the Bible.[1] In fact, it is tied to our new identity:

> **Disciple:**
> A believing learner or follower who becomes attached to their teacher in doctrine and conduct of life.

---

1   Matt. 28:19–20; Mark 16:15; Luke 24:47; John 20:21; Acts 1:8. More details are included later on fulfilling the Great Commission.

Therefore, if anyone is in Christ, the new creation has come: The old has gone, the new is here! All this is from God, who reconciled us to himself through Christ and gave us the ministry of reconciliation: that God was reconciling the world to himself in Christ, not counting people's sins against them. And he has committed to us the message of reconciliation. We are therefore Christ's ambassadors, as though God were making his appeal through us. We implore you on Christ's behalf: Be reconciled to God. (2 Cor. 5:17–20 NIV)

No matter what you have done or what has been done to you, you are made new in Christ and sent into the world on a mission. You have become a citizen of heaven (Phil. 3:20), and you are now an ambassador of God's kingdom here on earth. Like Joseph and Moses, you represent God in a foreign land.

To represent any kingdom well, we need to know it well so that we can represent it with integrity. We can start by knowing what God's kingdom is not; it is not an earthly kingdom (John 18:36) or a political kingdom (Mark 12:13–17) meant to replace our current systems of government. We need to still obey the rule of law unless it violates God's law (Rom. 13:1). Jesus told His disciples to pay taxes (Matt. 22:21). He never pursued political power. Quite the opposite—He fled when a crowd tried to make Him king by force (John 6:15). But Jesus did exercise spiritual power. As Jesus's ambassadors, **we are vessels of His power** to make a real, positive impact on the spiritual heart of society. We can protect life and promote justice with God's help and guidance. Motivated by love, we represent Him well.

How do we do this? We start by remembering that the God we serve is unbelievably kind, good, and brave. Throughout history, many people have died to save their kings, but our King died to save us.

> ### The Great Commission
> Jesus came and told his disciples, "I have been given all authority in heaven and on earth. Therefore, go and make disciples of all the nations, baptizing them in the name of the Father and the Son and the Holy Spirit. Teach these new disciples to obey all the commands I have given you. And be sure of this: I am with you always, even to the end of the age."
>
> Matthew 28:18–20

Before He called us to represent Him, He represented us by suffering the penalty for our sins. "'He himself bore our sins' in his body on the cross, so that we might die to sins and live for righteousness" (1 Pet. 2:24 NIV). Because He loves us, we love Him and want to represent Him well. As Jesus's ambassadors, we show the world that in God's kingdom

- love (not hate) rules;
- forgiveness (not revenge) heals;
- humility (not pride) reaps blessing; and
- grace (not performance) reigns.

As Jesus's ambassadors, we represent His wisdom. God's wisdom seems strange, even foolish, to the world (1 Cor. 1:20–25). But when we follow God by faith, the world will notice the results: "Wisdom is shown to be right by the lives of those who follow it" (Luke 7:35). Sometimes even unbelievers live by biblical principles without realizing it. Truth is truth regardless of whether someone believes God's Word. God's Word calls us to point people to the source of all wisdom and speak God's truth "in love" (Eph. 4:15). The most brilliant minds can find answers to their most profound questions in God's Word.[1]

We represent Jesus's love. By loving and serving others in practical ways, we spread God's love to a love-starved world. God's love flows through us to others (John 15:12). We love not "with words or speech but with actions and in truth" (1 John 3:18 NIV). We do not just wish people well; we meet their physical needs (James 2:16). Jesus takes all acts of love personally. When we serve others, we serve Him too:

"'For I was hungry, and you fed me. I was thirsty, and you gave me a drink. I was a stranger, and you invited me into your home. I was naked, and you gave me clothing. I was sick, and you cared for me. I was in prison, and you visited me.'

"Then these righteous ones will reply, 'Lord, when did we ever see you hungry and feed you? Or thirsty and give you something to drink?

---

1 Find answers to commonly asked Bible questions at GotQuestions.org.

Or a stranger and show you hospitality? Or naked and give you clothing? When did we ever see you sick or in prison and visit you?'

"And the King will say, 'I tell you the truth, when you did it to one of the least of these my brothers and sisters, you were doing it to me!'" (Matt. 25:35–40)

Our tangible expressions of love make the invisible God visible. "No one has ever seen God. But if we love each other, God lives in us, and his love is brought to full expression in us" (1 John 4:12). God's kingdom is all about real love—not only a feeling but also an action. God's kingdom is about the kind of love that focuses on others and then does something about it.

Even the laws of God's kingdom flow out of His great love for us. In the **Great Commandment**, our King teaches that we are to love God with everything—our heart, soul, mind, and strength. And, we are to love others as we love ourselves (Mark 12:29–31). The Ten Commandments provide specific guidelines on how to do that. The first four show us how to love God (Exod. 20:1–11), and the last six show us how to love others (Exod. 20:12–17). (When God says, "Do not . . ." He is saying, "Do not harm yourself or others.") When we start with a genuine love of God, we can then pour that love into our relationships. That is how we invite others into God's kingdom to experience God's love *personally*. "We are Christ's ambassadors; God is making his appeal through us. We speak for Christ when we plead, 'Come back to God!'" (2 Cor. 5:20).

> **The Great Commandment:**
> Jesus replied, "The most important commandment is this: 'Listen, O Israel! The LORD our God is the one and only LORD. And you must love the LORD your God with all your heart, all your soul, all your mind, and all your strength.' The second is equally important: 'Love your neighbor as yourself.' No other commandment is greater than these."
>
> Mark 12:29–31

Allow others to experience God's power, wisdom, and love through you.

Let the Bible Speak:
2 Corinthians 5 (Optional: Exodus 20:1–17)

Let Your Mind Think:
1. How does knowing you are an ambassador change the way you see your life?

2. Reread the Great Commission (Matt. 28:18–20). List the commands of Jesus. What promise did Jesus give the disciples?

3. How can you share God's love with someone today? Can you share food with a sick friend, smile and greet a lonely child, or encourage a weary soul?

Let Your Soul Pray:
Jesus, thank You for my mission as Your ambassador. What a joy it is to share the love You lavish on me! Help me clearly represent Your love to this love-starved world. Your Word says that You draw us to Yourself with unfailing love (Jer. 31:3). Please draw lost people to Yourself as I share Your love with them . . . In Jesus's name, amen.

Let Your Heart Obey:
(What is God leading you to know, value, or do?)

Look Down to Disciple Generations

Let each generation tell its children of your
mighty acts; let them proclaim your power.
Psalm 145:4

Let's return to the story of Moses and the Israelites. After a massive display of God's power, Pharaoh released the Israelites from the bonds of Egyptian slavery. Soon after their departure, he changed his mind, and the Egyptian cavalry pursued them. Backed against the Red Sea, the nearly two million Israelites panicked. They thought they were trapped, until God miraculously split the sea and provided dry passage. God then closed the walls of the water on top of the horsemen and war chariots to protect His chosen people (Exod. 14).

The journey to the land God promised should have taken them roughly fourteen days. Instead, it took them forty years. Only a few days after their rescue, they complained, "We are thirsty! We are hungry!" They even wished to be back in Egypt (Exod. 15–16). When God met their daily needs in the most astonishing sudden appearance of divine food (called manna), the people still complained. They forgot who God was. They forgot His love and kindness. They believed Satan's ancient lie that God was withholding good, tricking them, and leading them to failure (Gen. 3:1–5). Doubt and fear paralyzed them, and they refused to go into the Promised Land (Num. 13–14). So, they lost the privilege and had to wander in the wilderness for four decades. **Forgetting is dangerous.**

When the time came for their children to enter the Promised Land, **God protected the Israelites from their forgetfulness** (Josh. 3–4). He parted waters again, this time the Jordan River, which was at its dangerous flood stage. After the Israelites crossed the Jordan on dry land, God instructed them to build a memorial of twelve stones chosen from the middle of the river. Joshua explained the purpose of this stone memorial:

> He said to the Israelites, "In the future when your descendants ask their parents, 'What do these stones mean?' tell them, 'Israel crossed the Jordan on dry ground.' For the LORD your God dried up the Jordan before you until you had crossed over. The LORD your God did to the Jordan what he had done to the Red Sea when he dried it up before us until we had crossed over. He did this so that all the peoples of the earth might know that the hand of the LORD is powerful and so that you might always fear the LORD your God." (Josh. 4:21–24 NIV)

God knew hard times were ahead and His people may feel hopeless. His loving solution was not to reprimand them for their lack of faith but to remind them why they could trust Him. The twelve stacked rocks were a visual reminder of God's faithfulness for all people for all times. No more forgetting who God is or what He has done. No more questioning God's goodness and love, but remembering His total trustworthiness. In another way, this stone memorial helps us today fulfill our purpose. If we look closely at the passage, the memorial was for three groups of people:

1. **All future generations**.
   "In the future when your descendants ask their parents . . . tell them" (Josh. 4:21–22 NIV). Every person decides whether to love God or reject Him (Josh. 24:15). A mother's faith does not save her children. Faith is personal, and every person in every generation faces the same choice. That's why God instructed believers to teach their faith to the next generation (Deut. 6:7). And the most effective way to do that is to model authentic faith. Jesus instructed us to teach obedience to

all He commanded, not just to teach what He commanded (Matt. 28:20).

2. **All nations.**

   "*He did this so that all the peoples of the earth might know that the hand of the* LORD *is powerful*" (Josh. 4:24 NIV). As His ambassadors, we share God's love with all people, whether they live across the road or halfway around the world (Acts 1:8). God does not place boundaries on His love. So, we do not place boundaries on how, where, or whom God chooses to pour out His love. Tomorrow, we'll learn how we reach our neighbors and nations.

3. **All believers**.

   "*. . . that you might always fear the* LORD *your God*" (Josh. 4:24 NIV). God desires that we love Him with genuine affection and respect Him with inward awe and wonder. From a healthy and reverent relationship with God, we "fear" to grieve Him ever. Out of heartfelt gratitude, we adore and obey Him. On Day 19, we'll learn more about how we glorify God.

So even today, these memorial stones of the ancient Israelites can show us *how* to live our purpose to love and obey God, love everyone, and make disciples. An easy way to remember our change *in* position is to change *our* perspective: look down, look out, and look up. We *look down* to disciple the next generation, *look out* to reach our neighbors and nations, and *look up* to glorify God.

Today, let's learn how we can take steps to disciple the next generation. From the beginning, God made this a priority because each individual has a choice to trust Him. He specifically chose Abraham because he would instruct the next generation (Gen. 18:19 NIV). Even if you have not had a child of your own, God will give you *spiritual* children to nurture. Disciple and love them so that they become like your own children. The apostle Paul did not have biological children, but he called the many believers he mentored (like Timothy and Titus) his "children." Paul knew firsthand that people without families have the freedom to invest in many lives (1 Cor. 7:32–34).

Most people think discipling others is complicated, but look at the apostles' examples. They discipled believers by visiting people, writing letters, and praying for them. We can do that too. The best way to mentor others is by giving them your time. Meeting weekly for encouragement and loving accountability is powerful and effective– for your growth as well. (See "Weekly Gatherings" as an example.)

You do not need to be an expert before discipling others. Simply read a passage of Scripture together and answer questions. Share what you are learning, but do so humbly and gently (not with pride or bossiness). If you can't answer a question, it's okay to admit you don't know. Look up passages of Scripture and ask the Holy Spirit to reveal His wisdom. While sharing wisdom is important, it is equally important to share encouragement. Cheer others on as they walk with God. One of the best ways to help someone is by sharing your struggles. Talk about how God has healed your heart and answered your prayers.

To share our stories, we need to remember how God has worked in and through our lives. But remembering can be hard. We tend to

---

Weekly Gatherings

Whether connecting on the phone, online, or in-person, weekly gatherings are effective for spiritual growth. Consider using this simple agenda for each meeting:

1. **Past**—What are you grateful for from this past week? What is a concern? Each person shares briefly. One person prays and invites God to lead this time together. Then, review the goals set from the prior week to lovingly hold each other accountable.

2. **Present**—What is God teaching you today? Read a passage of Scripture together twice and answer the following questions from the passage:

    a. What do we learn about God?

    b. What do we learn about people? Good? Bad?

    c. What does God want us to know, value, or do?

3. **Future**—How can we act on what we learned today? Each person sets goals. End with prayer.

(See Appendix for Outline)

forget about God's love lavished on us in Jesus. Instead, we may dwell on unmet wants or unanswered prayers. God tells us repeatedly to remember—like He did with the Israelites. "Remember the things I have done in the past. For I alone am God!" (Isa. 46:9). **Jesus knew we'd struggle to remember. That's why He lovingly commanded us to observe a memorial—Communion, also called the Lord's Supper.** When we take Communion, the wine (or juice) reminds us of Jesus's blood, which was poured out for us. The bread reminds us of Jesus's body, which was broken for us (Luke 22:17-20; 1 Cor. 11:23-26). Although Communion is only for believers (1 Cor. 11:27), when unbelievers see and ask about this practice, we have an opportunity to explain Jesus's sacrifice for them, too.

You can create a family treasure for your children by creating your own "memorial stones." Keep a faith journal or display symbols that remind you of God's faithfulness in your life. These memorials will help you weave faith lessons into everyday conversations with the next generation. Those unplanned, daily conversations—"when you are at home and when you are on the road, when you are going to bed and when you are getting up" (Deut. 6:7)—are often when the greatest spiritual insights are shared. Faith is passed down in continual dialogue and lived out each day in our relationships with one another (1 Thess. 2:8). The next generation needs the knowledge of God more than anything else we can give them.

The most convincing memorial of God's power is your own changed life.

Let the Bible Speak:

Deuteronomy 6:1–7 (Optional: Psalm 145)

Let Your Mind Think:

1. We are to teach others to *obey* all Jesus commanded (Matt. 28:20). What is essential for us to keep in mind when we teach?

2. How has God worked in your life? Create a "memorial list" of events or answered prayers that remind you of God's faithfulness in your life.

3. Weekly gatherings are essential for growth, encouragement, and accountability. If you are not a part of a weekly gathering, pray to find one or start a group. Who could you mentor?

Let Your Soul Pray:

Father, You call to every generation (Isa. 41:4). Your Word says, "Future generations will be told about the Lord. They will proclaim his righteousness, declaring to a people yet unborn: He has done it!" (Ps. 22:30–31 NIV). As I look down to the next generation, show me people to mentor. Help me pass on my knowledge of You and live out true faith before them . . . In Jesus's name, amen.

Let Your Heart Obey:

(What is God leading you to know, value, or do?)

DAY

18

Look Out to Reach Neighbors and Nations

Therefore go and make disciples of all nations, baptizing them in the name of the Father and of the Son and of the Holy Spirit, and teaching them to obey everything I have commanded you.
Matthew 28:19–20 NIV

God had a bigger plan for the stone memorial than only the Israelites and their descendants remembering His goodness. People in the surrounding nations noticed the memorial too. That pile of twelve stones was a painful reminder of their gods' inferiority. Israel's God had parted both the Red Sea and the Jordan River, "so all the nations of the earth might know that the Lord's hand is powerful" (Josh. 4:24). When God dried up the Jordan River at flood stage, He disgraced the river god that the local people worshiped. In that moment, God demonstrated to the nations, "I am God, and there is no other; I am God, and there is none like me" (Isa. 46:9 NIV). "For great is the Lord, and greatly to be praised; he is to be feared above all gods" (Ps. 96:4 ESV). The one true God put all false gods to shame when He delivered His people.

As King Jesus's ambassadors, we proclaim an even more amazing deliverance: deliverance from sin (Days 3 and 4). God's power in parting waters was nothing compared to the power God "exerted when he raised Christ from the dead" (Eph. 1:20 NIV). Making a way for people to cross a river is miraculous. Making a way for sinful people to return to God is even more incredible. But God did it, and not just for a single nation, but for *all* nations, even nations who worship false gods. Because God sacrificed His Son for all nations, we tell all nations about His Son's sacrifice.

We tell the world until no place is left that has not heard (Matt. 24:14). "For God so loved *the world* that he gave his one and only Son" (John 3:16 NIV, emphasis added). **Jesus came for the whole world, not just Israel. God told Jesus**, "It is too small a thing for you to be my servant to restore the tribes of Jacob . . . I will also make you a light for the Gentiles, that my salvation may reach to the ends of the earth" (Isa. 49:6 NIV). Jesus came to rescue all people, so we all—both men and women—go to all people. We go regardless of nationality, gender, or social class. We are all God's image-bearers, all sinners in need of grace. We cannot allow prejudice, shame, or social discomfort to keep us from telling anyone about Christ. Think of the most difficult people to love, the people most different from you. Jesus loves them just as much as He loves you. He died for them and longs to rescue them. *So tell them.* How? You *listen, learn,* and *love.*

LISTEN

Listen for the *Holy Spirit* to lead you. You can pray:

- Lord, give me an opportunity to share Your love with _____. Open their heart. Give me Your words (Luke 12:12).
- Lord, is there anyone searching for You near me? Help us connect.

Listen for *needs.*

- Life transitions are often moments in people's lives when they are searching for guidance and are ready to hear God's True Story.
- During trials, people are often more aware of their need for God. Listen for hardship, hurt, stress, worry, big decisions, or anxiety.

LEARN

You listened, and the Holy Spirit prompted you to share Jesus's love. Now what should you do? Ask questions. Learn more about their story and ask permission to share your story.

1. Learn *their* story, including what they believe.

The most effective way to understand someone, or to start spiritual conversations, is to ask questions. Take time to listen to the responses you receive. Don't correct what they say when they respond. Listening well is a form of loving well. Ask one or more of the following questions:

- Do you have any spiritual beliefs?
- Do you believe in God?
  - If yes, ask, "Who is God to you?"
  - If no, ask, "Has there ever been a time when you thought there might be a God?" (Even if they say no, you can ask the next question to continue the conversation in a spiritual direction.)
- Who do you think Jesus is? Factual versus relational answers can give insight into a person's spiritual condition ("Jesus is God's Son" is different from "Jesus is *my* God").
- Has anyone shared the good news of Jesus with you before?
- Have you had a desire to go to heaven? Do you know how to get there?

2. Listen for a connection and ask to share *your* story.

Listen for a way you can connect your story to their story. Your purpose is not to talk about yourself or make the conversation about you. Your purpose is to find a way to say, "I understand" or "I thought that way, too." Then, share how your life changed when someone shared God's Story with you.

You can ask one of the following permission questions to determine whether to continue:

- May I share some good news that changed my life?
- Can I share how I found a personal relationship with God?
- For someone experiencing difficulties, ask, "Can I share with you something that got me through a difficult time in my life?"

If you do not receive permission to continue, do not push the discussion. Just encourage them and let them know you're available should they want to

Sharing Your Story in Seconds

Do you know how to share your God story (also called your testimony)?

Describe your life in two words before following Jesus, then describe your life in two words or a phrase afterward. Example:

"There was a time in my life when I was [fearful] and life felt [hopeless].

Then I was forgiven by Jesus and chose to follow Him. My life changed.

Now I have [peace] and [purpose] in my life. Best of all, I have a friendship with God. Do you have a story like that?

Source: #NoPlaceLeft

talk in the future. You have not failed; you have done what God called you to do. Pray silently for that person and wait for a time when your words might be welcome. Take a deep breath and remember it's God's responsibility to draw them to Him (John 6:44). Your responsibility is to be His witness.

LOVE

Sharing your story leads to sharing God's Story—the greatest love story. The most natural way of doing this is by sharing your story and God's Story *together*. God gave you a unique story that can help others, so do not be afraid to tell it. Your story might include healing from abuse, joy in suffering, or an awakening to God's purposes for you. As you share your story and Jesus's story of salvation, remember to include four essential components. The gospel message is similar to the four parts of God's Story we learned in Week 1. To remember them easily, let's think of it as a recipe. **Gospel Bread** requires four ingredients for the full meaning of the message to come out just right. Let's take a closer look at each ingredient:

1. **God loves us:** Share how we were created by God to glorify Him and experience His perfect love. God desires that we know Him and have a close relationship with Him—now and forever. "For God so loved the world, that he gave his only Son, that whoever believes in Him should not perish but have eternal life" (John 3:16 ESV).

2. **Sin separates us:** Share how sin broke our loving relationship with God. Sin means turning from God's will in our attitude or actions. Living life our own way, rather than God's way, separates us from Him and results in death (Isa. 59:2; Rom. 6:23). No one is without sin. "All have sinned and fall short of the glory of God" (Rom. 3:23 ESV).

3. **Jesus saves us:** Share how God loves us so much that He did not want us to remain separated from His love. God sent His only Son, Jesus, to save us from the penalty of sin and give us new, eternal life. "But God showed his great love for us by sending Christ to die for us while we were still sinners" (Rom. 5:8). Salvation is by God's grace through Jesus Christ, not our efforts or good works (Eph. 2:8-9).

4. **Repentance and faith change us:** Share that when we turn from our sins and trust Jesus alone as the Forgiver and life Leader, He makes us new (2 Cor. 5:17). God restores our relationship with Him now, and one day we'll be with Him in heaven—our perfect home. "If you openly declare that Jesus is Lord and believe in your heart that God raised him from the dead, you will be saved. For it is by believing in your heart that you are made right with God, and it is by openly declaring your faith that you are saved" (Rom. 10:9-10). Faith and repentance go together.

It's similar to the four-part framework of God's Story in Week 1. The most significant difference you may have noticed was the fourth ingredient. Repentance and faith are the choice to receive Jesus's free gift of salvation, which leads to new life (re-creation). Like making bread without flour, the gospel without these four parts comes out wrong. (Think about removing one element to see how it affects the message.) The Holy Spirit may lead you to share Jesus's message in different ways with different people in different places. But no matter how you share it, include all ingredients. (Remember the key words: *love, sin, Jesus, repentance and faith*.)

Sharing Jesus's message takes courage. The first few times you have a gospel conversation may seem a little uncomfortable, but it gets easier each time you introduce others to Jesus. If sharing your faith scares you, remember the Israelites. They stepped into a raging river to cross it *before* God made a dry path through it. God met their step of faith, and He will do the same for you. So do not believe the lie that people do not want to hear about Jesus. With many world religions being fear-driven, the love-driven message of Jesus is truly good news—the best news—you can share with a hurting world.

> **Tools to Share Your Faith**
> In the appendix, you'll find tools called **3 Circles** and **Listen, Learn, Love, Lord** to help you with these steps. Similar versions of these tools are used worldwide. (Download digital copies at allinmin.org.)

In heaven, we will see a "vast crowd, too great to count, from every nation and tribe and people and language, standing in front of the throne and before the Lamb . . . shouting with a great roar, 'Salvation comes from our God who sits on the throne and from the Lamb!'" (Rev. 7:9–10). Let's invite as many people as we can to gather with us on that day.

DAY 18

Let the Bible Speak:
Romans 10:9–17 (Optional: 1 Peter 3:15)

Let Your Mind Think:

1. Jesus came for all. Is there any person or group of people you find hard to love? Take a moment to confess and repent from this prejudice. How can you show them God's love?

2. Complete the Listen, Learn, Love, Lord tool found in the appendix to prepare and practice sharing Jesus with others. Review this tool in your weekly gatherings for accountability, practice, and prayer.

3. Practice sharing your story along with God's Story three or more times with a friend.

Let Your Soul Pray:
Father, You are the Creator of the ends of the earth. You want to rescue all nations. Your Word says, "The harvest is great, but the workers are few. So pray to the Lord who is in charge of the harvest; ask him to send more workers into his fields" (Matt. 9:37–38). Please send out more workers to share Your love, starting with me. Show me where to go and what to say . . . In Jesus's name, amen.

Let Your Heart Obey:
(What is God leading you to know, value, or do?)

Look Up to Glorify God

I give thanks to you, O Lord my God, with my whole
heart, and I will glorify your name forever.
Psalm 86:12 ESV

Today we will discover the greatest purpose of all, the final purpose
of the Israelites' memorial stones, the purpose that motivates us to
reach generations, neighbors, and nations,
the purpose of all creation,
the purpose of all creatures, and
the purpose of Christ Jesus Himself:
To Glorify God.

As we learned at the beginning of this faith journey, **God's Story
and your story are all about God's *glory***. God's devotion to His glory
may sound arrogant, selfish, or even tyrannical—but it is not. God is
not one of us; His ways are higher than our ways, and His thoughts
are higher than our thoughts (Isa. 55:9). When we are devoted to
ourselves first, we are arrogant, but when God is devoted to Himself
first, He is right. He is the furthest thing from a tyrant.

- A tyrant takes, but God gives (Acts 17:25).
- A tyrant demands work, but God offers rest (Matt. 11:28).
- A tyrant clings to power, but God gave up His power (Phil.
  2:5–11).
- A tyrant kills his enemies, but God (in the human form of
  Jesus) died to save His enemies (Rom. 5:10).

God is not a tyrant. That is a lie from the enemy who has lied about God from the beginning. He tells us lies that are similar to this. Please do not believe them. God does not trick us, manipulate us, keep good things from us, or take advantage of us (Num. 23:19).

When we look up to glorify God, we do not bow to a tyrant; we delight in a kind Father. We celebrate His love, stand in awe of His power, and rest in His peace. He is so good and so worthy of our praise. Let's take a moment to think deeply about who the one true God is. **Read these verses out loud** to guide your thinking. Below them, you will find space to add your favorite biblical descriptions of God.

My God is . . .

- the Alpha and the Omega, the first and the last, the beginning and the end (Rev. 22:13 ESV).

- the compassionate and gracious God, slow to anger, abounding in love and faithfulness (Exod. 34:6 NIV).

- God of gods and Lord of lords, the great, the mighty, and the awesome God (Deut. 10:17 ESV).

- Wonderful Counselor, Mighty God, Everlasting Father, Prince of Peace (Isa. 9:6 ESV).

-

-

-

Do you feel humbled? Grateful? Amazed? Take a moment to sit quietly and worship God. He is the only one worthy of all our praise (Deut. 10:21). He is everything good, lovely, wise, pure, beautiful, heroic, and true. As the psalmist wrote, "You are my Lord; apart from you I have no good thing" (Ps. 16:2 NIV).

Why do we glorify God? God created us for His own glory (Isa. 43:7). He alone is worthy of our praise (Ps. 145:3).

How do we glorify God? We glorify God by loving Him, praising Him, obeying Him, and *fearing Him.*

We may wonder how fearing God glorifies Him. The word **fear** in the Bible has many meanings, but in this context *fear* means respect and awe of God's person, power, and position. How can we love someone we fear or fear someone we love? Both loving God and fearing Him work together.

> **Fear of God:**
> Respect and awe of God's person, power, and position. With authentic affection for God, believers "fear" to grieve Him.

Consider the result when we do one without the other. Think through what might happen if we fear God but do not love Him. We will keep our distance. We will do what God requires, but we might not seek a relationship. When we hear that God is majestic in holiness and awesome in deeds (Exod. 15:11), we might feel unworthy. We know that God's position allows Him to judge sin, so we might worry about what He will do if we make a mistake.

We see in the pages of Scripture that God is not glorified in fear without love. A teacher of the law confronts Jesus with the ultimate question: "What is the most important commandment?" Jewish law contained an additional 613 commandments[1] that were added to the Ten Commandments over time, and this teacher of the law was probably exhausted trying to keep them all. He feared God, but did he love Him? Consider Jesus's answer:

---

1 "The number 613 was first given in the third century CE by Rabbi Simlai, who divided the 613 mitzvot into 248 positive commandments (what to do) and 365 negative commandments (what not to do). Since this figure was first announced, many have undertaken to enumerate the 613 commandments. Easily the one with the most lasting significance is the 12th-century list by Maimonides in his Book of the Commandments." "Mitzvot," ReligionFacts.com, June 22, 2017, www.religionfacts.com/mitzvot.

"The most important one," answered Jesus, "is this: 'Hear, O Israel: The Lord our God, the Lord is one. Love the Lord your God with all your heart and with all your soul and with all your mind and with all your strength.'" (Mark 12:29–30 NIV)

Although this God-fearing teacher kept the law, Jesus told him loving God was most important. He said this because fear without love lacks relationship. **Remember the purpose of loving and fearing God is not to get into heaven but to get into a relationship with your heavenly Father**. Fear of an eternity apart from God may have led you to follow Jesus. But as you receive Him and know Him, love grows and fear changes. No longer are you afraid of God because perfect love casts out fear (1 John 4:18). Instead, a reverential fear of God wells up inside, causing you to love and adore God with all you are.

Let's consider what happens if we love God but do not fear Him: We treat God casually, with little regard to His position or His commands and dismiss the consequences of sinful choices. We might take Him for granted. Often we see this in human relationships. We sometimes treat those whom we love most worse than we treat strangers.

This explains why the last purpose of the Israelites' memorial stones was "so you might fear the LORD your God forever" (Josh. 4:24). God wanted a right relationship with His chosen people and with the generations that came after them. Great blessings—treasures—were promised to those who fear God (Isa. 33:6) both then and now:

- **Fearing God protects us from people-pleasing**. Jesus focused His disciples on fearing God rather than fearing other people (Matt. 10:28). Fearing God can save you from the dangerous trap of seeking approval or praise from people instead of glory for God (Prov. 29:25; John 5:44).
- **Fearing God makes us brave**. Other fears fade when we truly fear God (Matt. 10:28; Heb. 13:6).
- **Fearing God makes us wise**. "The fear of the LORD is the beginning of wisdom" (Prov. 9:10 NIV).

- **Fearing God protects us from sin**. If we fear God, we will hate sin because it violates His nature and hinders our relationship with Him. When we fear God, we flee from sin (Prov. 16:6). Fearing God and fleeing from sin will protect us from sin's dangerous consequences and may even lengthen our lives (Prov. 10:27).

But fearing God, revering Him, does not always come naturally to us. Our sin nature leads us to ignore God's glory and inflate our own. So what steps can we take to develop a loving fear of God?

- **Ask God for help**. Ask Him to make you reverent by teaching you His ways (Ps. 86:11).
- **Think deeply about God's Word**, especially verses, like the ones listed above, that describe His character. The revelation of God in His Word should make us tremble (Ps. 119:120).
- **Enjoy the beauty and power of creation**. Read Psalm 19 and observe how the glory of God in creation moves our hearts to fear Him.[1]
- **Remember God's mighty works**. Like the Israelites, remember all God has done for you. Think about His mighty works—in creation, in human history, and in your own life—every day (Ps. 77:11–12).

Loving God and fearing God work powerfully together to glorify and obey God. Jesus said, "Whoever has my commands and keeps them is the one who loves me. The one who loves me will be loved by my Father, and I too will love them and show myself to them" (John 14:21 NIV). As we keep God's commands to reach generations, neighbors, and nations with God's love . . .

God's glory is our motivation,
God's glory is our message,
God's glory is our goal, and
God's glory is our reward!

---

1 For a humbling look at the majesty of God in the universe, read God's response to Job describing the design and administration of creation (Job 38–42).

DAY 19

Let the Bible Speak:
Psalm 19 (Optional: Psalm 128)

Let Your Mind Think:
1. Read Psalm 19 and notice where and when God's glory is revealed. Fearing God is pure (v. 9) and the right response to His glory. Why do you think God deserves glory?

2. Why is it important to love God and to fear Him?

3. How does loving and fearing God motivate you to fulfill your purposes?

Let Your Soul Pray:
Lord, Jesus cried out to You, "Father, glorify your name!" (John 12:28 NIV). I, too, want to glorify You. Teach me to love You with reverence and to do Your work . . . in Your strength . . . for Your glory alone. "Be exalted, O God, above the heavens! Let your glory be over all the earth!" (Ps. 108:5 ESV) . . . In Jesus's name, amen.

Let Your Heart Obey:
(What is God leading you to know, value, or do?)

Glorify God in Worship

All the nations you have made shall come and worship
before you, O Lord, and shall glorify your name.
Psalm 86:9 ESV

If you've spent any time at a church service, you've probably experienced a call to worship. Someone announces, "Come, let us worship the Lord." In gatherings around the world, the music begins, and everyone stands to sing together. While musical worship involves instruments and singing, there is much more taking place. It's not a warm-up to the sermon. It's not a time to be entertained. We unite our hearts and voices as an offering of praise for God's infinite worth. But worship is more than only *musical* worship. It's more than singing a song. When we worship God, we bring ourselves to God. All that we are. All that we do. We offer it—all—to God to glorify Him.

Yesterday we learned how loving and fearing God work together to glorify Him. **This combined loving fear of God—our reverent awe and deep love for Him—overflows in worship**. On Day 9, we learned:

- Worship is the admiration of whatever rules our hearts.
- Worship is adoring who God is and what God has done.
- Worship is offering ourselves to God. All things—singing, speaking, working, playing, serving, and even suffering—become acts of worship when we do them to glorify God.
- Worship is reserved for God alone.

Now that we have defined worship, let's describe what worship–*God-glorifying* worship–looks like in practice. How can you glorify God in worship?

Worship passionately. Our worship flows from our intimate relationship with God, embracing both Truth, what we know about Him, and Spirit–who enables us to fully delight in Him (John 4:23–24). The Bible invites us to praise God with joy and thanksgiving. But *when the Bible mentions worship*, the tone changes. "Come, let us worship and bow down. Let us kneel before the LORD our maker, for he is our God" (Ps. 95:6–7). Worship is often described with the act of kneeling or bowing, an external posture representing the internal heart shift of humility and surrender. We humble ourselves realizing who we are worshiping–the One of whom stars declare His glory. The One before whom mountains quake. The One in whose presence the earth trembles (Nah. 1:5). If all of nature worships passionately, so can we. Passionate, personal worship is a heartfelt acknowledgment of God as the rightful Lord of our lives.

Worship attentively. We can glorify God by ignoring or silencing distractions and directing all our attention on the One we worship. Close your eyes. Bow your head. Do what you need to do to focus on God. Invite the Holy Spirit to heighten your awareness of His presence. Learn to recognize His thoughts shaping your thoughts as you worship and read God's Word. Allow God to convict you, encourage you, and comfort you as you grow in your relationship with Him. "[Look] to Jesus, the founder and perfecter of our faith" (Heb. 12:2 ESV) so that you glorify God in worship.

Worship generously. We worship whatever rules our hearts, but we can influence what rules our hearts through our resources. "For where your treasure is, there your heart will be also" (Matt. 6:21 NIV). Giving is a privilege we embrace because we love the Lord and want to see His kingdom advance. "The point is this: whoever sows sparingly will also reap sparingly, and whoever sows bountifully will also reap bountifully. Each one must give as he has decided in his heart, not reluctantly or under compulsion, for God loves a cheerful giver" (2 Cor. 9:6–7 ESV).

God wants us to enjoy the good things He gives us, but He also commands us to use those resources to support those who preach His Word.[1] As we learned on Day 16, when we meet others' needs, we serve Jesus Himself (Matt. 25:40). Use your money to do good and help those in need (2 Cor. 8–9; 1 Tim. 6:17–19). But how much and how often? "On the first day of every week, each one of you should set aside a sum of money in keeping with your income" (1 Cor. 16:2 NIV). Give individually, regularly, and proportionally. Keep in mind that God owns it all (Pss. 24:1; 50:10).[2] **We are to be good stewards, responsible to Him for how we spend what He has entrusted to us**. "Give as freely as you have received!" (Matt. 10:8). God understands our circumstances and looks at the heart behind the giving.

Money is not our only resource. **We also have time to give and talents to share**. "Be rich in good works . . . generous and ready to share" (1 Tim. 6:18 ESV). As God's ambassador, spend your time investing in relationships. When we care for the sick, speak hope to weary souls, and share Jesus with others, we are giving in ways that build up God's kingdom.

Worship honestly. God knows us better than we know ourselves. He knows when you feel dry, apathetic, or even angry. Be honest with Him and express your feelings in prayer. (Read the book of Psalms for soul-stirring examples.) On our faith journey,

---

1   Matt. 10:10; Luke 10:7; 1 Cor. 9:6–14; and 1 Tim. 5:17–18.
2   Ron Blue, *Never Enough? Three Keys to Financial Contentment* (Nashville: B&H Publishing Group, 2017), 20.

Giving is a matter between you and God. He understands your circumstances and looks at the heart behind the giving. Jesus recognized the generosity of two worshipers: one gave little, and one gave much, but *both* gave sacrificially. The first, a poor widow, gave only a few pennies, but that was all she had to live on. Jesus noticed and praised her sacrificial gift (Luke 21:3–4). The second woman poured out an entire jar of extremely expensive perfume as an act of worship to her Deliverer (John 12:3–9). Some saw her generosity as an extravagant waste, but Jesus recognized the sacrificial heart behind her gift. **God does not focus on the size of your gift; He focuses on your heart.**

we will experience different seasons in life that affect our worship. Consider how you might worship God in the three seasons listed below:[1]

- **The Satisfying Season: Do you delight in God?** Are you absolutely satisfied with God and full of joy? Give thanks and rejoice in Him for this. "You satisfy me more than the richest feast. I will praise you with songs of joy" (Ps. 63:5). "I will rejoice in the LORD, I will be joyful in God my Savior" (Hab. 3:18 NIV).

- **The Longing Season: Do you desire God?** Do you long for Him but lack a deep sense of joy in His presence because your circumstances are consuming you? "As a deer pants for flowing streams, so pants my soul for you, O God. My soul thirsts for God, for the living God" (Ps. 42:1–2 ESV). Pray that God will fill you with joy in His presence (Ps. 16:11) so that you will delight in worshiping Him (Ps. 43:4).

- **The Lowest Season: Do you feel dry?** Do you feel spiritually barren, although you're repentant? Admitting your struggles and asking God for help is honest worship: "Then I realized that my heart was bitter, and I was all torn up inside. I was so foolish and ignorant—I must have seemed like a senseless animal to you" (Ps. 73:21–22). Ask God to rekindle your love for Him, reenergize your relationship with Him, and help you obey Him: "Restore to me the joy of your salvation, and make me willing to obey you" (Ps. 51:12).

---

1 Adapted from Dr. Michael Sharp and Dr. Mike Miller, "Worship Leadership" Intensive Class Notes: Three Stages of Worship, New Orleans: New Orleans Baptist Theological Seminary, May 2014.

What we focus on expands (Day 9).
Watch what consumes your thoughts so you do not waste your time, talents, and money on things that do not matter. You may end up worshiping those things instead of God. If you worship something, you become like it (Ps. 115:8 NIV). If you worship money, you will become greedy. If you worship beauty, you will become vain. So, stay away from idols (1 John 5:21).
Do not worship false gods (things as well as false teaching).

Worship together. When we find ourselves in the lowest season, we might be tempted to detach ourselves from others. Solitude and silence are good forms of worship. But extended isolation leaves us more vulnerable to the enemy's attacks. The exact opposite approach is the solution: worship together with believers. God gives us the local body of believers to gather together to worship Him and help each other. God instructs us to "consider how to stir up one another to love and good works, not neglecting to meet together, as is the habit of some, but encouraging one another" (Heb. 10:24–25 ESV). As we come together to worship God, we offer ourselves to God and each other. The early church beautifully modeled corporate worship, and the Lord added to their number (Acts 2:42–47). Active commitment to a local church is essential to our spiritual health and a high priority to Jesus.[1] "Christ loved the church and gave himself up for her" (Eph. 5:25 ESV). We are designed to worship together as a part of God's family—here and in heaven.

Friend, no matter what season of worship you are in today . . .

worship God passionately, withholding nothing;
worship God attentively, fixing your eyes on Jesus;
worship God generously, offering all you have to His service;
worship God honestly, expressing the true state of your heart;
worship God together, encouraging one another to love God, love everyone, and make disciples.

That is worship that glorifies God.

---

1 Read "How to Find a Good Church" on Day 12.

Let the Bible Speak:
Psalm 103 (Optional: Psalm 100)

Let Your Mind Think:

1. Do you worship passionately, attentively, generously, and honestly? Which of these is easiest for you? Hardest for you? Reflect on the reasons for your ease or difficulty.

2. Describe which season of worship you are in right now: Satisfying, Longing, or Lowest?

3. Are you worshiping with other believers as a part of a local church? If not, pray for God to lead you to a Bible-teaching church (Day 12) or start a weekly gathering (Day 17).

Let Your Soul Pray:
Father, as I worship You, make everything else—all the people around me, all the problems I face—fade away. Keep my eyes fixed on You, my heart loyal to You, and my resources devoted to You, for Your glory alone. . . In Jesus's name, amen.

Let Your Heart Obey:
(What is God leading you to know, value, or do?)

Worship God Through Pain

Why, my soul, are you downcast? Why so disturbed within me? Put your hope in God, for I will yet praise him, my Savior and my God.
Psalm 42:5–6 NIV

Worshiping can seem easy when life is calm and going well, but when life is hard, worshiping can be hard too. When we suffer, we may not feel the goodness of God. Sometimes, all we feel is pain. But that very pain makes the praise of suffering hearts pure because it displays a fierce loyalty to God—a loyalty to Him alone and not simply loyalty to what He can do for us. Worship given despite discomfort is often free of selfish motives, and it sends the enemy running.

Satan wars against worship. He was banished from heaven because he tried to steal God's glory, as if that were even possible. He has been retaliating ever since (Day 3). He continues to wage war on God's glory by trying to steal our worship. Suffering puts us on the front line of this battle for glory; the enemy tries to capitalize on our weakness (1 Pet. 5:8). He lies to us about God to keep us from worshiping (John 8:44). He questions God's goodness, slanders God's motives, and ignores God's glory (2 Cor. 4:4). "And he [Satan] knows the heart of love God has for the human race, so he wants to defeat God's purpose to turn them into joy-filled, great and good worshipers of Him. He wants to frustrate the great desire of God's heart."[1]

---

1   Tim Keller, *Walking with God through Pain and Suffering* (New York: Dutton, Published by the Penguin Group, 2013), 273.

Worship defeats darkness. When darkness overshadows you and evil breaks your heart, the last thing you may want to do is worship. But worshiping God is exactly what you should do.

You are telling God that you believe Him for who He says He is:

Your Protector (Ps. 91).
Your Comforter (2 Cor. 1:3–4).
Your Provider (Phil. 4:19).
Your Healer (Ps. 103:2–4).
Your Faithful and True Judge (Rev. 19:11).
Your Good Shepherd (John 10:11).
Your Lord and Your God (John 20:28).

If the enemy strangles you with anxiety, worship God by thanking Him, asking Him for help, and trusting Him with the outcome. Pray, "Jesus, You decide what is best," and surrender all your burdens to Him because He cares for you (1 Pet. 5:7). "Don't worry about anything; instead, *pray about everything*. Tell God what you need, and *thank him for all he has done*" (Phil. 4:6 ESV, emphasis added). **This verse holds the key to overcoming anxiety, worry, and stress—prayers of thanksgiving**. Gratitude reminds us of who God is and what He has done. The next verse continues, "Then you will experience God's peace, which exceeds anything we can understand" (v. 7). When we respond with worship, thankful for God's greatness, our problems seem smaller in comparison.

If the enemy smothers you with depression, worship God by lifting your voice to Him. Your focus will shift from yourself to the all-powerful, all-loving God. Trust God to lift you up out of darkness and exchange your "spirit of despair" for "a garment of praise" (Isa. 61:3 NIV). "He lifted me out of the pit of despair, out of the mud and the mire. He set my feet on solid ground and steadied me as I walked along" (Ps. 40:2). When you feel down, read through the book of Psalms. Highlight every verse that soothes your soul with its words of hope. Verses put our sorrows into words and wrap them up in God's love and faithfulness. **Worship declares the unshakable goodness of God, the victory He has already won** (1 Cor. 15:57).

Praising God through pain does not mean ignoring your pain. Praising in pain means you deal with pain by pouring it out to the One who knows you, loves you, and draws close to you. The psalms frequently swell with emotional outbursts. These can be negative as well as positive, but they are always directed toward God.

Being honest with God about our pain also helps us guard against any bitterness that tries to take root in our hearts (Heb. 12:15). There is a vast difference between bitterness, which curses God and those we deem responsible for our pain, and godly grief, which honors Him. Bitterness turns us *away* from God; godly grief turns us *toward* God. It is far better to cry out to God and tell Him everything than it is to turn away from Him. Turning away usually leads to a self-centered mindset and negative behaviors; we take matters into our own hands and perpetuate the bitterness. If you feel confused and hurt, it is okay to ask God, "Why?" Jesus did. On the cross, He cried out, "My God, my God, why have you abandoned me?" (Matt. 27:46).

Jesus asked questions, but He never questioned God's goodness. He knew His Father's will was for the best—even if that meant temporary suffering—and He never wavered in that trust. Down to His very last breath, He entrusted His pain to God (Luke 23:46).

If God seems silent, it does not mean He is absent. Worshiping through pain will lift your focus toward God and make you more aware of His presence. There is an intimacy with God experienced through suffering. "The Lord is close to the brokenhearted; he rescues those whose spirits are crushed" (Ps. 34:18). Praising God through pain draws us closer to Him and brings blessings that only come in those times when our faith is put to the test. Sin and the suffering it causes were never part of God's original plan. Yet, in His perfect love, He was willing to come to earth and experience the pain personally—suffering in our place to end it once and for all. When Christ returns, His victory over sin and suffering will be fully realized. Until then, God gives us the strength to endure—and even find joy (James 1:2)—in our present pain as we look forward to that day when He will take away our pain forever (Rev. 21:4).

Have you experienced loss? In what is believed to be the oldest book of the Bible, a man named Job lost all his possessions, his children, and his health, but Job still expressed his grief by bowing and praising God: "He fell to the ground in worship and said: 'Naked I came from my mother's womb, and naked I will depart. The LORD gave and the LORD has taken away; may the name of the LORD be praised'" (Job 1:20–21 NIV). Worshiping despite pain proved Job's loyalty to God.

Have you been betrayed? One of the twelve disciples, Judas, betrayed Jesus by handing Him over to people who would crucify Him. Jesus knew He would be betrayed, but He still praised God (Matt. 26:14–30). When a dear friend betrayed David, he prayed and told God about his feelings. He wrote, "If an enemy were insulting me, I could endure it; if a foe were rising against me, I could hide. But it is you, a man like myself, my companion, my close friend . . . As for me, I call to God, and the LORD saves me" (Ps. 55:12–13, 16 NIV). Worshiping despite betrayal demonstrated David's trust in God.

Are you persecuted? The apostle Paul suffered persecution, but Paul still praised God. Even while in chains, he wrote, "Rejoice in the Lord always; again I will say, rejoice" (Phil. 4:4 ESV). Worshiping despite persecution proved Paul's confidence in God.

Are you poor? God warned Habakkuk that poverty would soon afflict his people, but Habakkuk still praised God. "Though the fig tree does not bud and there are no grapes on the vines, though the olive crop fails and the fields produce no food, though there are no sheep in the pen and no cattle in the stalls, yet I will rejoice in the LORD, I will be joyful in God my Savior" (Hab. 3:17–18 NIV). Worshiping despite poverty proved Habakkuk's faith in God.

You are not alone in your pain and suffering. Many in past generations have praised God through pain (Heb. 11). Many in this generation worship through suffering too. Reach out to others who follow Jesus. Be careful not to isolate yourself; loneliness only opens the door to temptation and discouragement. When you suffer, stay connected to believing friends in your church family (Heb. 10:25). When God restores you, offer the comfort you received from Him to comfort others (2 Cor. 1:3–7).

Worship God through pain, and trust Him to bring you through your most difficult days. He is working, even if we do not see it or feel it. He is always worthy of your worship.

Let the Bible Speak:

Psalm 42 (Optional: Romans 8:18–39)

Let Your Mind Think:

1. Are you currently in pain or suffering? If you are, what does it mean to you to worship God through your pain? If not, how might a past experience with suffering have been different if you had worshiped God through it?

2. Answer Week 3 Discussion Questions.

Let Your Soul Pray:

Father, You see my suffering. You catch my tears and keep them in a bottle (Ps. 56:8). I bring You my pain. Help me worship You through suffering, knowing that You are my Healer, my Comforter, and my Deliverer. Deepen my friendships with other believers so that we can share the comfort we receive from You . . . In Jesus's name, amen.

Let Your Heart Obey:

(What is God leading you to know, value, or do?)

WEEK 3 DISCUSSION QUESTIONS:

**Review this week's lessons and answer the questions below.
Share your answers with your friends when you gather this week.**

1. Are you an ambassador for Jesus? What does that mean to you?

2. The biblical patriarchs shared our same purpose, but they each fulfilled it differently. What gifts, skills, or talents has God given you? Is He calling you to do any particular work or to reach any particular group of people? What are your next steps in fulfilling your specific purpose?

3. Jesus commands us to make disciples. Review and practice each step in the Listen, Learn, Love, Lord tool found in the appendix. (If you have not completed it, please do so now.) When can you share Jesus with those on your relationship map? Pray for opportunities. Practice telling your God story.

4. Read Matthew 6:19–21. Why do you think God tells us to store up treasure in heaven? How can you let go of earthly rewards and work for heavenly rewards instead?

PART II:

LIVING OUT YOUR STORY WITH GOD

The Bible's true stories inspire us as we learn about God's Story. We see God's rescue plan lived out through the fathers of the faith. We read how God parted the sea for Moses (Exod. 14) and the raging river for Joshua (Josh. 3). We discover how God sees Hagar and calls her by name (Gen. 16) and rescues Daniel from the lions' den (Dan. 6). These are just a few of the many miraculous stories we might read with wide-eyed wonder as we reflect on the powerful God we serve.

While these stories inspire us, we tend to forget the ordinary days between the God moments. Often people think that unless God displays Himself in extraordinary ways every day, or every week, or at least every month, something must be wrong.

So what do we do with those *ordinary* days that turn into ordinary months that turn into ordinary years? What did the men and women living in Bible times do? Do you ever wonder what daily life was like for Moses during the forty long years he spent as a shepherd in Midian before God called Him to go back to Egypt?[1] What was life like for Moses's sister, Miriam, as she spent decades praying for God to deliver her people from slavery? Moses and Miriam lived out their stories with God—day after ordinary day. They spent much of their lives waiting—and trusting God. The same is true for us. Burning bushes and parted seas may not fill our lives, but **our ordinary days can glorify our extraordinary God as we trust Him**. King David provides us with a similar example.

David was a shepherd chosen by God at a young age to become

---

1 Acts 7:23–30.

Israel's future king. Imagine going back in time and talking with this young man who was anointed as a ruler many years before he came to power. The conversation might go something like this:[1]

"What are you doing, David?"

"Tending sheep."

"Yes, I see that."

"My parents gave me this job to do. It's the worst job in the house. Usually slaves tend the sheep, but I'm the youngest son of many children, so that's probably why I'm the one out here, day after day, watching animals."

"What do you do to pass the time?"

"Well, I talk to God a lot. There's no one else to talk to out here. And I like to play the harp, so I've been working on some prayer songs."

"Prayer songs?"

"Yes, my conversations with God set to music. I've been writing them down because they seem special. It seems like God is giving me the words to say back to Him."

"Really?"

"Yes, but that's not all I do. I have to stay alert because we have a lot of wild animals around here that would love to have one of these sheep for lunch. I've been practicing with my sling. Every day I'm getting better at hitting the targets."

"So, you're singing while practicing your sling around sheep?"

"Well, yes. That's my life. Kind of ordinary, but I'm not always going to be shepherding. I'm really a king."

"You're a king? Really?"

"Yes, I've been anointed the future king of Israel."

"Where is your robe? And your servants? And your throne?"

"I don't have any king privileges yet."

"When are you going to have them, and where are you going to get them?"

"I don't know."

---

1   Adapted from a sermon illustration by James MacDonald on Walk in the Word Radio, AM 550, Jacksonville, FL, 2009.

"You don't know?"

"No."

"So what are you going to do in the meantime?"

"Well, I guess I'll sing prayers, practice my sling, and tend sheep."

Do you think David knew his sling skills would one day defeat the giant warrior named Goliath (1 Sam. 17)? Do you think he knew his prayer songs (many of which are in the book of Psalms) would comfort millions of people for thousands of years? Even King David, who was called "a man after [God's] own heart" (1 Sam. 13:14), had ordinary days—lots of them.

You may not be an earthly king, but in King Jesus, you are part of the royal family of God. **He wants to do extraordinary things through you as you give Him your ordinary days**.

But how do we glorify God, day by day, for a lifetime?

We start by developing daily habits that help us grow our relationship with God and keep us focused on His purposes. We need to learn to pay attention to God throughout the day as David did and trust the Holy Spirit to help us keep our eyes on Him. Obeying God, day after ordinary day, for years produces extraordinary results.

In Weeks 4–7, you will learn about daily spiritual disciplines that will help you connect with the Author of your true story. During the next few weeks, you will understand what it means to live out your story with God, in His strength and for His glory, day by day.

It is not enough for us to know *about* God. We must know God *personally*. The lessons in the upcoming weeks will teach you how to grow closer to God through abiding in Him and by setting aside intentional time to commune with Him. You'll be learning and practicing what is in the Bible and communicating with God through prayer. You'll also learn about your relationship with the Holy Spirit and how He equips you to serve others and share the love of Jesus. The end of this journey will be the beginning of another as you go out into the world, in your community, and maybe even beyond it, to invite others into God's True Story.

As a Jesus-follower, you do not need to practice these disciplines to build up your own righteousness. Remember that your

Spiritual Disciplines: Personal and interpersonal activities given by God in the Bible as a means of attaining closeness, devotion, and conformity to Jesus.

right standing before God is the result of your salvation through Jesus Christ *alone*. You cannot add to the finished work of Jesus on the cross.

Neither do you need to practice these spiritual disciplines to earn God's love. He *already* loves you. In fact, God is loving you right now. He cannot love you any more than He already does.

Instead, think of spiritual disciplines as daily rhythms to walk with God as He works in and through you. **They are not about striving; they are about abiding**. Practice them to grow stronger in your relationship with God. Use the disciplines to recognize His voice, follow where He leads, trust Him through trials, and enjoy Him as you learn to live out your story in His strength.

Let's take another step together on our faith journey . . .

WEEK FOUR

ABIDING—STAYING
CONNECTED TO GOD

DAY
22

Know God as Your Friend

Greater love has no one than this: to lay down one's
life for one's friends. You are my friends if you do what
I command. I no longer call you servants, because a
servant does not know his master's business. Instead,
I have called you friends, for everything that I learned
from my Father I have made known to you.

John 15:13–15 NIV

Jesus knew He had only a few uninterrupted moments left with His disciples before He would be arrested. The dreaded prophecies of His betrayal and brutal execution were upon Him. He knew His closest followers and friends were about to see Him accused, beaten, and hung on a cross to die. And that He would do nothing to stop it. He had been trying to prepare them for this (Luke 22:31–37). He reminded the disciples they were chosen for a mission, and Father God would answer their prayers to fulfill the mission (John 15:7–8). But there was more. A change needed to take place in their relationship with Him. From followers to friends. From merely obeying commands to understanding His true purpose and their part in it. Jesus explained how this intimate union with Him would be the *only effective approach to ministry—and life.* As hours dwindled to minutes left with His disciples, Jesus instructed them repeatedly to **abide in Him**.

This week we will learn what it means to abide in Christ. For now, think of abiding as togetherness or oneness with Jesus. It's the idea that we live in Him and dwell with Him through all of life. We share Jesus's thoughts, emotions, intentions, and power.[1]

Like the disciples' altered relationship with Jesus, a change needs to occur in *your* relationship with Him. In Week 1, we learned God's Story and that we have a choice to be a part of it. In Weeks 2 and 3, we learned our identity and purpose in Christ. Now that we know *why* God created us, it's time to learn how to live differently to *fulfill* our purpose. It starts with growing an *intimate friendship* with God.

Your story with God is a story of friendship. Stop for a moment and think about that. God created you to be friends with Him. When Jesus called His disciples "friends" (John 15:15), this may have surprised them.[2] The only previous example in the Scriptures of a person being called a friend of God was Abraham.[3] But Jesus knew what was about to happen the next day and in the coming weeks and years, and He invited them—invites us—to draw closer to Him.

Yes, the God of the universe, who spoke galaxies into existence, wants to be your friend. No other religion describes a relationship with God as a friendship.

Friendship with God is no ordinary friendship. We do not treat Jesus casually, as if He is our equal. The remainder of the New Testament refers to Jesus as Lord, God, Savior, and King. We obey Jesus. Not the other way around. What Jesus is inviting us to experience is intimacy—knowing Him, His heart, His mission, His companionship. Servants are expected to obey without explanation. But Jesus calls us friends; He says, "Everything that I learned from my Father I have made known to you" (John 15:15 NIV).

Jesus shares not only His mind and His will but also His very life. He says, "There is no greater love than to lay down one's life for one's friends. You are my friends if you do what I command" (John 15:13–14). Obeying His commands proves our friendship with God, and that starts with abiding in Him.

The secret to this intimacy is quality time—the more time we spend engaging with Jesus, the more we get to know Him, His ways,

---

1 Rodney A. Whitacre, *John*, vol. 4, The IVP New Testament Commentary Series (Westmont, IL: IVP Academic, 1999), 376.
2 Kenneth O. Gangel, *John*, vol. 4, *Holman New Testament Commentary* (Nashville, TN: Broadman & Holman Publishers, 2000), 285.
3 2 Chron. 20:7; Isa. 41:8; James 2:23.

His thoughts. Just as time spent together grows human relationships, quality time with God will grow your relationship with Him too. Set aside time each day to be still before Him, just like Jesus did.

Jesus often withdrew from His busy life to spend time alone with His Father, usually in the morning while it was still dark (Mark 1:35). We can follow Jesus's example. Like musicians who tune their instruments before a concert, we need to tune ourselves—heart, soul, mind, and strength—to be Spirit-led and Jesus-centered before we begin our daily activities.

You will find that the more time you spend alone with Him, the more time you'll want to be with Him. **To make a daily devotional time a reality, it's good to have a plan**. Decide on a time (early, if possible) and a place (quiet, if possible). If getting up early is hard, try going to bed earlier, or find a time before or after the morning rush. Start with fifteen minutes and build up from there. Here are some reminders of how to approach your time with Him:

1. **Quiet yourself.** The Bible describes this as waiting on the Lord in hope and rest (Ps. 62:1, 5). Invite God to meet with you and lead your time together as He wishes. "Open my eyes that I may see wonderful things in your law" (Ps. 119:18 NIV). As you linger with Him, ask Him to increase your awareness of His voice.

2. **Listen to God's Word.** Read passages from the Bible slowly so you absorb what you are reading. Try the 10-1-1 approach. Start with reading just *ten verses*, and focus on what God is saying to you through them. Slow down and keep reading until *one verse or phrase* catches your attention. Focus on *one word* within that verse

---

Do you own a study Bible?

If your Bible has a concordance (see pp. 70–71) or topical index, look up an attribute of God that relates to a need or a key word that relates to a concern in your life. Read the passage slowly. If a word or phrase seems important, write down the verse. If your Bible has cross-references, read the suggested passages. Write down what you are learning. Follow the suggestions in your Bible to other verses that explore the same idea. Pray about what you are learning and listen for God's promptings. The Holy Spirit will never prompt you to do anything contrary to God's Word.

to remember that day. This is how your conversation with God begins. He will reveal His will through His Word. (Though God rarely speaks audibly, He often speaks to one's heart through His Word.) What you are reading may remind you of a circumstance or a relationship in your own life. You may feel prompted to act in obedience to a biblical command. When God speaks, listen and respond. Let the key verse or key word be spiritual food for your day. Think about it as you go through your day. Every word in the Bible is inspired by God, or "God-breathed" (2 Tim. 3:16 NIV). Even the genealogies and history have meanings we can explore and from which we can learn about God, His will, and His purposes.

3. **Pray.** Respond to God through prayer. Talk to Him about what you read in His Word and listen for His thoughts in your thoughts. From what you read, ask God:

- What do You want me to know *about* You today?
- What do You want to *do* together today?

These questions will help you absorb and apply what you are reading. As you think through your answers, you can pray God's Word (the key word or phrase) to Him. When you speak His Word in prayer, your mind is renewed to His. As you pray, thank Him, and ask for His help.

4. **Journal.** Write down key Bible verses, prayers, and any insights that God gives you. Writing down what you learn will help you remember what God has said so that you can apply and share it with others. If a distracting thought comes to mind (for example, if you think of something you need to do later that day), write it down and release it so you can return to focusing on your conversation with God.

Your daily devotional time (quiet time) grows your friendship with God. As your most dependable friend, God is always there for you. He rejoices with you when you rejoice, and He comforts you when you are hurting. Jesus walked this earth as "a man of sorrows and acquainted with grief," so He empathizes with your pain (Isa. 53:3 ESV). You experience God's joy, even when life is hard, because you never walk alone.

DAY 22

Let the Bible Speak:
John 10:11–18 and Psalm 23 (Optional: Psalm 27)

Let Your Mind Think:
1. All relationships need time to grow, and we protect time for those relationships we value most. What steps will you need to take to set aside daily time with God?

2. Jesus describes Himself as our Good Shepherd, and we are His sheep who listen to His voice (John 10). With this in mind, **read Psalm 23 slowly**. How do you depend on Him to lead you today?

3. How does your obedience to Jesus's commands demonstrate your friendship with Him (John 14:21)?

Let Your Soul Pray:
God, thank You for calling me Your friend. Deepen my relationship with You as I learn to abide in You. Help me discern Your thoughts within my thoughts, so that I may obey Your commands. Please give me quality time with You each day to restore my soul . . . In Jesus's name, amen.

Let Your Heart Obey:
(What is God leading you to know, value, or do?)

Rest In, Rely On, Release All to God

*I am the vine; you are the branches. Whoever
abides in me and I in him, he it is that bears much
fruit, for apart from me you can do nothing.*
John 15:5 ESV

Imagine boarding an empty bus with Jesus as the driver. You have a choice as to where you sit. You can sit up front near Jesus and enjoy a close relationship with Him as He navigates you through life. Or, you can distance yourself from Jesus and take a seat in the back of the bus. In the back, the ride is bumpy with a limited view of where you are going. You cannot see Jesus's actions or clearly hear His voice from the back seat. Once you board the bus, and regardless of where you choose to sit, Jesus will take you to where He wants you to go. The choice is what type of relationship you want with Him on the journey. Will your choice be to abide in Him or to sit in the back without a close connection to the Driver?

Yesterday we learned how to grow our friendship with Jesus during a daily devotional time. But how do we abide through the rest of our day?

Abiding in Jesus is more than spending time with Him. **Abiding in Jesus is releasing control and remaining connected in order to rest and receive**. Like a passenger riding on a bus, we are not in control of our lives. But abiding means we are no longer alone—we're with Jesus. The word *abide* is translated "to remain," "to stay," "to live," or "to dwell."[1] Abiding in Jesus combines faith, obedience, trust, rest, grace, and Spirit-led living. This oneness—communing—with Jesus is a mysterious unity with God and the only way to abundant life (John 10:10).

> **Abide** is also translated "to remain" or "to dwell." For this study, abiding in Jesus means to
>
> • rest in God;
> • rely on God;
> • release all to God;
> • receive all we need from God.

Jesus says, "Abide in me, and I in you" (John 15:4 ESV). He gives the example of a grapevine: "I am the vine; you are the branches" (John 15:5 ESV). Jesus is the Vine, the source of abundant life, rooted in the earth and giving nourishment to the entire plant. We are the weak, dependent branches, unable to produce fruit on our own. But as we receive grace-filled nourishment from the Vine, He bears life-changing fruit through us.

Think about how much a weak little branch depends on the vine for everything it needs to survive and thrive. In fact, Jesus said, "My power works best in weakness" (2 Cor. 12:9). **Our weakness can help us recognize our dependence on God**. That's the goal. That's why Paul wrote, "I am glad to boast about my weaknesses, so that the power of Christ can work through me" (2 Cor. 12:9). So we stay connected to the Vine—believing in Jesus, trusting Him, and knowing that everything we have and everything we need is coming from Him. If we stay connected to Him, the Holy Spirit will run like sap through us, and God will bear much fruit in our lives.[2] Jesus says in John 15:5, "If you remain in me and I in you, you will bear much fruit" (NIV). That's good news. But the second part of that verse mentions the consequence of losing that connection: "Apart from me you can do nothing."

If abiding in Jesus means bearing good fruit, then not abiding in Jesus means just the opposite: **nothing**. Not producing anything of eternal significance. No amount of good works, if done apart from God, qualify as the good "fruit" Jesus is talking about in this passage.

---

1   William Arndt et al., *A Greek-English Lexicon of the New Testament and Other Early Christian Literature* (Chicago: University of Chicago Press, 2000), 630.

2   R. Kent Hughes, *John: That You May Believe*, Preaching the Word (Wheaton, IL: Crossway Books, 1999), 357.

He invites us into His work for us to accomplish—with love—what He has planned for us to do (John 15:9; Eph. 2:10). Works done without love, to please ourselves, to earn recognition, and to feed our pride will have no lasting value (1 Cor. 13:1–3).

We are meant to be strong branches through which the very life of God flows. Life flows from God, not from us. This is why **Jesus does not command us to bear fruit; He commands us to *abide* in Him. Producing fruit is the Holy Spirit's work**, so if we depend on Jesus, the Vine, as the source of our nourishment, God's fruit *will* form, and we will glorify God with it (John 15:8). But if we turn our hearts toward worldly things to give us life, we become empty and lifeless, like dry deadwood (John 15:6 NIV).

God does not want us to shrivel up and wither, fruitless and life-less, detached from Jesus, our life source. He is the Gardener who cares for us (John 15:1). First, He cleans us and connects us to the Vine. In Christ, we are clean and have the potential to bear fruit (John 15:3). But we occasionally need pruning, just like any good fruit-bearing tree does. For example, sins such as gossip, unfor-giveness, worry, selfishness, and addiction are like deadwood. They block the flow of Jesus's life-giving nourishment. They drain our en-ergy and keep us from bearing fruit, so the Gardener cuts them off (John 15:2). He wants to see us healthy, fruitful, and connected to the Vine, but we need to cooperate. **How do we abide in God? We *rest***

Worldly Christianity

Abiding in God separates worldly Christians from Spirit-led, fully devoted Jesus followers. Worldly Christians think and act like the world. The apostle Paul called the Corinthian believers "worldly" or "fleshly" (1 Cor. 3:1–4 NIV and NASB, respectively).

Worldly Christians continually grieve the Holy Spirit by not doing what the Bible says. They are easily offended, worrisome, irritable, unforgiving, prayerless, easily angered, selfish, or overly concerned about what others think. They do not aggressively fight sin; instead, they allow their old sin nature to influence their lives more than the Holy Spirit (Rom. 8:5–8, 13). Because of their weak faith and spiritual immaturity, they are driven primarily by their own desires and worldly thinking rather than by God's desires and biblical truth.

If this describes you, confess your weakness and give Jesus the rightful position of supremacy in your life.

in God. We *rely* on God. We *release* all to God. As we do, we *receive* all we need from God.

1. **Rest in God**. Believe *in* God, but also *believe* God to rest in Him (Heb. 4:9–11). Believe who He is, what He has done, and who you are in Him.

- Rest in Jesus's love for you. Jesus says, "As the Father has loved me, so have I loved you. Abide in my love" (John 15:9 ESV).
- Rest in Jesus's provision for you. God is fully aware of your needs, cares, and worries. "And my God will supply every need of yours according to his riches in glory in Christ Jesus" (Phil. 4:19 ESV).
- Rest in what God has done for you through Christ. Do not worry about what to do for God. Instead, serve Him because you love Him, not out of obligation. No more working for God's favor. No more defining yourself by your circumstances. No more grasping for control. Receive His comfort. Will you rest in Jesus?

2. **Rely on God**. Believe God is telling the truth. Rely on His Word and depend on His Holy Spirit. The question is not whether the Vine will provide all we need but whether we will receive it from Him. Will you seek other sources of nourishment from the world and block His provision? Don't pull back from God. Receive all that the Vine has to give each day. Have faith and allow Him complete access to your life so that He can flow through you. He is always worthy of our trust and always ready to provide. Will you rely on Jesus?

3. **Release all to God**. Believe God is in charge of results and outcomes. Give your past, present, and future to Him. There is freedom, healing, and wholeness when you release your grip. That's because God changes hearts and lives—not us. So lay down your will, your emotions, and your circumstances, and allow grace to flood your life. Lay down your life for others like Jesus did (John 15:12–13), and lay down your plans as well. God will never ask you to follow Him

without giving you His grace for every step of the way. Jesus promises, "If you keep my commandments, you will abide in my love" (John 15:10 ESV). To abide in Jesus, you need to surrender and obey. Will you release everything to Jesus?

Resting in, relying on, and releasing all to Jesus may seem like a risky step of faith. But look at the promised blessings we receive when we stay connected to Jesus. In John 15 Jesus said if you abide in Him and His words abide in you . . .

- you will bear much fruit (v. 5),
- your prayers will be answered (vv. 7, 16),
- you will obey Him (vv. 10, 14),
- you will experience His love (vv. 9–10),
- you will experience His joy (v. 11),
- you will show that you are His disciple (v. 8), and
- you will be His friend (v. 14).

This seems too good to be true, but it is true. And you have a choice to make each day, each moment. Friend, will you live dependent on Jesus?

Let the Bible Speak:
John 15:1–17 (Optional: 1 John 3:11–24)

Let Your Mind Think:
1. How did the imagery of the bus or the vine change how you see your relationship with God?

2. Reread the definition of a worldly Christian. In what areas do you depend on things of the world instead of God? Take time to ask God for help in those areas.

3. What steps can you take to rest in God, rely on God, and release all to God? Begin with your first step today.

Let Your Soul Pray:
Lord Jesus, You are my Source of life. I want to abide in You. Help me rest in You, rely on You, release all things to You, and receive all I need from You. Bear much fruit in my life to Your glory . . . In Jesus's name, amen.

Let Your Heart Obey:
(What is God leading you to know, value, or do?)

Receive from God– Grow Deep Roots

Blessed are those who trust in the LORD and have made the LORD
their hope and confidence. They are like trees planted along a
riverbank, with roots that reach deep into the water. Such trees are
not bothered by the heat or worried by long months of drought.
Their leaves stay green, and they never stop producing fruit.
Jeremiah 17:7–8

On your faith journey, Bible passages may become personal favorites.
In your times of discouragement, you discover passages that consistently refresh your soul. And in your joyful times of worship, you
find verses that declare God's majesty and splendor. It is common
for believers to return to well-loved passages for hope and encouragement. Take for example Isaiah 55. We quote verse 11 to remember
God's Word "will not return to [Him] empty" (Isa. 55:11 NIV). But we
forget to keep reading. We pull out our favorite parts of the chapter but miss the context. If you look closely, the passage reveals an
incredible transformation: "Instead of the thorn shall come up the
cypress; instead of the brier shall come up the myrtle" (Isa. 55:13 ESV).
God's Word will accomplish its purpose to take thorns and briers, the
consequence of sin (Day 3), and transform them into lush trees–new
life. This passage symbolizes not only the fourth part of God's Story
but also that we are like those thorns and trees.

God's work of salvation completely changes us. We do not go from
being like a weak thorn bush to a better thorn bush. When we receive

Jesus, we become fundamentally different.[1] Our new life in Jesus makes us like mighty trees: strong and fruitful, "great oaks that [He] has planted for his own glory" (Isa. 61:3). But trees grow slowly, and so do we. It takes time to develop deep spiritual roots in God, fully anchored and ready to draw on His power as we live out our stories with Him each day. **The strength and fruitfulness of our lives depend on our roots**.

Roots matter the most. Broken branches can grow back, but broken roots can kill a whole tree. That is why "the godly have deep roots" (Prov. 12:3). **Unseen roots supply visible fruit**. We "take root below and bear fruit above" (2 Kings 19:30 NIV). In the same way, our time alone with God is unseen but supports our faith and supplies outward evidence of our faith. Just as roots continually drink in water and nutrients, we need to continually draw on God's strength, wisdom, grace, and love. We cannot earn these gifts. Only God can give them freely, but we need to receive them.

Abiding in Jesus is all about developing deep, healthy roots in Him, watered by the living water of the Holy Spirit (John 4:10; 7:38–39). Through daily devotional time, we become rooted in God's Word, rooted in prayer, rooted in grace, and rooted in love. Receiving all we need from God takes faith and trust to grow spiritual roots ready to absorb God's provision.

What nourishment do you need to receive from God today?
Grow roots in God's Word to receive His WISDOM.

Wisdom is a divine gift from God offered generously to those who ask (James 1:5). But often we do not ask for it, so we do not receive it (James 4:2). When we spend time with God, when we read or listen to His Word, it becomes an opportunity to draw from His wisdom and strength. He guides our paths, our conversations, and our relationships.

> Oh, the joys of those who . . . delight in the law of the LORD, meditating on it day and night. They are like trees planted along the riverbank, bearing fruit each season. Their leaves never wither, and they prosper in all they do. (Ps. 1:1–3)

---

1 Paul Tripp, "Why Do I Need the Bible?" Paul Tripp Ministries, Inc., May 13, 2019. https://www.paultripp.com/app-read-bible-study/posts/001-why-do-i-need-the-bible.

Anchor yourself in God's Word like roots anchor trees firmly into the ground. Begin by reading a verse each day from the book of Proverbs, one of the wisdom books in the Old Testament. By spending time in God's Word, we learn God's will, and our foundation will be firm through life's fiercest storms (Matt. 7:24–25). Abide in His Word.

Grow roots in prayer to receive His PEACE.

Prayer, especially private prayer, grows deep spiritual roots. Just as plant roots drink in water continually, we "pray continually," drinking in the Holy Spirit's refreshment and strength (1 Thess. 5:17 NIV). And no matter what is happening in the world around us, when we offer prayers *with gratitude*, God gives us His supernatural peace (Phil. 4:6–7). His peace is greater than anything we can understand or try to produce on our own. **Our peace is fueled by our prayer life**. God's peace is how believers who experience a loss or endure chronic illness can say through it, "I'm all right. God is with me." The peace they receive through prayer becomes a powerful testimony to God's provision and care. They receive all they need from God as they place their trust in Him through prayer.

> You will keep in perfect peace all who trust in you, all whose thoughts are fixed on you! (Isa. 26:3)

Jesus knew the value of living in this state of continual peace and dependence on His Father, so He modeled for us what personal prayer time looks like. He "often withdrew to lonely places and prayed" (Luke 5:16 NIV). He also taught us explicitly about prayer: "But when you pray, go into your room and shut the door and pray to your Father who is in secret. And your Father who sees in secret will reward you" (Matt. 6:6 ESV). Perhaps the Lord's Prayer provides the most detailed and frequently memorized prayer model.[1] No matter what our personal prayer life looks like, know that the more time

---

1 This Lord's Prayer is based on Matthew 6:9-13: "Our Father in heaven, hallowed be your name. Your kingdom come, your will be done, on earth as it is in heaven. Give us this day our daily bread, and forgive us our debts, as we also have forgiven our debtors. And lead us not into temptation, but deliver us from evil" (ESV).

we spend talking with God, the deeper our roots will grow into His patience and peace. Abide in prayer.

Grow roots in God's grace to receive HIS LOVE. It is difficult to give love away if you have not received it yourself. Abiding in Christ is intentionally absorbing God's unconditional loving-kindness every day. When we remember there is nothing we can do to earn or lose God's love, we root ourselves in God's grace. Rather than assume the worst in others, we believe the best. We become less judgmental and extend love more quickly. Through faith, our "roots will grow down into God's love and keep [us] strong" (Eph. 3:17). The apostle Paul knew the power of God's love. He prayed:

> May you have the power to understand, as all God's people should, how wide, how long, how high, and how deep his love is. May you experience the love of Christ, though it is too great to understand fully. Then you will be made complete with all the fullness of life and power that comes from God. (Eph. 3:18–19)

When we receive God's immeasurable love, we become more secure in who we are in Christ. This experience changes us, and we become a conduit of God's love toward others. Growing roots deep into Christ's love is how we fulfill our purpose to love others well (Day 16). Know who *you* are because you know *Him* so well. Abide in His love (John 15:9).

God is limitless. As we abide in Christ, He provides all we need at the right time and in the right way. "So then, just as you received Christ Jesus as Lord, continue to live your lives in him, rooted and built up in him, strengthened in the faith as you were taught, and overflowing with thankfulness" (Col. 2:6–7 NIV). Our time with God roots us in Him so that we soak up His strength, even as we move forward with each day's challenges. **As we grow roots downward, we will also grow branches upward**. Our branches will grow broad and strong, sheltering others, surviving storms, and bearing much fruit. We'll learn more about fruit tomorrow, but for now, remember that your daily time apart with God is root work—and roots are the key to abiding in God.

DAY 24

Let the Bible Speak:
Psalm 1 (Optional: Isaiah 55)

Let Your Mind Think:
1. How does trusting God to provide all you need change the way you endure hardships?

2. What distracts you from spending time with God each day? What changes can you make to be rooted in God and His Word?

3. What do you need to receive from God today? Joy? Comfort? Discernment? Ask God to help you; He will.

Let Your Soul Pray:
Father, I want to grow healthy roots in You. As I spend time with You each day, help me grow in Your Word, in prayer, and in Your love. Anchor me in You so I will receive all I need and be strong in times of trouble . . . In Jesus's name, amen.

Let Your Heart Obey:
(What is God leading you to know, value, or do?)

Bear Fruit as You Abide

The fruit of the Spirit is love, joy, peace, patience, kindness,
goodness, faithfulness, gentleness, [and] self-control.
Galatians 5:22–23 ESV

If there were one word to describe what happens in the life of a believer between now and heaven, it would be *change*. Having faith in Jesus places us in a lifelong process of transformation. We are completely made new spiritually, but the evidence of change may take time to show results. It's like a seed that takes time to grow before it produces fruit. Our lives genuinely change over time and eventually produce spiritual fruit. In both cases, God is the one who causes the growth. The apostle Paul said it this way: "I planted the seed in your hearts, and Apollos watered it, but it was God who made it grow" (1 Cor. 3:6).

The beautiful reality is that someone planted the gospel seed in your life, whether it was days or years ago. But God causes the seed to grow (Mark 4:26–28). He wants you to experience true love, freedom from addictions, peaceful confidence, excitement for the future, and so much more. No matter what you've done or what has been done to you, God will complete what He started in your life (Phil. 1:6). He will transform *every part of you:*[1]

1. Your **mind** into the mind of Christ as you read God's Word
2. Your **affections** for God as you receive His unconditional love

---

1   Zane Pratt, "Making Disciples in Another Culture." Breakout, Send Conference, Orlando, FL, July 26, 2017.

3. Your **will** as you learn to abide in, trust, and obey God
4. Your **relationships** as you love others, even those who are difficult or different from you
5. Your **purpose** as you learn to live for God's glory, not your own

Are you starting to see some of these changes? Be encouraged by and grateful for God's good work in your life. Remember, it's not how far you have to go but how far you've come that matters. We'll learn more about this change process (called sanctification) in Week 7. But for today, know that bearing fruit is the evidence of change and the result of abiding faith.

Bearing fruit is a precious gift God gives us to know we belong to Him. We do not have to wait to meet Jesus to know we have an authentic relationship with Him. Remember, salvation is by faith alone, "but faith that saves is not alone."[1] Jesus told His disciples:

> I am the vine; you are the branches. Whoever abides in me and I in him, he it is that bears much fruit, for apart from me you can do nothing. If anyone does not abide in me he is thrown away like a branch and withers; and the branches are gathered, thrown into the fire, and burned. If you abide in me, and my words abide in you, ask whatever you wish, and it will be done for you. By this my Father is glorified, that you bear much fruit and so prove to be my disciples. (John 15:5–8 ESV)

You and I might read this passage and think the command is to bear fruit. But in the original Greek language of the New Testament, we discover the command is to abide in Jesus. Bearing fruit is the evidence of our close friendship with Him. We can rest knowing we're responsible not for the *quantity* of fruit but for the *quality* of our relationship with God.

All believers can bear fruit abundantly. A poor widow can bear as much fruit as a lifelong pastor if she is abiding in Christ and using what God has given her for His glory (Luke 16:10). God changes us into His nature as we cooperate (Day 5): "Put off your old self, which

---

1 Norman L. Geisler, *Systematic Theology: In One Volume* (Minneapolis, MN: Bethany House Publishers, 2011), 890.

belongs to your former manner of life and is corrupt through deceitful desires, and to be renewed in the spirit of your minds, and to put on the new self, created after the likeness of God in true righteousness and holiness" (Eph. 4:22–24 ESV). Cooperating is not about self-improvement and **legalism**. It's about putting on the new you God created. No matter where we live or how many years we have lived, God bears abundant fruit through us when we abide in Jesus.

> **Legalism:**
> Obsessive rule following. People fall into legalism when they strive to earn God's favor or impress others through outwardly good behavior or good works. Jesus condemns legalism. We cannot serve Jesus if we are still trying to impress other people (Gal. 1:10), and we cannot earn God's favor through anything we do. Instead, we receive God's favor through what Jesus did for us (Eph. 2:8–9). Godly obedience flows not from legalism but from gratitude and love for God and all He's done for us.

Now that we've learned the significance of bearing fruit, it's time to define what it is. The Bible describes fruit in different ways: Christlike character (Gal. 5:22–23), righteous behavior (Phil. 1:11), praise (Heb. 13:15), and leading others to faith in Christ (Rom. 1:13–16). Jesus spoke about bearing fruit by *our love* for God and one another (John 15:9–17).

Today, let's focus on the fruit of our Christlike character, budding first in our hearts and then blossoming in our actions. Love, joy, peace, patience, kindness, goodness, faithfulness, gentleness, and self-control are all connected—different aspects of the same fruit, grown by the Spirit, in you. If we have love, we will have joy. If we have joy, we will have peace. The same is true for when we lack fruit. Without peace, we cannot have patience. Without patience, we cannot have self-control, and so on. The fruit of the Spirit will increase or decrease just as our relationship with God increases or decreases.

Sometimes we're tempted to think that we can cultivate some aspects of this fruit and not others. Someone might say, "I've just never been a patient person, but I can grow in the other aspects." Or, "My father was harsh, so I never learned how to be gentle." But we cannot stop growing in some aspects of godly character because they are difficult. We also do not want to limit God's work in our lives because of our personalities, our pasts, or our cultures. *All* aspects of spiritual fruit are *essential*. Thankfully, if we are sincerely growing in any one of these aspects, we will grow in the others as well.

If we want to know if faith is authentic, look at the fruit. Jesus says, "A good tree produces good fruit, and a bad tree produces bad fruit. . . . Yes, just as you can identify a tree by its fruit, so you can identify people by their actions" (Matt. 7:17, 20). Ask Jesus to help you rid yourself of bad fruit. He can help you cultivate the good fruit that shows you belong to Him. "Get rid of all bitterness, rage, anger, harsh words, and slander, as well as all types of evil behavior. Instead, be kind to each other, tenderhearted, forgiving one another, just as God through Christ has forgiven you" (Eph. 4:31–32). Yes, forgive one another.

Forgiveness is part of all good fruit. As we learned on Day 10, if God forgives us, we can forgive others who hurt us. This is a critical step in our faith journey and why we want to mention this again. Because receiving God's forgiveness and extending forgiveness to others softens our hearts and allows us to grow the fruit of the Spirit. Forgiveness does not condone or excuse offenses but releases the resentment that poisons good fruit. We are no longer easily offended when we remember that *we* are forgiven. Forgiving hearts are patient, kind, and loyal.

In contrast, the weed of unforgiveness chokes out good fruit. It blocks love, kills joy, and steals peace. It can lead to a bitterness that makes us impatient, unkind, and even hateful. We might give up on people, becoming harsh and careless with our words and actions. When we withhold forgiveness from others, it is usually because we do not understand or remember how much God has forgiven us (Luke 7:47). The hard truth is that when we refuse to forgive, we remain in bondage and betray God's grace. (Read Matthew 18:21–35, a parable about an unforgiving debtor.) Friend, **forgiveness does not set the offender free; it sets us free on a path out of our pain**. This hard step brings healing and health to bear good fruit.

Good fruit reveals real faith. Bearing fruit is not only evidence of internal heart change, but it also reveals itself in outward actions.

James says that real faith produces good deeds—good fruit (James 2:26). "We are saved *by* faith, but *to* works (Eph. 2:8–10; Titus 3:3–8)."[1] And God is also at work in your life right now, transforming you to produce spiritual fruit. Do not get discouraged if change is not happening fast—this is part of the root work necessary for your true story (Day 24). So, "Let us not become weary in doing good, for at the proper time we will reap a harvest if we do not give up" (Gal. 6:9 NIV). Keep getting nourishment from the Vine. Don't give up. God will produce a harvest through you when the time is right, and it will be delicious.

---

1 Ibid., 1041.

DAY 25

Let the Bible Speak:
Galatians 5:13–6:10 (Optional: James 2:14–26)

Let Your Mind Think:
1. What does the fruit you see in your life tell you about your faith?

2. Think about who planted gospel seeds in your life and thank God for them. Who in your life is far from God that you could lovingly sow gospel seeds in?

3. Is there someone you need to forgive? List the people or injuries that need your forgiveness. Ask the Holy Spirit for help to forgive and release each offense or person that comes to mind. **Forgiveness is a necessary step in your faith journey**. If you are unable to forgive, seek a trusted pastor or wise Christian friend to help you.

Let Your Soul Pray:
Father, produce good fruit in my life for Your glory. I pray that when others spend time with me, they will taste Your goodness. Show me any fruit in my life that does not please You; take it away and clean my heart so I can grow good fruit—the fruit of love, joy, peace, patience, kindness, goodness, gentleness, faithfulness, and self-control. Help me forgive others as You have forgiven me. Thank You for all You are doing in and through me . . . In Jesus's name, amen.

Let Your Heart Obey:
(*What is God leading you to know, value, or do?*)

Resist Temptation

Do what is good and run from evil so that you may live!
Amos 5:14

Resisting temptation is more complicated than we think. Most people are not good at anticipating the power of urges and unintentionally expose themselves to temptation. Like yesterday's sometimes difficult but necessary step of forgiveness, today, we take a hard step to guard against sin—because sin is serious.

We will never fully comprehend sin's harmful effects on creation. But we can realize how severe it is when we understand God's harsh response to it. Our sin cost Him Jesus, His only Son, nailed to a cross. Naked, bleeding, mocked, and abandoned so that we could be forgiven, healed, favored, and adopted. Jesus not only paid the price for our sin, but He also broke its *power* over us. We were once slaves to sin, but now we are free (Rom. 6:22). We can live *for* God, *with* God, and *in* God. **Nothing will ever separate us from God's love** (Rom. 8:38). Not even sin.

But sin still hurts. It hurts us and all our relationships, especially our relationship with God. **Sin blocks our connection to the Vine**. Cut off from our Life Source, our peace, strength, and joy will wither. We won't produce any good fruit. God will seem distant—prayer will be lifeless and His Word, boring. Sin breaks our abiding, and we suffer the consequences of that separation.

If we are still trying to get away with sin, we have missed the point. Sin always has consequences, terrible consequences, that block the abundant life—the blessings—Jesus died to give you.

Worry robs rest. Jealousy crushes peace. Gossip hurts friendships. Fear smothers faith. Complaining kills joy. Lying breaks trust. Unfaithfulness destroys relationships.

We all want rest, peace, friendship, faith, and joy. We all want trustworthy relationships. So let's understand the facts and activate a plan.

The reality is our unhealthy desires can lure us into sin (James 1:14), and our enemy knows our weaknesses: "[our] craving for physical pleasure, [our] craving for everything we see, and [our] pride in our achievements and possessions" (1 John 2:16). Satan also tempted Jesus in each of these areas, but Jesus stayed faithful. Let's learn from Jesus's perfect example.[1]

First, Satan used physical temptation to urge Jesus to do what felt right (Luke 4:3–4). When Jesus fasted for forty days, Satan tempted Him to turn stones into bread. "Jesus answered, 'It is written: "Man shall not live on bread alone"'" (Luke 4:4 NIV). Jesus trusted God to satisfy His needs *at the right time*. Friend, the enemy whispers, "You're missing out. No one will know. It will only be one time," or, "Everyone sins and all sins are equal; besides, God wants you to be happy." Do not listen to these lies. Apart from God, we have no good thing (Ps. 16:2). Trust God to satisfy you. "Since he did not spare even his own Son but gave him up for us all, won't he also give us everything else?" (Rom. 8:32). God will provide in the right way.

Next, Satan used emotional temptation for Jesus to question God's love (Luke 4:5–8). Satan showed Jesus all the kingdoms of the world and offered them to Him. All Jesus had to do was worship Satan, but Jesus refused. Jesus trusted God to give Him what was rightfully His *at the right time*. Friend, the enemy will show you worldly wealth, beauty, and power. He will say, "You're not enough. You're not smart enough. You don't have enough. You're not attractive." He'll try to convince you that you'll be complete and satisfied once you focus everything on those things. Do not listen—resist him. He's trying to direct your worship away from God and spin you into a constant frenzy. If we're not content without those things, we will not be content with

---

1   Read Luke 4:1–13 for the full account of Satan tempting Jesus in the wilderness. Notice that although Jesus was sinless, He still experienced temptation. This demonstrates that the temptation to sin is not sin itself.

those things. The enemy breaks promises and steals blessings. God keeps His promises and gives true blessings—not always fleeting earthly wealth, but eternal heavenly riches; not fading physical beauty, but unfading inner beauty; not worldly power, but godly influence.[1] Be faithful with little, and God will entrust you with much (Matt. 25:23).

Finally, Satan used the temptation of pride to question Jesus's identity (Luke 4:9–12). Satan wanted Jesus to jump from the temple roof to prove His identity as the Messiah, knowing angels would catch Him. Jesus refused. Jesus did not need to prove Himself. He trusted God to reveal His true identity *at the right time*. Satan will question your identity in Christ and tempt you to seek validation from others. He will whisper, "Are you genuinely God's child? Does He actually love you? Then prove it. Work harder. Perform. Strive." Do not listen—resist him. Of course you are God's child. There is no need to prove your identity to others or yourself.

Satan tempts us like he tempted Jesus. He is the father of all lies, and he has one mission: to steal, kill, and destroy (John 8:44; 10:10). He hates God, and he hates our abiding connection with God. He wants us to give in to temptation so he can break that connection. **Temptation itself is not sin; it is a call to battle**. Here's how to fight and win:

1. **Rely on the Holy Spirit, not your willpower**.[2] You are never alone. God is with you, *in* you, and He "is able to keep you from stumbling" (Jude v. 24 ESV). "God is faithful. He will not allow the temptation to be more than you can stand. When you are tempted, he will show you a way out so that you can endure" (1 Cor. 10:13). Through the power of the Holy Spirit, we can *always* make the right choice. We are no longer a slave to sin, and we now have the power and authority to make better choices. Rely on the Holy Spirit and activate the promise: "Resist the devil and he will flee from you" (James 4:7 NASB).

2. **Speak God's Word**. Words are powerful (Prov. 18:21; Matt. 12:37). Every time Satan tempted Jesus, Jesus quoted Scripture in return. Jesus knew Scripture for each specific temptation. He was ready

---

1   Matt. 5:13–14; 6:19–20; 1 Pet. 3:3–4.
2   In Week 7, you will learn more about the Holy Spirit and how to work with Him.

before the attack; we can be too. Jesus has already given you victory, so speak that truth out loud: "I am a child of God with victory over _____" (see 1 Cor. 15:57). Take authority over temptation. We may not have control over a first ungodly thought, but we do have control over our second thought and potential wrong action through the power of the Holy Spirit.

3. **Remove temptations.** Jesus prayed, "Lead us not into temptation" (Matt. 6:13 ESV). He also taught that we should get rid of our eyes, hands, and feet if they cause us to sin (Mark 9:43–48). Jesus was not talking about actual amputation, but He *did* want to portray how serious we should be about avoiding temptation. What tempts you? Do not look at it, do not touch, and do not go there. "And don't let yourself think about ways to indulge your evil desires" (Rom. 13:14). The fleeting pleasures of sin are not worth the consequences.

4. **Ask for help.** Satan targets loners like predators target isolated prey. Find friends; connect with local believers in a church. Help each other pay attention to God and hold each other accountable for resisting the temptations we all face. Share your sin struggles. Memorize empowering Scriptures together. Encourage one another and meet regularly. "Confess your sins to each other and pray for each other so that you may be healed" (James 5:16).

Sin is dangerous. Do not let Satan tell you otherwise. No physical pleasure, possession, or achievement in this life is worth breaking fellowship with God.

But when you do sin—and we all do—confess and repent right away. "If we claim we have no sin, we are only fooling ourselves and not living in the truth. But if we confess our sins to him, he is faithful and just to forgive us our sins and to cleanse us from all wickedness" (1 John 1:8–9).

Jesus not only rescues us from the penalty of sin but also rescues us from temptation. Abide in Him.

> When you **CONFESS**, you admit your sin and agree with God that it is evil. When you **REPENT**, you turn away from your sin and obey God by doing what is right.

DAY 26

Let the Bible Speak:
Colossians 3:1–17 (Optional: James 4)

Let Your Mind Think:
1. What people, places, and things tempt you? How can you avoid them?

2. Identify, write out, and memorize specific Scriptures that will help you resist the temptations you face most frequently.

Let Your Soul Pray:
Lord, thank You for paying the ultimate price to rescue me from sin. Oh God, may I never use Your grace as an excuse to sin. Free me from sinful habits, and deliver me from temptation so I can enjoy close friendship with You . . . In Jesus's name, amen.

Let Your Heart Obey:
(*What is God leading you to know, value, or do?*)

Fight with the Armor of God

Lead me in the right path, O Lᴏʀᴅ, or my enemies will
conquer me. Make your way plain for me to follow.
Psalm 5:8

Picture a path leading to God, winding up hills, through valleys, and across rivers. As we follow Jesus, we need to stay on this path even though it is narrow and difficult (Matt. 7:14)–narrow because Jesus is the only Way to the Father (John 14:6), and difficult because our bodies are hindered by our old sin natures. We live in a world full of temptations, distractions, false religions, and sin–all of which the enemy uses to lure us away from the path with Jesus. Thankfully, we do have a way to stay on track, a way to follow the good path set for us.

Abiding faith.

As we've been learning all week, abiding in Jesus connects us to Jesus, the only Way to the Father. When we abide in Him, we stay on His path because we are one with Him. Satan knows the incredible power of abiding in Jesus, and he will do anything to break our oneness with God. But we know his age-old strategy and how to resist his temptations. Today, we learn more about his approach and how to stand firm in our faith:

> For our struggle is not against flesh and blood, but against the rulers, against the authorities, against the powers of this dark world and against the spiritual forces of evil in the heavenly realms. (Eph. 6:12 ɴɪᴠ)

People are not our enemies; Satan is. Because we are in Christ, Satan cannot control us, but that doesn't keep him from lurking beside God's path. Sometimes he whispers lies. Or screams insults and accusations. Other times, he works through forbidden practices, like the occult or witchcraft (Gal. 5:19–21). He tries to disrupt our communication with God and sends distractions to lure us away. He sends people to divide us and plant doubts in our minds. *Satan is the author of confusion and division*. Be watchful; his activity does not always immediately appear evil (2 Cor. 11:14). Jesus called him the father of lies (John 8:44). But do not be afraid, because Satan is no match for God: "He who is in you is greater than he who is in the world" (1 John 4:4 ESV). Satan is *not* omnipresent (everywhere, all the time) or omniscient (all-knowing) or omnipotent (all-powerful). He cannot read our minds, and he has no authority over us. We can walk in total peace, fully enjoying God on the journey, because He is not only *with* us but also *equips* us for victory with special armor:

> Therefore put on the full armor of God, so that when the day of evil comes, you may be able to stand your ground, and after you have done everything, to stand. Stand firm then, with the belt of truth buckled around your waist, with the breastplate of righteousness in place, and with your feet fitted with the readiness that comes from the gospel of peace. In addition to all this, take up the shield of faith, with which you can extinguish all the flaming arrows of the evil one. Take the helmet of salvation and the sword of the Spirit, which is the word of God. And pray in the Spirit on all occasions with all kinds of prayers and requests. With this in mind, be alert and always keep on praying for all the Lord's people. (Eph. 6:13–18 NIV)

God goes forward to fight for His people and gives us His armor (Isa. 59:17). Each piece of armor symbolizes an important reality of His protection over us. In the book of Ephesians (ch. 6), the apostle Paul used the imagery of a Roman soldier's set of armor to illustrate our spiritual armor. Let's look at how each piece protects us as we abide in Christ:

1. **Belt of Truth:** This belt steadies you as you walk God's path. The ancient Romans believed the area around the waist was the seat of emotions. Some cultures still hold this view. Girding (encircling and securing) this area symbolizes keeping emotions in check by aligning them with truth. When we put on the belt of truth, we align our thoughts, attitudes, and actions with the truth of God's Word (John 17:17). Satan lies about everything. He distorts God's Word and twists our emotions. He sends false teachers to pull us from God's path. He uses fear and self-pity to make us stumble. Yet the more we gird ourselves with God's belt of truth, the less likely we are to trip over the enemy's deception. "Know the truth, and the truth will set you free" (John 8:32 ESV). Strap on your belt of truth.

2. **Breastplate of Righteousness:** The breastplate covers your chest, generally thought of by the Romans as the place your soul resides, with Jesus's righteousness—His perfect obedience and virtue. It also defends you against two of the most vicious enemies of your soul: self-righteousness *and* self-condemnation:

   - *Self-righteousness dismisses Christ's righteousness as unnecessary, saying,* "I don't need a Savior. I am good enough. God owes me His favor."
   - *Self-condemnation, the other extreme, dismisses Christ's righteousness as too little,* saying, "Christ's work on the cross was not enough. I am too sinful. I must try harder to earn God's favor."

Both are dangerous forms of pride, revealing a belief in self-sufficiency, the ability to earn God's favor ourselves. Both ignore the reality of God's grace (Gal. 2:21). In His grace, **God transferred our sins onto Jesus at the cross and transferred Jesus's righteousness onto us (2 Cor. 5:21; 1 Pet. 2:24). The greatest exchange!** Now Christ's righteousness—which is both necessary and sufficient—covers us. Place your faith in Jesus's righteousness alone. Be confident that in Him you are *already* righteous, and *live* in a way that honors your calling. Sin gives the enemy a foothold in your life, an opportunity to pull you off God's path (Eph. 4:27). Guard your heart by continually putting on the breastplate of righteousness.

3. **Shoes of Peace:** During the first century AD, Roman soldiers wore spiked sandals tied on with thick leather thongs. They offered a solid foundation for intense battle. Shoes stabilize your footing. Satan tries to knock you off balance by causing relational divisions, especially within the church. Do not let him. God has given us a foundation of peace (Luke 21:26; John 16:33). Be a peacemaker. Jesus said the unity among His followers would show the world that God sent Him (John 17:21). Live at peace with God and others, and when others ask about the peace they see in your life, "always be ready to explain it" (1 Pet. 3:15). "How beautiful are the feet of those who bring good news!" (Rom. 10:15 NIV). Strap on the shoes of peace.

4. **Shield of Faith:** Roman soldiers would first soak their shields in water to protect against the fiery darts of their enemies. The shield of faith extinguishes our enemy's fiery arrows of doubt, shame, fear, and guilt. He may shout, "You can't trust God! God doesn't really love you! You are worthless!" But you can stop these arrows with faith in God's goodness, faith in God's love, faith in Jesus. "We achieve . . . victory through our faith" (1 John 5:4). Faith comes by hearing God's Word, so listen to God (Rom. 10:17). Meditate on His Word as you walk with Him. "For we walk by faith, not by sight" (2 Cor. 5:7 ESV).

5. **Helmet of Salvation:** This helmet protects your thoughts—it's the assurance of salvation to protect your mind from Satan's deceptions. Knowing that you are saved is a strong defense against doubt, fear, confusion, and insecurity (1 John 5:11–13). The enemy cannot steal your salvation from you (John 10:28). God has rescued you from sin and adopted you as His own child. You are His forever. You are forgiven forever. You are loved forever. He covers you and protects you. "O LORD, my Lord, the strength of my salvation, you have covered my head in the day of battle" (Ps. 140:7 ESV). You have nothing to fear.

6. **Sword of the Spirit:** The sword of the Spirit is the Word of God. In Ephesians 6:17, "word" means the sayings of God.[1] We need to take

---

1 Vine's *Complete Expository Dictionary of Old and New Testament Words* (Nashville: Thomas Nelson, 1984), 683.

hold of the sayings that are in the Bible and use them to fight the enemy. God's Word abides in you as you abide in Him (John 15:7). **Scripture helps us discern what is almost true from what is actually true. Almost true is still false**. And dangerous. Satan looks attractive at times (2 Cor. 11:14), but do not be fooled. When the enemy presents good-looking detours from God's path, God's Word lights up the right path so we can follow it (Ps. 119:105). The sword of the Spirit is the only offensive weapon in our armor. It's "living and active, sharper than any two-edged sword, piercing to the division of soul and of spirit, of joints and of marrow, and discerning the thoughts and intentions of the heart" (Heb. 4:12 ESV). Use it to slash the enemy's lies, the way Jesus did.

The sword of the Spirit is always sharp and effective in battle. But how firm is our grip on it? Would we go into battle holding a deadly weapon with only two fingers? Of course not. If we did, we would be easily defeated. Similarly, holding loosely to the sword of the Spirit, leaving our Bibles unopened and unread as we go out into the world each day, is a dangerous choice. Why would any of us go into battle ignorant of our most effective weapon? Friend, we need to learn to handle this weapon well (2 Tim. 2:15). Keep God's Word close at hand and strengthen your grip on it.

7. **Constant Prayer:** No soldier goes to battle without some way to communicate with leaders, and neither should we. We need to be in constant communication with our Leader for direction. "I will instruct you and teach you in the way you should go; I will counsel you with my eye upon you" (Ps. 32:8 ESV). Always pray for yourself and others—that you would stay firm in faith and boldly proclaim Jesus's message (Eph. 6:19). Talk to God and listen for His instructions.

Thinking about life as a constant battle might seem intense, exhausting, even frightening. But it is not. Battling is not about bleeding or surrendering to the enemy. It is about abiding in Jesus. He has already bled for us and won the victory (1 John 5:4). Rest in His ability to fight for you (Exod. 14:14). **The battle belongs to God** (2 Chron. 20:15).

DAY 27

Let the Bible Speak:
Psalm 91 (Optional: Isaiah 59:17–19)

Let Your Mind Think:
1. How does knowing God is with you change the way you see your journey?

2. What pieces of armor would be most helpful to you in resisting the enemy?

3. How can we be certain victory is ours (Ps. 91; Eph. 1:19–23)?

Let Your Soul Pray:
Lord, help me abide in You and trust You to lead me. Remind me to put on Your armor in Your strength so I can resist the devil and encourage other believers who walk with me. Help me enjoy this journey with You and grow closer to You with every step I take . . . In Jesus's name, amen.

Let Your Heart Obey:
(What is God leading you to know, value, or do?)

DAY
28

Enter God's Rest Through God's Word

So then, there remains a Sabbath rest for the people of God, for whoever has entered God's rest has also rested from his works as God did from his. Let us therefore strive to enter that rest.

Hebrews 4:9–11 ESV

In the beginning, God created the heavens and the earth (Gen. 1). He powerfully spoke into existence all of creation and breathed life into Adam's formed body. When it was all said and done, God created once more–He created a day of rest. From the opening pages of our Bible, we see a rhythm of work and rest that continues throughout God's Story:

- "You have six days each week for your ordinary work, but on the seventh day you must stop working" (Exod. 23:12).
- "Six days you shall labor, but on the seventh day you shall rest; even during the plowing season and harvest you must rest" (Exod. 34:21 NIV).
- "Rest in the LORD and wait patiently for Him" (Ps. 37:7 NASB).
- "Cease striving and know that I am God" (Ps. 46:10 NASB).
- "Come away by yourselves to a desolate place and rest a while" (Mark 6:31 ESV).

It might seem strange that God has to command us to rest, but humans have a long history of resisting rest. Why do we fight it?

Maybe it's because we do not understand it. As we learn in Genesis, God was the first one to rest. "On the seventh day God had finished his work of creation, so he rested from all his work. And God blessed the seventh day and declared it holy, because it was the day when he rested from all his work of creation" (Gen. 2:2–3). The first thing God declares holy is not a person or an object but a day. He rested after He completed His work, and He called His day of rest "holy," or set apart. Based on these verses, we might define rest as time set apart to enjoy God's completed work.

But there is more to this concept of rest than a break from work. Another verse offers more insight: "Only in returning to me and resting in me will you be saved. In quietness and confidence is your strength" (Isa. 30:15). In this case, rest is returning to God, quieting our hearts in His presence, and putting our confidence in Him. **Rest is demonstrating our trust in God**. Although God instructed the Israelites to pause from physical work with a Sabbath day of rest to remember His deliverance (Deut. 5:15), we see God's rest is not just physical inactivity.

In Jesus's day, religious leaders misunderstood rest. When they accused Jesus's disciples of breaking the Sabbath, Jesus responded to them, saying, "The Sabbath was made for man, not man for

A Day of Rest

For believers, spiritual rest in Jesus is a way of life. However, in addition to spiritual rest, God made our bodies to need physical rest. It is wise to take a Sabbath day of rest each week if possible. As we empty ourselves in serving, we must take time to be refilled.

After God used Elijah to demonstrate His mighty power on Mount Carmel, Elijah became exhausted and depressed (see Day 12). God knew Elijah's spiritual depression came from physical exhaustion, so God met Elijah's physical needs. After God gave Elijah rest and food, Elijah was able to return to God's work (1 Kings 18–19).

What restores you? If your job involves physical work, you may need to rest physically by reading a book or sitting down to visit with friends. If your work is not physically active, you may need to rest by getting outside to enjoy God's creation. Jesus taught, "The Sabbath was made to meet the needs of people, and not people to meet the requirements of the Sabbath" (Mark 2:27). There's no need to be legalistic about a weekly day of rest. Just remember that God gave you a physical body with physical limitations. Rest.

the Sabbath" (Mark 2:27 ESV). They later attacked Jesus for breaking their man-made Sabbath rules. But the Sabbath rest was meant to help them, not burden them. Their obsession with the rules of rest blinded them to the heart of rest—and the only real source of rest—Jesus, the Lord of the Sabbath (Matt. 12:8).

Through Jesus, we enjoy ultimate rest—peace with God. We can rely on Him and release all to Him, finding rest in Him. He invites us to join Him in the true rest that only He can provide:

> "Come to me, all of you who are weary and carry heavy burdens, and I will give you rest. Take my **yoke** upon you. Let me teach you, because I am humble and gentle at heart, and you will find rest for your souls. For my yoke is easy to bear, and the burden I give you is light." (Matt. 11:28–30, emphasis added)

Yoke: A fitted frame worn across the shoulders to help a person or an animal carry a load in two equal parts.

Rest, in the fullest sense of the word, flows from our relationship with God, a relationship made possible only through Christ. **Rest, then, means more than one work-free day each week; it also means abiding in Jesus as a way of life.** Physical, mental, emotional, and spiritual rest is a priceless gift from God.

> We rest physically from our labor.
> We rest from our anxiety, fear, or worry.
> We rest in God's salvation.

God's grace makes it possible to work and rest. But if we seek our value in work, resting will be difficult. If we find our worth in Jesus, we place our confidence no longer in what *we* do but in what *He* has done. We rest in Him. And when we work, we work not to earn God's love but in response to His love. Work and rest stay in balance when we are abiding in Him.

So why do we resist rest? We learn from the Israelites how they refused to enter God's rest when they refused to enter the Promised Land (Heb. 3:17–19). They did not believe He would take care of them, and as a result, they worried and wandered restlessly through the wilderness. On a larger scale, all sin follows this same pattern. We doubt that God will satisfy us, so we look for satisfaction outside of His will. And we doubt God is in control, so we hold on to our problems. Then we worry and wander restlessly, estranged from God. It's like pacing back and forth, wearing ourselves out, and going nowhere. We stay in the wilderness.

Today, God invites us to enter His rest, not through the Promised Land, but through the Promised One–Jesus. When people do not trust Christ, they reject His gift of rest. They doubt Him, disobey Him, and wander restlessly through life. Even as believers, we can fall into a similar pattern. When we doubt God's promises and disobey His commands, we block our abiding connection with Him and fail to enter His rest.

Are you restless? Whether you have never trusted Jesus for your life or have trusted Him but wandered away, the solution is the same: return to God and rest in Him. "In returning and rest you shall be saved" (Isa. 30:15 ESV). Ask God to prune (or cut away) any deadwood that keeps you from abiding in Him. Believe God and believe what He says. Hebrews 4:3 says it this way: "For only we who believe can enter his rest." You can rest and relax in God's warm embrace, knowing He is always with you, always loves you, and is always worthy. So when life seems overwhelming and worries try to consume you, take a deep breath. Breathe in God's love; breathe out anxiety. Get your focus back on God (Col. 3) and enter His rest once again.

Let the Bible Speak:
Hebrews 3:7–4:12 (Optional: Matt. 12:1–14)

Let Your Mind Think:
1. How would you define God's rest? In what ways do you need to enter His rest?

2. Answer Week 4 Discussion Questions.

Let Your Soul Pray:
Father, You are my refuge. You say, "Come to me, all you who are weary and burdened, and I will give you rest" (Matt. 11:28 NIV). *I am weary and burdened. Give me Your rest. Quiet my heart and rescue me from all that blocks my connection with You . . . In Jesus's name, amen.*

Let Your Heart Obey:
(What is God leading you to know, value, or do?)

WEEK 4 DISCUSSION QUESTIONS:

**Review this week's lessons and answer the questions below.
Share your answers with your friends when you gather this week.**

1. How does abiding in Jesus grow your relationship with God and help you live out your story in His strength?

2. How has God pruned you in the past? What hindrances to abiding in Christ does God want to free you from?

3. "The fruit of the Spirit is love, joy, peace, patience, kindness, goodness, faithfulness, gentleness, [and] self-control" (Gal. 5:22–23 ESV). Which of these do you seem to bear in abundance? Which of these aspects do you want to grow more fully?

4. How does sin cause suffering? Why does sin block your connection with Jesus? What practical steps can you take to resist temptation?

5. How can you put on the armor of God each day? Which piece of armor is especially reassuring to you? Which one(s) might you neglect to put on regularly?

WEEK FIVE

GOD'S WORD—LISTENING
TO THE AUTHOR OF LIFE

Cherish God's Word

They are not just idle words for you—they are your life.
Deuteronomy 32:47 NIV

If we really want to know God, if we really want to understand how to change our lives and the world, the Bible needs to be a high priority. But it is not enough to know the truths of the Bible. We need to live the truths of the Bible *with* God. Lives transform and communities change when we lovingly apply biblical truth through the power of the Holy Spirit. We're dedicating this week to the Bible—our most precious earthly possession. We'll take a tour of the Bible, learn how to study and memorize it, discover why we can trust it, and more. Let's get started.

The Bible is unlike any other book in all of history. God inspired more than forty human authors from different backgrounds to write it. They were shepherds, religious leaders, kings, government officers, and fishermen. They wrote over a period of more than 1,600 years on three different continents—Asia, Europe, and Africa.[1] But here is the wonder of it all: These diverse authors all point to the same theme. Why? Because *God Himself* guided them to tell *His* Story. Who else could weave a unified message of truth through such different times, personalities, and cultures? Who else could write such a life-changing book consistent within itself? No one but God. It is His Book—His True Story.

---

1 Howard G. Hendricks and William D. Hendricks, *Living By the Book: The Art and Science of Reading the Bible* (Chicago: Moody Publishers, 2007), 26.

How do we know? His Word tells us, and His life flows through it.[1] "All Scripture is inspired by God" (2 Tim. 3:16), for "no prophecy in Scripture ever came from the prophet's own understanding, or from human initiative. No, those prophets were moved by the Holy Spirit, and they spoke from God" (2 Pet. 1:20–21). Through His Word, God speaks to us, teaches us, corrects us, and prepares us for what lies ahead (2 Tim. 3:16–17). On every page of Scripture, God reveals *Himself* to us, and our love for Him grows deeper. **To love God more, we get to know Him in His Word.**

That is why accepting *every part* of the Bible is so important. And why altering Scripture is so dangerous. Picking and choosing what parts of it we believe and discarding the parts we disagree with are like crafting our particular religion or carving out a false god. Just as life-saving medication can become ineffective or dangerous if altered, so can life-giving Scripture. Jesus warned against ignoring the parts of the Bible we do not like:

> Not even the smallest detail of God's law will disappear until its purpose is achieved. So if you ignore the least commandment and teach others to do the same, you will be called the least in the Kingdom of Heaven. But anyone who obeys God's laws and teaches them will be called great in the Kingdom of Heaven. (Matt. 5:18–19)

Do not edit God's Word.

Do not add other material to God's Word, either. "Every word of God is flawless . . . Do not add to his words, or he will rebuke you and prove you a liar" (Prov. 30:5–6 NIV). In Revelation, we see an even stronger warning against altering God's Word:

> I warn everyone who hears the words of the prophecy of this book: if anyone adds to them, God will add to him the plagues described in this book, and if anyone takes away from the words of the book of this prophecy, God will take away his share in the tree of life and in the holy city, which are described in this book. (Rev. 22:18–19 ESV)

---

1 Day 31 addresses the validity of God's Word.

The consequences of changing or twisting God's Word are severe, so "refuse to practice cunning or to tamper with God's word" (2 Cor. 4:2 ESV).

Even with these warnings, people still add to or take away from the Bible to justify their beliefs or avoid offending others. That's why studying the Bible for ourselves is critically important. We can know God and His Word. We do not need to be surprised about future events the Bible reveals, like our judgment (Day 6). We can safeguard ourselves from false teaching and learn God's wisdom as we study the Bible.

> ### Bible Translations
> Today's Bible translations are superb. The original manuscripts of the Bible were carefully hand copied for generations. Small copy errors have been found (e.g., misspelled words, missing or duplicate letters). Of the less than 1 percent of Scripture that was copied incorrectly, no doctrinal teaching or command was compromised.
>
> Source: Geisler, Norman L. "Bible, Evidence For," *Baker Encyclopedia of Christian Apologetics*, Baker Reference Library (Grand Rapids, MI: Baker Books, 1999).

Your Bible study time might be separate from your devotional time. During devotional time (Day 22), you may want to meditate on a few Bible verses, pray, and listen for the Holy Spirit's promptings (Gal. 5:16). **In Bible study, our reading of the Bible is more intense: we research it, memorize it, and study it carefully to learn more about God**. Whether you study the Bible during your quiet time or do this separately, the point is to be intentional and consistent.

Sometimes we struggle to study the Bible. Schedules get changed. Family members get sick. Life gets complicated. The result is we get distracted and Bible study seems burdensome. Let's learn some of the blessings that only come when we persevere to know God's Word:

1. **Know God**—Scripture weaves God's person, position, and power on all the pages for you to know, worship, and love God. Without spending time in God's Word, we tend to forget Him. And as we remember from Day 17, forgetting is dangerous.

2. **Know yourself**—God's Word is like a mirror reflecting the reality of our hearts. We see what God wants us to see about ourselves and how He blesses us when we walk in His ways (James 1:22–25).

3. **Know God's plan**—The Bible reveals an origin-to-destiny perspective of the world (Week 1) and our part in it. Living only in the here and now without understanding God's bigger True Story, we can get discouraged and distracted.

4. **Know how to live well every day**—Today, you decided to read this faith journey. In a few minutes, you'll choose to apply what you learned. After that, you'll make another decision and another. Every day you make thousands of decisions, and God's Word guides you like light on a path to help you make wise choices (Ps. 119:105).

Just as a daily rhythm of exercise and eating healthy changes us slowly physically, regularly studying the Bible gradually transforms us spiritually. Whether or not we're aware of the change, we do strengthen our spiritual muscles. But unlike with physical food, when we fill ourselves with God's Word, we never become too full. Our capacity for God's Word just expands, and we crave more of it. God's Word is the only feast that can truly satisfy the hunger of our souls. As you learn this week how to study the Bible, you'll discover its immeasurable value, often described in word pictures:

- God's Word grows you like a **seed** (1 Pet. 1:23).
- God's Word guides you like **light** (Ps. 119:105).
- God's Word washes you like **water** (Eph. 5:25–26).
- God's Word anchors you like **bedrock** (Matt. 7:24–25).
- God's Word **rains** on you, nourishing growth that bears fruit (Isa. 55:10–11).
- God's Word prunes you and protects you like a sharp **sword** (Eph. 6:17; Heb. 4:12).

- God's Word **teaches, rebukes, corrects**, and **trains** you (2 Tim. 3:16–17).
- God's Word is your **very life** (Deut. 32:47).

God's Word is life-giving and heart-changing. No wonder the enemy relentlessly attacks it. Getting us to question Scripture is his oldest trick. Remember when he tempted Eve in the garden, he asked, "Did God really say . . . ?" (Gen. 3:1). If he can plant doubt, he can start a chain reaction that leads us away from God:

- Satan knows that if we do not trust God's Word, we will not read it.
- If we do not read God's Word, we will not discover God's Story and the story He has written for us.
- If we do not discover God's Story, we will not know when the enemy is deceiving us.
- And if we are deceived, we will not resist temptation, nor will we worship God.

Yes, the enemy desperately wants us to doubt God's Word. But as we learned, we can extinguish these flaming arrows of doubt with our shields of faith. *Believe* God's Word. Confidently take up that sword of the Spirit and "destroy the devil's work" (1 John 3:8 NIV). That is why Jesus came, and that is why we are here. We destroy the devil's work when we liberate generations, neighbors, and nations with the truth of God's Word. Let's wield our swords well.

DAY 29

Let the Bible Speak:
Psalm 19:7–11 (Optional: 2 Peter 1)

Let Your Mind Think:
1. Which word picture of the Bible means the most to you right now? Why?

2. What is the difference between devotional time and Bible study? How can you make time for both?

3. On Day 19, we read Psalm 19. Reread verses 7–11 and list the different descriptions and purposes of God's Word. What are some specific ways God's Word has changed you?

Let Your Soul Pray:
Father, You are the Author of life, the Author of the Bible, and the Author of my story. As I read Your Word, reveal Yourself to me. Give me wisdom and understanding. Show me how to apply Your Word to my daily life as I live out the story You've written for me. "Open my eyes that I may see wonderful things in your law" (Ps. 119:18 NIV) . . . In Jesus's name, amen.

Let Your Heart Obey:
(What is God leading you to know, value, or do?)

DAY

30

Receive God's Word–The Parable of Seeds and Soil

A farmer went out to plant his seed. . . . The seed is God's word.
Luke 8:5, 11

Between the moment you receive Jesus and the instant you receive your new residence in heaven, few things are more nourishing and satisfying to your soul than feasting on–receiving–God's Word. The more we read God's Word, the more we will want to read it. That's because as we absorb and apply the truths of Scripture to our lives, we radically change (Rom. 12:2). The presence of sin loses its potency. The grace of God penetrates our hearts. **But to unleash the power of God's Word in our lives, we need to read it *and receive it.***

Jesus illustrates how we receive God's Word in a parable about seeds and soil. As you read, *remember God's Word is the seed* (Luke 8:11):

> "A farmer went out to plant his seed. As he scattered it across his field, some seed fell on a footpath, where it was stepped on, and the birds ate it. Other seed fell among rocks. It began to grow, but the plant soon wilted and died for lack of moisture. Other seed fell among thorns that grew up with it and choked out the tender plants. Still other seed fell on fertile soil. This seed grew and produced a crop that was a hundred times as much as had been planted!" (Luke 8:5–8)

Notice all the seed was good. The seed in this parable is perfect. It's the condition of a person's heart and how they receive God's

Word that makes the difference between a life of fruit and a life that's stuck and not growing in faith. The condition of the soil limits or promotes growth. God's Word is true and powerful and ready to bear fruit, but *we* determine how fruitful it will be in our lives. As you read Jesus's explanation of the four different soils, think about the condition of your own heart. Which soil are you?

1. **Are you a footpath, hardened and exposed to the enemy?** "The seeds that fell on the footpath represent those who hear the message, only to have the devil come and take it away from their hearts and prevent them from believing and being saved" (Luke 8:12).

Is your life a highway hardened by past hurts, emotional doubt, or sinful living? If so, the world may crush the seed of God's Word as soon as it falls on you. The enemy may snatch away what's left. If we harden our hearts, harboring spite or indulging in sinful behavior, we expose ourselves to the enemy and make it harder for God's Word to grow. The Old Testament prophet Hosea gave these instructions to the Israelites whose lives had been hardened by sin:

> Sow righteousness for yourselves, reap the fruit of unfailing love, and *break up your unplowed ground*; for it is time to seek the LORD, until he comes and showers his righteousness on you. (Hosea 10:12 NIV, emphasis added)

The Israelites' lives were like the unplowed ground, which was unused and unusable. The solution, then, was to open up their hearts, like breaking up unplowed ground preparing the soil, to receive God's righteousness. It is the same now for us. If God is speaking to you right now, do not harden your heart (Heb. 4:7). Ask God to heal emotional wounds or remove harmful habits that harden your life. No matter how neglected or hard those areas of our lives may be, God can still produce a harvest. He will give us His grace for every step of change and healing along the way.

2. **Are you like rocky soil with shallow roots?** "The seeds on the rocky soil represent those who hear the message and receive it with

joy. But since they don't have deep roots, they believe for a while, then they fall away when they face temptation" (Luke 8:13).

Does this describe you? Do you feel good when you hear the good news of Jesus but lose your resolve to follow Him when faith seems hard and another path seems easier? Momentary enthusiasm for Jesus is not the same as abiding in Him (see Week 4). Some people seem spiritually passionate for a while, but inwardly, they do not abide in Jesus. Spiritual feelings are not the spiritual roots we need to sustain us through suffering and temptation. Shallow faith fades over time.

We humans are often shallow, living out of our emotions. Shallowness is living in what we think and feel instead of being led by the Holy Spirit. We need to say, "I believe it, and no one can steal it from me." If our soil is rocky, we need to dig out the rocks of apathy or laziness. They are boulders that weigh us down and prevent our spiritual growth. Instead, let your roots grow deep into God. "From his glorious, unlimited resources he will empower you with inner strength through his Spirit. Then Christ will make his home in your hearts as you trust in him. Your roots will grow down into God's love and keep you strong" (Eph. 3:16–17). Look back on Day 24 to review how to grow deep roots.

3. **Are you like thorny soil, tangled up in worry and wealth and pleasure?** "The seeds that fell among the thorns represent those who hear the message, but all too quickly the message is crowded out by the cares and riches and pleasures of this life. And so they never grow into maturity" (Luke 8:14).

Are you consumed with worry about your life, your appearance, or your success? Do you think about money often, always wanting more? Do you want happiness, entertainment, or leisure more than you want God? If so, these lesser things will grow up like thorns and strangle your spiritual growth. We miss so much of what God has for us when we're distracted by pleasure, false glamour, money, and other lesser things.

Jesus warned us not to worry: "These things dominate the thoughts of unbelievers, but your heavenly Father already knows all your needs. Seek the Kingdom of God above all else, and live righteously, and he will give you everything you need" (Matt. 6:32–33).

4. **Are you the good soil?** "Still other seed fell on fertile soil. This seed grew and produced a crop that was a hundred times as much as had been planted! . . . And the seeds that fell on the good soil represent honest, good-hearted people who hear God's word, cling to it, and patiently produce a huge harvest" (Luke 8:8, 15).

Now we come to the desired soil. The "fertile soil" that produces a harvest from God's Word. But as we did with the other soils, let's put our hearts to the test: Do you love God's Word and apply it to your life? Do you depend on it for wisdom and strength? Do you trust God more than you trust your own understanding (Prov. 3:5)? If so, God's Word will flourish in you and bear much fruit (Day 25).

Jesus invites us to pray for the harvest: "If you abide in me, and my words abide in you, ask whatever you wish, and it will be done for you. By this my Father is glorified, that you bear much fruit and so prove to be my disciples" (John 15:7–8 ESV). Notice the disciple-making context of these verses. Jesus promises to give us whatever we ask, *if we stay connected to Him and His Word.* When we do, we want what He wants and make requests in line with His will.

Revisit this parable of seeds and soil to remember what it takes to become good soil: "Hear God's word, cling to it, and patiently produce a huge harvest" (Luke 8:15). If you find an aspect of your life that is unplowed ground, surrender it to the Lord for His cultivation. God is the great Gardener (John 15:1), and His will is to bear fruit in your life.

Let this parable also encourage you as you sow the seed of God's Word into other people's lives. When you share God's Word, the seeds you plant are good. If they do not take root and grow in someone's life, the soil—the condition of their heart—may be the problem. **God will measure our lives not by the harvest but by the seeds we sow in love**. Our job is to sow God's Word lovingly and to water it as we disciple new believers, but *God alone* makes it grow (1 Cor. 3:6–8).

DAY 30

Let the Bible Speak:
Luke 8:4–15 (Optional: Jeremiah 4:1–4)

Let Your Mind Think:
1. Most of us identify with more than one kind of soil in our hearts. What kinds of soil do you find in your heart?

2. What unplowed ground or thorny distractions threaten your growth and fruitfulness?

3. Where do you see God bearing fruit in your life now? Take a moment to celebrate His faithfulness and commitment to your growth in Him. Write down where you are experiencing fruit so you can remember it (make a memorial stone—see Day 17).

Let Your Soul Pray:
Father, thank You for the good seed of Your Word. Please keep the enemy from snatching it away from me. Help me grow deep roots to draw on Your endless stores of refreshment and strength. Make my heart fertile ground for Your Word to grow and bear fruit . . . In Jesus's name, amen.

Let Your Heart Obey:
(What is God leading you to know, value, or do?)

Trust God's Word– Reasons to Believe

Your word is truth.
John 17:17 NASB

How do you know the Bible is not a made-up story? Has anyone ever asked you that? Maybe you've wondered yourself whether God's Word really *is* God's Book. As you will discover today, we can have confidence in the authority of Scripture.

Not only does the Bible claim to be the Word of God thousands of times . . .

Not only does God tell us He inspired men to write the books of the Bible . . .

Not only do the authors attribute the words they were writing to God . . .

But there also are many other reasons to trust the Bible. For now, we'll explore just eight:

1. **Jesus trusted God's Word and testified personally to its authenticity.** Jesus began His ministry by reading Isaiah 61:1–2, which described the Rescuer God promised to send. He then announced, "Today this scripture is fulfilled in your hearing" (Luke 4:21 NIV). Jesus taught God's Word, the Law, and lived it. He said, "Do not think that I have come to abolish the Law or the Prophets; I have not come to abolish them but to fulfill them" (Matt. 5:17 NIV). As we learned on Day 26, Jesus also resisted temptation by quoting Scripture, prefacing each response to

Satan with "It is written" (Matt. 4:4, 7, 10 NIV). On Jesus's resurrection day—the first Easter—He led two disciples through the Bible, explaining "all the Scriptures concerning himself" (Luke 24:27 NIV). If Jesus, the perfect Son of God, trusted God's Word, how much more should we?

2. **The Bible is full of historical and geographical references**. An imaginary work would not likely include so much historical detail. The historical books of the Old Testament are filled with specific details on places, dates, times, people, and the ancient Near East culture. In his account of Jesus's life, Luke included every detail necessary to provide the full context for Jesus's birth. What details can you find in these verses?

> At that time the Roman emperor, Augustus, decreed that a census should be taken throughout the Roman Empire. (This was the first census taken when Quirinius was governor of Syria.) All returned to their own ancestral towns to register for this census. And because Joseph was a descendant of King David, he had to go to Bethlehem in Judea, David's ancient home. He traveled there from the village of Nazareth in Galilee. He took with him Mary, to whom he was engaged, who was now expecting a child. (Luke 2:1–5)

In these verses, Luke lists the names of two rulers, a specific historical event, three geographical locations, the name and family history of Joseph, and the reason why Joseph had Mary with him. Luke was not afraid of fact-checkers. In fact, this level of detail invites people to examine the facts for accuracy.

3. **Historical documents and archaeology confirm the Bible is accurate**. Not only does the Bible include truthful spiritual content, but also it records historical and geographical details with remarkable accuracy. For example, archaeologists discovered evidence of the destruction of Jericho that correlates to the biblical account found in Joshua.[1] Aramaic inscriptions that record the "House of

---

1 Walter A. Elwell, *Evangelical Dictionary of Theology: Second Edition* (Grand Rapids, MI: Baker Academic, 2001).

David" were discovered from Tell Dan.[1] A siege ramp and a mass grave were unearthed that match the Assyrian invasion during Hezekiah's reign.[2] Much more archaeological evidence than this has been found.

There are also ancient historical documents recording details of events described in Scripture. For example, Matthew and Mark both describe unusual darkness and an earthquake that occurred when Jesus was crucified:

> From noon until three in the afternoon darkness came over all the land. . . . And when Jesus had cried out again in a loud voice, he gave up his spirit. At that moment the curtain of the temple was torn in two from top to bottom. The earth shook, the rocks split and the tombs broke open. (Matt. 27:45, 50–52 NIV)

Secular historians described similar events. The Greek historian Phlegon wrote that during Tiberius Caesar's reign, around the time Jesus was executed, it became like night in the middle of the day and earthquakes shook the region.[3] Another historian named Thallus wrote that dreadful darkness covered the land and earthquakes split rocks in Judea.[4] These secular records agree with the biblical report of darkness and earthquakes at the time of Jesus's death.

4. **Bible prophecies accurately predicted historical events long before they happened**. The Bible contains hundreds of prophecies, most of which have already been fulfilled. (Those that haven't happened yet apply to the end times when Jesus will return.) Events predicted in the Old Testament and described in the New Testament are some of the most specific prophecies that have ever come true. Here are just a few:

---

1   Ibid.
2   Nicholas R. Werse, "Hezekiah, King of Judah," ed. John D. Barry, David Bomar, Derek R. Brown, Rachel Klippenstein, Douglas Mangum, Carrie Sinclair Wolcott, Lazarus Wentz, Elliot Ritzema, and Wendy Widder, *The Lexham Bible Dictionary* (Bellingham, WA: Lexham Press, 2016).
3   Gary R. Habermas, *The Historical Jesus: Ancient Evidence for the Life of Christ* (Joplin, MO: College Press Publishing Company, 1996), 218.
4   Ibid., 196–197.

- About 700 years before Jesus's birth, Micah wrote that the Messiah would be born in Bethlehem (Mic. 5:2; Matt. 2:1–6).
- Zechariah predicted that Jesus would be betrayed for thirty pieces of silver (Zech. 11:12; Matt. 26:14–15).
- David prophesied that Jesus's hands and feet would be pierced (Ps. 22:16; John 20:24–28).
- Isaiah predicted that Jesus's body would rest in a rich man's tomb (Isa. 53:9; Matt. 27:57–60).
- Jesus's resurrection was also predicted multiple times (Ps. 16:8–11; Acts 2:24–31).

Perhaps a person could try to manipulate some life details to fulfill Scripture, but no one could change where they would be born, how they would die, or what would happen to their body after death. People cannot know or control the future, *but God can and does*. The Bible accurately predicts future events because its Author knows "the end from the beginning" (Isa. 46:10).

5. **The Bible includes embarrassing information about its "heroes."** Many ancient historians exaggerated leaders' victories and down-played or eliminated failures in an attempt to promote ideologies or causes. But the Bible's writers made no such adjustments. Scripture openly reports that Abraham fathered a son with his wife's servant and lied about his wife, calling her his sister. Jacob lied and stole. Moses committed murder. David committed murder and adultery. Jonah ran from God and then hated that the people of Nineveh re-pented. Peter denied Christ three times. Paul arrested and condoned the murdering of followers of Jesus. If the Bible were man-made, it would probably not expose the flaws of its heroes, but thankfully, the Bible was divinely inspired to glorify God, not people.

6. **The Bible includes multiple eyewitness accounts**. Four different people—Matthew, Mark (under Peter's guidance), Luke, and John—wrote accounts of Jesus's life. If their stories were entirely different, we could not trust them. But their stories are very similar, with only minor variances that seem to be based on their personalities, the

details they noticed, and the people to whom they spoke. The variations that some call "inconsistencies" are another reason why we *should* trust that these stories are authentic.[1] Identical stories from four very different men would strongly suggest copying or heavy editing. When we read the Gospels of Matthew, Mark, Luke, and John, they are similar, but not identical. That is what we would precisely expect from multiple, true accounts of the same events.

7. **The Bible values women and relies on their testimony**. The cultures in which the Bible was written did not respect women. Yet the Bible praises, rewards, and celebrates women over and over again. The Bible reports that women were the first to discover Jesus's empty tomb while the men hid in fear behind locked doors. If the male biblical authors had invented the story of the resurrection, they would not have described themselves as cowards, much less chosen female witnesses to Jesus's resurrection, since a woman's testimony in their culture was considered worthless. The Gospels also readily report that Jesus spoke not only to women (including some who were prostitutes) but also to foreigners, children, lepers, and tax collectors. He openly spoke with all sorts of people that the culture found offensive or worthless. Though these interactions were shocking, Jesus's followers—divinely inspired to write God's Story with unfailing accuracy—recorded them anyway. The Bible is not a product of their culture. It is a product of God.

8. **Finally, you can know the truth of the Bible personally through your own experience**. As you read the Bible every day, truths will stand out to you at just the right time. You will begin to notice the depth and clarity and beauty of God's Word. The Holy Spirit will help you see connections between different portions of Scripture, giving you a fuller understanding of spiritual truths. Often, reading the Bible will provide you with peace even if what you are reading does not directly describe the sources of your stress. That is because every time you read it, you meet with the Author, and encountering God gives you peace.

---

1 J. Warner. Wallace, *Cold-Case Christianity: A Homicide Detective Investigates the Claims of the Gospels* (Colorado Springs, CO: David C Cook, 2013).

But what happens when you don't *feel* God's peace? What happens when you experience uncertainty? It's normal to have questions and doubts, especially when we suffer. Even John the Baptist doubted Jesus. This man who God sent to prepare the way for Jesus—who boldly confronted hypocrisy, preached repentance, and declared, "Look, the Lamb of God, who takes away the sin of the world!" (John 1:29 NIV)—was the same man who doubted Jesus from a prison cell. John the Baptist sent his disciples to ask Jesus, "Are you the Messiah we've been expecting, or should we keep looking for someone else?" (Luke 7:19). Alone, hungry, and imprisoned by the evil King Herod, John wondered if Jesus would establish the kingdom since it hadn't happened.

In response, Jesus presented evidence *through Scripture*: "Go back and report to John what you have seen and heard: The blind receive sight, the lame walk, those who have leprosy are cleansed, the deaf hear, the dead are raised, and the good news is proclaimed to the poor" (Luke 7:22 NIV). Jesus was saying He was doing all that the Scriptures said He, the Messiah, would do (Isa. 35:5–6).

If doubt causes you to question the truth, go back to the evidence, as Jesus encouraged John the Baptist to do. Remember how you've experienced God. Let creation convince you again of God's existence. Immerse yourself in God's Word. Pray like the man who cried out to Jesus, "I do believe; help me over-come my unbelief!" (Mark 9:24 NIV).

But doubts do not have to be a part of your story. Another man of God, Paul, also found himself in a prison cell with

> ### Doubts? Consider Luke 11:9–10:
> "So I say to you: Ask and it will be given to you; seek and you will find; knock and the door will be opened to you. For everyone who asks receives; the one who seeks finds; and to the one who knocks, the door will be opened." (NIV)

his execution quickly approaching. Still, he did not waver in his faith. Why was he so confident? Faith. Factual evidence is essential, but it pales in comparison to confidence born of faith, which grows through an abiding relationship with God. Paul wrote, "This is no cause for shame, because I know whom I have believed" (2 Tim. 1:12 NIV). *Whom* he believed steadied his heart, not *what* he believed. When you suffer, or have doubts, remember *whom* you have believed. Abide in Him.

Let the Bible Speak:

2 Timothy 3:14–4:8 (Optional: Exodus 24:4)

Let Your Mind Think:

1. What do you think is the most persuasive reason to trust the Bible?

2. Why do you think people believe the Bible is not accurate or relevant? Do you believe the Bible is accurate and relevant? Why or why not? Take time to allow the Bible to help you in any area of unbelief.

3. How might abiding in Jesus help someone grow in their trust in God's Word?

Let Your Soul Pray:

Father, Your Word is true. All of it. Help me believe it and follow it fully. I pray that I will know, really know, the truth. Only Your truth will set me free (John 8:32). Your Word is truth (John 17:17). Lord, make our personal relationship so real, so close, so full, that it leaves no room for doubt . . . In Jesus's name, amen.

Let Your Heart Obey:

(What is God leading you to know, value, or do?)

Tour the Bible– Book by Book

Your promises have been thoroughly tested,
and your servant loves them.
Psalm 119:140 NIV

If your Bible could speak, what would it say to you? Would it share how you are beginning your journey through its pages? Or would it welcome your return after a long time away? Maybe it would share how it delights in your daily moments together. But if your Bible seems neglected, today we can help you become more acquainted. If you feel a little intimidated with the Bible's library of sixty-six books, you're not alone. Where do you begin? An excellent way to feel more comfortable in unfamiliar territory is to take a guided tour.

Yes, our faith journey today includes a tour of the Bible. By overviewing its basic context and content, we will discover how God's Story fits together. We'll also get a better sense of where to read to find the help we need. We'll end our tour with suggestions on which parts you may consider reading first. Let's go.

We will start where the Bible starts: the **Old Testament**. Originally written mostly in Hebrew, the Old Testament was compiled over a period of one thousand years.[1] It can be divided into four parts:

---

1 The Old Testament books were originally written in Hebrew, except for portions of the book of Daniel, which were originally written in Aramaic.

1. **The Torah (Genesis–Deuteronomy):** The Torah, or Jewish Written Law, consists of the first five books of the Bible. These books were given by God to Moses and include within them the stories of creation, the flood, the Patriarchs, and the wanderings of the Hebrew nation before entering the Promised Land. They also include the biblical laws of Judaism, beginning with the Ten Commandments. The Torah is also referred to as the Pentateuch or the Five Books of Moses.

2. **Story of God's People (Joshua–Esther):** The next twelve books of the Bible continue to tell the story of God's people in roughly chronological order. We've already walked through their story from the time of creation through the crossing of the Jordan River into the Promised Land (Genesis–Joshua). Let's return to the point where we left the story.

In **Joshua**, we read about God leading the Israelites to conquer the Promised Land. At first, the Israelites did not have a king; they had judges. In the book of **Judges**, we see cycles of rampant sin and short-lived repentance, for "there was no [earthly] king in Israel. Everyone did what was right in his own eyes" (Judg. 21:25 ESV). As it often does, the people's sin led to suffering. God remained faithful and continually delivered His people through leaders, the judges, but sadly, the Israelites repeatedly returned to doing evil.[1] They ignored God and worshiped idols. Against this backdrop of sin, we find the book of **Ruth**. Some scholars believe Ruth is written from a women's perspective. This book teaches us how God includes a woman from outside of Israel in His rescue plan, making her part of the family line of Jesus.

Eventually, the Israelites demanded a king so they could be like all the other nations. God gave them what they asked for, and in **1 Samuel**, we meet the first king of Israel, Saul. This king quickly wandered from God's path and lost God's blessing. In 1 Samuel 13 we meet David, whose reign as king of Israel is documented in **2 Samuel**. David was a man after God's own heart (1 Sam. 13:14) who wrote

---

1   Judg. 2:2–3, 11–13, 17, 19; 3:6, 7, 12; 4:1; 6:1, 10; 8:24–27, 33; 10:6; 13:1; 17:6; 21:25.

roughly half of what we read in Psalms. He was also a man of war, and he had many flaws. Unlike Saul, David repented and turned back to God when he sinned. God blessed David, establishing his throne forever, with the Messiah coming from his family line (2 Sam 7:8–17).

In **1 Kings**, we read about David's son Solomon, who came to power next. He was the wisest of men, but not wise enough to avoid marrying many women who worshiped other gods.

In **2 Kings**, we see time after time that human kings were broken by sin. Many of these kings influenced their people to worship other gods, and everyone suffered the consequences. First, the nation of Israel split into two separate kingdoms—Judah to the south (the southern kingdom) and Israel to the north (the northern kingdom). Then, God sent both kingdoms into captivity because the people refused to repent of their sin and idolatry. The Assyrians eventually conquered Israel. The Babylonians eventually conquered Judah and took many of its people into **exile** in Babylon. The Babylonians were later conquered by the Persians. The time of the kings lasted approximately 345 years,[1] and **1 and 2 Chronicles** reexamine many key events from this time: 1 Chronicles retells much of 1 and 2 Samuel, and 2 Chronicles retells much of 1 and 2 Kings.

> **Exile:**
> A removal of a nation from their homeland. In both the Assyrian and Babylonian invasions, a remnant—or small group of people— was left to work the land.

Finally, after seventy years in exile in Babylon, God brought some of His people back home, just as the Scriptures prophesied.[2] In the book of **Ezra**, we read about a time of both physical and spiritual restoration. As the returning exiles rebuilt the temple in Jerusalem, Ezra the priest helped the people rebuild spiritually by restoring God's law and renewing God's covenant (a formal contract of the relationship between God and His people). The book of **Nehemiah** describes the rebuilding of the wall around Jerusalem, which restored security from nearby enemies. More

---

1 K. A. Kitchen, *On the Reliability of the Old Testament* (Grand Rapids / Cambridge: William B. Eerdmans Publishing Company, 2006), 30–32.
2 Isa. 23:15; Jer. 25:11–12.

importantly, the wall helped to restore the nation's identity and confidence as God's chosen people. In the book of **Esther**, we learn about an incredibly brave Hebrew orphan who became the queen of Persia. Through her royal position and her courage, she risked her life to save God's people from genocide.

3. **The Writings of God's People (Job–Song of Solomon):** The next five books of the Bible record human responses to God, but they are no less inspired by God. These books are also called the books of wisdom, or the Wisdom Literature. The language is often poetic, full of imagery and artfully crafted words. **Job** tells the story of a man's faithfulness to God despite intense suffering. **Psalms** is a collection of prayer songs and poems, devoted to God's glory, which often express raw human emotion in light of God's truth. King Solomon recorded some of his wisdom in **Proverbs** and described the emptiness of a godless life in **Ecclesiastes**. He also wrote a passionate love poem called the **Song of Songs**, also called **Song of Solomon**. This poetic song tells a romantic story between a bridegroom and his bride. Some scholars believe it symbolizes God's love for people and Jesus's love for the church.

4. **The Writings of the Prophets (Isaiah–Malachi):** The final seventeen books of the Old Testament are God's responses to His people. In these books, God expresses His great love and compassion, urging His people to repent and return to Him. God also warns that people who refuse to repent and trust Him will suffer His wrath.

Through the stories of God's people, their responses to God, and God's responses to them, the Old Testament teaches us about the devastating effects of sin on our relationships with each other as well as with God. But throughout these stories, God repeatedly promises to send a Rescuer. In this sense, the Old Testament is a story of hope and the New Testament is the fulfillment of that hope.

Not long after the resurrection of Jesus, nine human authors, inspired by God, wrote the **New Testament** books in Koine Greek, the common language of that time.[1] Just like the Old Testament, the New Testament can be divided into four parts:

1. **The Story of Jesus (Matthew–John):** The Gospels of Matthew, Mark, Luke, and John tell the story of Jesus's life, teachings, death, and resurrection.

2. **The History of the Church (Acts):** The book of Acts records the first thirty years of the early church and the spread of Christianity. Sometimes called the Acts of the Holy Spirit, the book includes the coming of the Spirit on Pentecost (see p. 1).

3. **The Letters of the New Testament (Romans–Jude):** These letters, written by leaders in the early church, explain Jesus-centered theology. They also describe how to live in community with other believers and how to represent Jesus to unbelievers.

4. **The Conclusion (Revelation):** This book describes the end times when Jesus will return to reign forever. We see the wrath of God released on those who remain separated from God by their sin. But we also see the full expression of God's love and His presence with His people in a new heaven and a new earth. It is a book of great hope in the life to come, an eternity with no more sorrow or suffering because Jesus makes all things new (Rev. 21:4–5).

Now that we've taken a quick tour of the Bible, here are suggestions to get started:

*   Start with the Gospels. As ambassadors of Jesus, the most important thing we can do is learn about Him—who He is, what He says and does, what He cares about. Follow Him by

---

1   James P. Sweeney, "Chronology of the New Testament," ed. John D. Barry, David Bomar, Derek R. Brown, Rachel Klippenstein, Douglas Mangum, Carrie Sinclair Wolcott, Lazarus Wentz, Elliot Ritzema, and Wendy Widder, *The Lexham Bible Dictionary* (Bellingham, WA: Lexham Press, 2016).

repeatedly reading through Matthew, Mark, Luke, and John in whatever order you choose. You will get to know your Rescuer, and you will become more like Him. As you read, you will also notice that Jesus frequently quoted from Deuteronomy and Psalms, so you may want to read those two books next. To better understand how to live according to Jesus's teaching, read the letters of the New Testament. Each New Testament letter was written to address a particular situation, so it is essential to read all the books repeatedly.

- When you start a book, make the time to read through it all in one or two sittings to get a good overview. Then, start reading the book again from the beginning, but this time read slowly. Focus on key ideas.

- Consider using a daily reading plan to guide you through the whole Bible. You can find several reading plans online. Also, many Bibles include reading plans on the front or back pages.

Whichever approach to reading you choose, **the goal is not for us to get through the Bible but for the Bible to get through to us**. Now you know *where* to read in the Bible. Tomorrow, you will learn in greater detail *how* to read it so that you strengthen your relationship with God.

DAY 32

Let the Bible Speak:
Psalm 119:1–56 (Optional: 2 Peter 3:18)

Let Your Mind Think:
1. On our Bible tour, what stop along the way was new to you or surprised you?

2. Read the first part of Psalm 119 (vv. 1–56). How are we blessed?

3. Talk with a friend about which book of the Bible to study first. You might agree on a reading plan to work through together. Then hold each other accountable and discuss what you learned. As you read each book, look for how it fits into God's larger story.

Let Your Soul Pray:
Father, Your Word is so rich, so full. Help me study it every day. As I read the Gospels, help me to begin to act, think, and speak like Jesus. Open my mind and heart, and "give me understanding according to your word" (Ps. 119:169 NIV) . . . *In Jesus's name, amen.*

Let Your Heart Obey:
(What is God leading you to know, value, or do?)

Study the Bible—
Step by Step

Open my eyes that I may see wonderful things in your law.
Psalm 119:18 NIV

The religious leaders waited their whole lives for this very moment. Year after year, they spent time learning and fulfilling the commands in Scripture. These men prided themselves on their memorization and interpretation of the Hebrew Bible (Old Testament). They taught their children, as their parents had taught them, to prepare for the coming Messiah. And when this moment came, when Jesus stood in front of them, many of these experts in the law did not recognize Him. Not because Jesus did not fulfill the prophecies—He did. Not because they were confused—they were not. They missed Him because they missed the meaning of Scripture. Jesus said to them:

> You search the Scriptures because you think that in them you have eternal life; and it is they that bear witness about me, yet you refuse to come to me that you may have life. (John 5:39–40 ESV)

They boasted in their understanding of Scripture when all along it pointed to Jesus (Luke 24:25–27). Jesus was saying to them, "How could you know Scripture and not know me?" Rather than worship the Word of God (Jesus), they worshiped God's words. They focused on rules, not a relationship with God—laws, not the love of God. Their heads were full of knowledge, but their hearts remained unchanged.

Today, as we learn how to study the Bible, let us take a different approach. Let's study Scripture with humility and the desire to know and follow Jesus. Let's grow in both truth and love. Let's exalt Jesus, not ourselves, with our new knowledge. Because when we open up the Bible, we can expect to meet with God. Experiencing God will deepen our sense of need for His grace and deepen our love of Jesus.

Now that we know to approach Bible Study with the goal of heart change, not just head knowledge, let's get started. There are many ways to study the Bible. Below is one approach using five steps:

1. **Pray.**

Before you start reading, PRAY. The Holy Spirit helps us understand God's Word (1 John 2:27). He guides us into all truth (John 16:13). Ask Him to give you wisdom and open your spiritual eyes as you read God's Word (Psalm 119:18). Then trust that He will do what you have asked (James 1:5-7). Now you're ready to read.

2. **Read.**
   - Read attentively. When you study the Bible, pay attention. Reading verses out loud may help you slow down and listen to the words. Writing out verses may help you slow down and focus. One approach is to draw a line down the middle of a piece of paper. On the left side, write out the passage, verse by verse. On the right side, write down notes and thoughts next to each verse. As you read and copy, look for clues about the message: Who is speaking? To whom are they speaking? What are they saying? Why? When?

   - Read repeatedly. This will help you find those clues. If you read the same passage multiple times, new details, meanings, and personal applications will emerge. It's the *living* Word of God, which means it's not static—it's active (Heb. 4:12). God's Word penetrates our lives to assess what is there.

   - Read diligently. Studying the Bible takes time and effort. **It is important to learn the context of Bible passages and stories,**

or we might misunderstand them. Take time to discover the historical/cultural setting, literal meaning (what it says), and literary nature of the passage (how it fits in the chapter and book). Think about how it relates to the overall story of God (Week 1) and how it may point to Jesus (Luke 24:13-17, 27). When we read to examine the context—the larger perspective—we can understand the meaning of the passage.

- <u>Read carefully.</u> Notice the details, too. What verbs are used? What words are repeated? When any word or verse stands out, write it down. If your Bible gives cross-references, explore them. Also, watch for transitional words. If you see *therefore*, read the previous section to better understand the text (What is it there for?). If you see *but*, look for a redirection of some kind. If you do not understand a word, look for it elsewhere in Scripture, and use context to determine the meaning, as we did for the words *holy* (Day 13) and *rest* (Day 28). Let the Bible help you interpret the Bible.

- <u>Read humbly.</u> Sometimes, the Bible will be difficult to read because we may not always agree with it. When that happens, remember that God's ways are higher than our ways (Isa. 55:9). Trust Him, and believe His Word. At other times, the passage will seem familiar, and we might assume that we already understand it fully. When that happens, humbly ask God to open your eyes to new details, or new applications. Finally, during those times when you can't find information or answers you want to find, remember: "The secret things belong to the LORD our God, but the things that are revealed belong to us and to our children forever, that we may do all the words of this law" (Deut. 29:29 ESV). Focus on what He *has* given you, knowing that it will be exactly what you need.[1]

---

1 This "Read" section is how I learned to study the Bible. I've found most of these concepts in this book: Howard G. Hendricks and William D. Hendricks, *Living By the Book: The Art and Science of Reading the Bible* (Chicago: Moody Publishers, 2007), 79–131.

3. **Ask Questions.**

- <u>What was God saying to the original audience?</u> Think about the facts. What actually happened in the passage? Let's not rush to apply the Bible to our own lives before understanding how it applied to the original audience. Try to understand what the Holy Spirit was saying in their particular situation.

- <u>What was the format?</u> How these words were presented is also important. Was the psalm meant to be spoken or sung? Was it to be read aloud to a group or intended for an individual? Paying attention to how each passage was first delivered gives context to better understand the meaning.

- <u>Are there timeless truths for believers today?</u> Is there a promise or a warning that is true for all people at all times?

- <u>What does the Scripture tell you about God?</u> His person? His character? His promises?

- <u>What does the Scripture tell you about humanity?</u> Our hearts? Our needs? Our behaviors?

If time is limited, you can simply ask, "What does God want me to know, value, or do?"

4. **Apply.**

- <u>What does the Bible tell you about yourself?</u> We need to personally apply God's Word to our lives: "Don't just listen to God's word. You must do what it says. Otherwise, you are only fooling yourselves" (James 1:22). Remember, **God does not just want to inform us; He wants to transform us. God's purpose is that we become more like Christ** (Rom. 8:29). With His help, we apply His Word to our daily lives to develop Christlike character, attitudes, and behavior.

- <u>Did you find a promise?</u> Thousands of promises are in the Bible, and many have specific conditions. For example, Romans 10:9 states that *if* we say and believe Jesus is Lord, *then* we will be saved. Conditional promises show us what to do.

- <u>Did you find a command?</u> Is there any action to take based on this passage?

- <u>Did you find a caution or warning?</u> God wants to protect us from danger. Often our sin nature is our biggest threat. His warnings help us avoid unnecessary pain.

5. **Pray and Journal.**
   - <u>Talk with God.</u> If He has given you direction, ask Him to clarify your next step and help you move forward in faith. If He has revealed sin, ask Him to forgive you and free you from it. If He has given you a promise, thank Him for His faithfulness. If He has shown you something about Himself, thank Him for revealing Himself to you. Pray verses back to God. (We'll discuss praying Scripture next week on Day 40.)

   - <u>Journal.</u> Write down verses, prayers, and personal reflections. Keeping a simple notebook where you can record what you learn will help you remember God's faithfulness. It may also remind you of things you've learned that can help

Promises and Laws in the Bible

As you apply God's Word to your own life, keep in mind that some promises were given only to specific people at a specific time. For example, God's promise that Mary would conceive and give birth to the Son of God applied only to Mary. Not all Bible promises are universal. In the same way, not all Old Testament laws still apply. Many Levitical laws were for the priesthood only and meant to demonstrate that the Israelites were set apart by God. After Jesus came and provided the way for people of all nations to join God's family, some laws changed. For example, spiritual circumcision of the heart, which occurs when people place their faith in Christ, replaced physical circumcision (Rom. 2:25–29). Also, God nullified dietary laws, declaring all food clean, just as all people—Jew and Gentile alike—could become spiritually clean through Jesus (Acts 10). While context is important, it's essential to remember that God never breaks His promises. He is faithful.

others along their way. And, don't hesitate to underline or make notes in your Bible. They can become memorial stones (Day 17) to mark what you've learned, how God helped you during a challenging time, and how far you've come on God's path.

After you finish, SHARE. Tell someone about your experience in God's Word. Share what God teaches you with a humble attitude. Ask others to share what they are learning. Pass on your knowledge as God creates opportunities.

More Tips for Bible Study:

1. Read the same passage in different Bible translations, if available, to understand it better.

2. If your Bible has cross-reference verses, look them up and see how key ideas or words may appear elsewhere in the Bible. When we compare Scripture with Scripture, we're protected from misunderstandings. Using cross-references helps us understand the meaning of a verse or passage and how it may be connected to other parts of the Bible.

3. When a verse seems important, slow your reading pace and examine each word. For example, Jesus taught His disciples to pray in Matthew 6:9–13. Think through each word starting

Bible Translations

Both Old Testament Hebrew and New Testament Greek are complex languages. Their grammar structures and literary styles may not exist in other languages, so translating the Bible is a complex task. Thankfully, because of advanced research, many modern translations are superb. If you have multiple translations to choose from, try to use a word-for-word translation when doing word studies (like the English Standard Version). When studying concepts for modern application, use thought-for-thought translations (like the New Living Translation). For a balanced approach, use mediating translations (like the New International Version or Christian Standard Bible).

with the first word, "Our." What does this plural word show you? Who is included in "Our"? Then go to the second word, "Father." What does that title tell you about your relationship to God? Keep inspecting each word slowly to unpack treasures. (Note: Use a word-for-word Bible translation when doing word studies.)

4.   Do not look for hidden meanings. The Bible is not a puzzle; it's God's revelation of timeless truths for all people. He wants us to read it and understand it with His help, not with our human temptation to manipulate Scripture to support our ideas or to justify our positions.

5.   There are many resources available both online and in book form.[1] Many people have a Bible dictionary (to define the many difficult words included in the Bible) and a concordance (to find the location of biblical words in the Bible). You may have one or both of these tools in the back of your Bible. When using commentaries, check your understanding *after* you do your analysis. If no one else has reached similar conclusions, you are probably off track.

If you're struggling with a lack of desire to study the Bible, tell God. Ask Him to give you a passion for His Word. That is a prayer He delights to answer. God wants us to enjoy our time with Him in His Word. He wants us to draw strength, wisdom, peace, and joy from its pages. As we do, we can guard against feelings of pride with how knowledgeable we become. Remember, Jesus wants you to know Him, not just know facts about Him. Invite God to transform your mind and heart as you learn His will in His Word.

---

1   Visit allinmin.org for more resources we've compiled to help you study and apply biblical truth to your life.

DAY 33

Let the Bible Speak:
Psalm 119:57–112 (Optional: Philippians 1:9–11)

Let Your Mind Think:
1. Which of the above Bible study steps do you already do?

2. Which steps are new to you?

3. What are some ways you can apply what you learn from study-ing the Bible? God isn't impressed by knowledge (gathering facts); He wants a relationship (doing what He says with Him). How do you think studying the Bible will add to your story of knowing and serving Him?

Let Your Soul Pray:
Father, may I never neglect Your Word (Ps. 119:16). Help me as I study the Bible. Guide me as I read it and apply it to my own life. Give me opportunities to share what You teach me with others . . . In Jesus's name, amen.

Let Your Heart Obey:
(What is God leading you to know, value, or do?)

Memorize God's Word

I have hidden your word in my heart that
I might not sin against you.
Psalm 119:11 NIV

Every day with every choice we make, you and I answer the following two questions: *What do I believe about God?* and *What do I believe about myself?* Whether we're aware of it or not, we view life through a lens of theology and identity. Most of the time, we don't even realize we're making assumptions and drawing conclusions about God, ourselves, and the world around us. Our set of beliefs (or worldview) shapes our conversations and priorities. Or, to say it another way, what is in our hearts "determines the course of all we do" (Prov. 4:23).

God's Word has much to say about guarding our hearts and setting our hearts on things above.[1] We need a worldview that can explain, guide, and motivate all things toward what God is calling us to do. Knowing God's four-part story (Week 1) helps us understand the world and respond appropriately. But we also need biblical principles for all areas and all times of our lives. That's why **hiding God's Word in our hearts is essential**.

Let's take a look today at why and how to memorize God's Word.

Memorizing God's Word makes it available at all times. No matter where we go or what we do, we're always ready for whatever comes our way. God's Word is our powerful, personal, and multipurpose tool of transformation. It's a light to our path, a hammer to

---

1   For examples on guarding your heart, see Prov. 4:23; 24:12; Phil. 4:7; Col. 3:1.

crush sin, a mirror to search our souls, a sword to defeat enemies, and so much more. When we memorize God's Word, no one can take it from us, and we make it available for God to use at any time. Scripture can permeate our prayers and conversations "when [we] are at home and . . . on the road . . . going to bed and . . . getting up" (Deut. 6:7). Powerful, life-changing prayer can come from Scripture or from our own hearts. When we memorize Scripture, we combine the two. The Holy Spirit reminds us of these truths written on our hearts that are often the answers to our prayers.

Memorizing God's Word comforts us and others with just the right words at just the right time. Because we've all been through difficult times, it feels so comforting to be supported by people who love us. When we have God's Word written on our hearts, God can encourage others through us. We can look into their eyes and share words of love and hope rather than look down at our Bible or phone to find a verse. Sometimes we're the one who needs encouragement. But no one can be with us every moment of every day. No other human can carry our pain for us. That's when God will remind us with the Scripture we have hidden in our hearts that He is there and He is working. God's Word eases our sorrow. "Your words were found and I ate them, and Your words became for me a joy and the delight of my heart; for I have been called by Your name, O LORD God of hosts" (Jer. 15:16 NASB).

Memorizing God's Word transforms our thinking. The principles in the Bible go against what the world promotes and our selfish desires. They are simply not natural for us, but they are essential for us to abide in Christ. Memorizing Scripture allows God's thoughts to nest deeply into our souls to strengthen us, correct us, and encourage us. When that happens, we can make choices that go against our natural tendency. Our thoughts are radically transformed (Rom. 12:2). Like when we are accused or betrayed, our natural response might be to defend or retaliate. God's Word reminds us to calm down: "Do not repay evil with evil or insult with insult. On the contrary, repay evil with blessing, because to this you were called so that you may inherit a blessing" (1 Pet. 3:9 NIV). When we're confronted with a difficult family member, coworker, or church member, God whispers, "Be patient, bearing with one another in love" (Eph. 4:2 NIV). When our eyes are opened to our own pride and self-righteousness, God reminds us, "Humble yourselves" (James 4:10). Rather than draw attention to ourselves, we draw attention to God. Our judgmental attitude turns into compassion. Being easily offended or angered reverses to being a peacemaker. We receive correction well and admit when we're wrong. Completely unnatural—that's Scripture at work in our hearts.

Memorizing God's Word helps us fulfill our purpose. The more we study Scripture, the more we discover God's character and our calling. God's Word penetrates our hearts, and our love for God expands and so does our love for others. We want them to experience an intimate friendship with Jesus. We want to see them rescued from the clutches of sin and thriving in new life—now and eternally. But our purpose to love God, love others, and make disciples means we need to always be ready to share our hope in Christ (1 Pet. 3:15). By memorizing God's Word, we can explain God's message with God's words. Do you remember "Gospel Bread" from Day 18? Start by memorizing a verse for each of these four essential ingredients:

- God loves us: "For God so loved the world, that he gave his only Son, that whoever believes in him should not perish but have eternal life" (John 3:16 ESV).
- Sin separates us: "For all have sinned and fall short of the glory of God" (Rom. 3:23 NIV).
- Jesus saves us: "But God showed his great love for us by sending Christ to die for us while we were still sinners" (Rom. 5:8).
- Repentance and faith change us: "If you openly declare that Jesus is Lord and believe in your heart that God raised him from the dead, you will be saved. For it is by believing in your heart that you are made right with God, and it is by openly declaring your faith that you are saved" (Rom. 10:9-10).

Memorizing God's Word helps us resist temptation. "I have hidden your word in my heart that I might not sin against you" (Ps. 119:11 NIV). Memorized Scripture is beyond doubt a powerful weapon that defeats sin when we use it: "For the word of God is alive and powerful. It is sharper than the sharpest two-edged sword" (Heb. 4:12). Though the Word of God is always sharp, sometimes our grasp of it isn't. Thankfully, we can strengthen our grip by committing it to memory. We have no better example than Jesus. As we learned on Day 26, He gripped the Word of God firmly to resist temptation. We can ready ourselves for spiritual battle by memorizing Scripture, especially verses that relate to our most common temptations and weaknesses. For example:

Temptation	Memorize
Temper	Fools vent their anger, but the wise quietly hold it back. Proverbs 29:11 Everyone should be quick to listen, slow to speak and slow to become angry, because human anger does not produce the righteousness that God desires. James 1:19–20 (NIV)
Pride	Pride leads to conflict; those who take advice are wise. Proverbs 13:10 God opposes the proud but gives grace to the humble. James 4:6
Lack of self-control in spending money, eating, or satisfying your physical desires	So humble yourselves before God. Resist the devil, and he will flee from you. James 4:7 No temptation has overtaken you that is not common to man. God is faithful, and he will not let you be tempted beyond your ability, but with the temptation he will also provide the way of escape, that you may be able to endure it. 1 Corinthians 10:13 (ESV)
Harsh tongue	Don't use foul or abusive language. Let everything you say be good and helpful, so that your words will be an encouragement to those who hear them. Ephesians 4:29 A gentle answer turns away wrath, but a harsh word stirs up anger. Proverbs 15:1 (NIV)

Craving material things	Yet true godliness with contentment is itself great wealth. After all, we brought nothing with us when we came into the world, and we can't take anything with us when we leave it. So if we have enough food and clothing, let us be content. 1 Timothy 6:6–8 Don't love money; be satisfied with what you have. For God has said, "I will never fail you. I will never abandon you." Hebrews 13:5
Gossip	A gossip betrays a confidence, but a trustworthy person keeps a secret. Proverbs 11:13 (NIV) Those who consider themselves religious and yet do not keep a tight rein on their tongues deceive themselves, and their religion is worthless. James 1:26 (NIV)
Worry/Fear	Be strong and courageous. Do not be afraid; do not be discouraged, for the LORD your God will be with you wherever you go. Joshua 1:9 (NIV) For God gave us a spirit not of fear but of power and love and self-control. 2 Timothy 1:7 (ESV)

We see the power of memorizing Scripture, but figuring out how to do it is where most people give up. If you want to memorize Scripture but don't know where to start, here are some suggestions that may help:

1. Choose a verse that means something to you. Pick a passage that God can use in a specific way for your life.

    "**Sanctify** them by the truth; your word is truth." John 17:17 (NIV, emphasis added)

2. Say the verse reference before and after the verse, so you will know where to find it.

    John 17:17 "Sanctify them by the truth; your word is truth." John 17:17

> **Sanctify:**
> to purify or make holy or sacred. The idea is for people or things to be set aside for the worship of God.

3. Break the verse into shorter phrases and memorize one phrase at a time. **Concentrate on what the passage is saying so it's written on your mind and in your heart:**

   Sanctify them by the truth / (Think: Truth transforms.)
   your word is truth. (Think: God's Word is the truth.)

4. Read the verse aloud many times, emphasizing key words. Repetition is the key to learning, so review often.

   SANCTIFY them by the truth / your WORD is truth.

5. Write the verse and, without looking at the verse, write the first initial of each word in the verse.

   John 17:17 Sanctify them by the truth; your word is truth.
   John 17:17
   John 17:17 S T B T T Y W I T. John 17:17

The key to memorizing Scripture is not to try to memorize data—letters, words, and sentences. We are not computers, and this is not data entry. We engage both heart and mind when making decisions, so memorize with both heart and mind. Learn not only what is written but also why it is written. Understand the connection or story or meaning. When you select a passage, concentrate on style and the substance of what is being communicated.

So often we think we cannot memorize Scripture, but all of us memorize things that matter to us—important dates, passwords, songs, even sports statistics. As we've already established, what we focus on expands. If we give our time and attention to it, we can do it. And you can make this fun. Try singing verses, using hand motions, or drawing pictures. Some people prefer memorizing by listening to God's Word. There are audio Bibles available online and in physical form that make listening and memorizing easier.

Memorizing God's Word is not about being able to recall a string of words. It is about preparing for whatever lies ahead on your journey. When you hide God's Word in your heart, you are packing a flashlight to light your path, water to refresh your soul, bread to nourish your spirit, and a sword to fight your enemy. Prepare your heart well.

DAY 34

Let the Bible Speak:
Psalm 119:113–176 (Optional: James 1:22)

Let Your Mind Think:
1. Why do you think people have a hard time memorizing some things? Why should it be easier for us to memorize God's Word?

2. Are there some areas of your life where you feel God is working to transform you? Find a verse to help you, strengthen you, or guide you in that area and begin to memorize it now.

3. Of the many benefits of memorizing Bible verses, which applies to you the most?

Let Your Soul Pray:
Lord, write Your Word on my heart. Make my mind like a sponge to soak up Scripture. Guide me to memorize the verses You know I will need on my journey. As Your Word takes root in my life, change my heart and transform my thoughts . . . In Jesus's name, amen.

Let Your Heart Obey:
(What is God leading you to know, value, or do?)

DAY

35

Review and Practice–
God's Word

Study this Book of Instruction continually. Meditate on it day
and night so you will be sure to obey everything written in
it. Only then will you prosper and succeed in all you do.

Joshua 1:8

In ancient times people would travel miles and stand in long lines
for days to meet with spiritual leaders. They were seeking help with
decisions, predictions for the future, divine revelation, or a blessing.
As Jesus-followers, we do not need to travel or wait for God's revelation. We open the Bible. When we do, the Author of the Book guides
us into truth. No matter what continent, culture, or generation,
God's Word is life-giving and life-changing for all people at all times.

We've learned a *lot* about God's Word this week, so let's take
some time to put into practice what we've learned (Matt. 7:24). Let's
apply Bible study strategies from this week's lessons to a passage of
Scripture and review the steps covered on Day 33:

1. Before you start, *pray*.
2. Read the passage carefully and repeatedly.
3. Ask questions about what you've read.
4. Apply it.
5. Pray and journal those prayers and reflections. This will help
   you to remember and share what you've learned with others.

As we'll see, new students of the Bible can learn important spiritual truths without any special background or education. Let's begin.

Step 1: Pray now.
Ask God for wisdom and spiritual discernment to understand and apply this passage of Scripture to your life.

Step 2: Read the passage.
Read it humbly and deliberately. Take notice of the careful details. Then read it a second time, underlining key words and making notes in the margin.

James 1:1–12 (NIV)

James, a servant of God and of the Lord Jesus Christ,

To the twelve tribes scattered among the nations:

Greetings.

Consider it pure joy, my brothers and sisters, whenever you face trials of many kinds, because you know that the testing of your faith produces perseverance. Let perseverance finish its work so that you may be mature and complete, not lacking anything. If any of you lacks wisdom, you should ask God, who gives generously to all without finding fault, and it will be given to you. But when you ask, you must believe and not doubt, because the one who doubts is like a wave of the sea, blown and tossed by the wind. That person should not expect to receive anything from the Lord. Such a person is double-minded and unstable in all they do.

Believers in humble circumstances ought to take pride in their high positions. But the rich should take pride in their humiliation—since they will pass away like a wildflower. For the sun rises with scorching heat and withers the plant; its blossom falls and its beauty is destroyed. In the same way, the rich will fade away even while they go about their business.

Blessed is the one who perseveres under trial because, having stood the test, that person will receive the crown of life that the Lord has promised to those who love him.

Step 3: Ask Questions.
(Important: The following answers serve as an example of Bible study interpretation. God can speak differently to different people using the same passage.)

- <u>Who is speaking?</u> *James, a servant of the Lord.*
- <u>Who is he speaking to?</u> *Believers scattered among nations.*
- <u>What is he saying?</u> (general idea) *James knows all believers will face trials of many kinds and provides a way for believers to see their trials in view of eternity.*

Answering these first three questions is a good start. Now, let's look more closely.

- <u>What was God saying to the original audience through James?</u>
  - *Trials can be tests of faith that produce perseverance.*
  - *Perseverance is needed for spiritual maturity.*
  - *If believers need wisdom for trials, they are to ask God.*
  - *God gives wisdom generously without hesitancy, so long as the believer asks without doubting that God will answer.*
  - *Poor or rich, no one escapes trials or death.*
  - *Blessing comes with having withstood the test.*

- <u>What was the format?</u> *The book of James is a letter from one leader to brothers and sisters in the faith.*

- <u>Are there any timeless truths for believers today? Promises? Warnings?</u>
  - *All believers will face trials.*
  - *Believers do not need to wonder about the purpose of trials. They can ask God for wisdom and He will give it generously.*
  - *Financial status has no bearing on eternal standing with God.*
  - *The promised crown of life (eternal life) is for those who love God, and the evidence of this love is shown by steadfast obedience in this life.*

- <u>What does this passage tell you about God?</u>
  - God wants us to grow spiritually strong so we are not shallow, weak, and easily swayed.
  - God does not waste pain. Trials can be used for our good.
  - God gives His divine wisdom generously to those who sincerely ask for it.
  - God grows our faith by helping us persevere through trials so we can withstand tests and enjoy eternity with Him.
  - God blesses us both here on earth (spiritual maturity through trials) and in eternity (crown of life, having withstood the test).

- <u>What does this passage tell you about humanity?</u>
  All believers need to mature in faith. Trials can be used to develop perseverance, but we need to choose how we view trials.

Step 4: Apply what you are learning.

- <u>What does this passage tell you about yourself?</u>
  This passage reminds me of how trials reveal the type of faith I have. My response to adversity and affliction shows what I believe and where I place my hope. When I trust God through trials, He provides His wisdom, power, and strength. This reliance on God produces perseverance to help me mature and endure to the end.

  I realize I have a choice as to how I face hardship: choose joy and trust God, knowing He is doing a work in me, or choose despair, believing Satan's lie to doubt God's goodness. Rather than see trials as a consequence for lack of faith, I can endure hardships knowing God is at work for my earthly and eternal good.

- <u>Is there a promise? Command? Warning?</u>
  God promises to give us wisdom during trials if we ask and do not doubt. We are not left alone trying to navigate adversity or wonder what God's purpose is for them. We can ask God, and He promises His wisdom. God also promises to bless us both here (spiritual maturity) and in eternity (crown of life).

- <u>What do you want to remember?</u>
  *Developing perseverance is like building muscles to grow
  strong in my faith to withstand hardships. I do not want to be
  a weak Jesus-follower who is easily moved and tossed around
  like waves or wind. I want to be strong in the Lord. I need to
  remember to trust God through trials because it leads to spiritual maturity. Eternal rewards are at stake. I choose joy.*

  *Memorize: "Consider it pure joy, my brothers and sis-
  ters, whenever you face trials of many kinds, because you
  know that the testing of your faith produces perseverance"*
  (James 1:2–3 NIV).

Step 5: Pray.
*God, thank You for helping me see trials from Your perspective. I'm
grateful trials are not wasted distractions but can be used for good,
eternal purposes. Please give me Your wisdom and strength so I can
learn and grow strong in You. Help me to persevere to the end with a
godly perspective–choosing joy. You are worth more than any trial I
must endure because You first loved me and suffered for me. I love You.
In Jesus's name, amen.*

Through the example above, did you see how you might study the
Bible? With careful reading, we were able to learn spiritual truth that
goes against what most of the world says about trials. Trials are not
necessarily because of lack of faith, but they can grow our faith. Consider reading the whole book of James to see how this theme of trials
and growing in faith is expanded. One major lesson from this passage
is that we can simply open God's Word and ask for His wisdom.

This week we explored the power of God's Word. Next week we'll
explore how God's Word empowers our prayers. Jesus promises, "If
you remain in me and my words remain in you, ask whatever you
wish, and it will be done for you" (John 15:7 NIV). **Studying and praying
God's Word fuels heart-changing, mountain-moving prayer.**

DAY 35

Let the Bible Speak and Your Mind Think:

Now, it's your turn. Take some time to practice studying God's Word. This week you've already read the longest chapter in the Bible, Psalm 119. For this exercise, read the shortest chapter in the Bible, Psalm 117.

1. Read Psalm 117 below. Follow the Bible study steps above. (For more detailed instructions, look back at Day 33.)
2. Underline, highlight, or circle key words right on this page. You can write notes about the verses in the margin.
3. When you have finished all the steps, you might choose a verse to memorize. In this case, you could memorize the whole psalm.
4. Answer Week 5 Discussion Questions.

Psalm 117

Praise the LORD, all you nations.
Praise him, all you people of the earth.
For his unfailing love for us is powerful;
the LORD's faithfulness endures forever.
Praise the LORD!

Let Your Soul Pray:

God, thank You for Your Word. I treasure it. "The law from your mouth is more precious to me than thousands of pieces of silver and gold" (Ps. 119:72 NIV). Help me study the Bible each day, and help me understand what I read. I pray that I will not just learn about Scripture but be transformed by it. Transform my heart, my thoughts, my words, and my actions. "Direct my footsteps according to your word" (Ps. 119:133 NIV) . . . In Jesus's name, amen.

Let Your Heart Obey:

(What is God leading you to know, value, or do?)

WEEK 5 DISCUSSION QUESTIONS:
Review this week's lessons and answer the questions below.
Share your answers with your friends when you gather this week.

1. When you read the parable about seeds and soil, what did you learn about your own heart? How can you become more receptive to God's Word?

2. We explored many reasons we can trust God's Word. Which reason was new to you?

3. In our tour of the Bible books, we followed the Story of the Bible from creation to eternity. How does your story reflect the greater Story we find in God's Word?

    ○ The people of Israel found themselves in a cycle of sin and repentance during the time of the judges. How can learning about this cycle and how to fight it in your life help you?

    ○ Have you ever felt distant in your relationship with God, like the Israelites did in exile? How can memorizing Scripture help you to feel more of His presence in your life?

    ○ How can studying God's Word help you to experience close fellowship with God, like the love expressed in Song of Solomon?

    ○ Studying God's Word will help us to know Jesus better, like the people in the Gospels. How can studying God's Word help you abide in Jesus?

4. After our time together in this *Your True Story* study, if possible, agree on a reading plan your group could do together and continue meeting to discuss what you learn.

WEEK SIX

PRAYER—TALKING
WITH THE AUTHOR OF LIFE

DAY 36

Talk with God, Change Your Heart

This is the confidence we have in approaching God:
that if we ask anything according to his will, he hears us.
And if we know that he hears us—whatever we ask—
we know that we have what we asked of him.
1 John 5:14–15 (NIV)

God loves to talk with you. He cherishes your prayers because they are evidence of the sweet friendship you share. Think about how you might keep a letter as a reminder of a significant person or occasion. The Bible says that God keeps your prayers in golden bowls, and they rise to Him like a sweet aroma (Rev. 5:8; Ps. 141:2). He whispers, "Never stop praying" (1 Thess. 5:17). Why? Because prayer deepens your relationship with God. Friends become closer the more they talk with each other.

Can you imagine friends who never spoke to each other? They would not have much of a friendship. Or a married couple who never spoke directly to each other but only communicated through a pastor or some other intermediary? They would still be legally married, but their relationship would be strained and impersonal. Without prayer, your relationship with God would be just as lifeless. Prayer keeps your friendship with God dynamic, living, and personal.

Prayer is a continual conversation that flows from an intimate friendship with God. When you talk to Him, "what you say flows from what is in your heart" (Luke 6:45). Parents and children do more than just repeat standard, memorized greetings to each other: "Hi." "Hello." "How are you?" "Good. How are you?" "Good." "Have a nice day." "Bye." No, in healthy relationships, people also speak from their hearts–spontaneously and sincerely. The Bible contains examples of prayer we can use to speak to God, but we can also speak to God in our own words. He does not judge or criticize our words; He looks into our hearts. He's not worried about grammar or wanting prayers that sound impressive. He cares for you, and He is interested in what you have to say from your heart.

But some people may find it hard to talk to someone they cannot see. Others may find it hard to pray because they believe God will do what He wants regardless of our prayers. Consider these ideas about the purpose and power of prayer.

Pray to get more *of* God, not just to get more *from* God. Yes, God delights to answer our prayers, and we can ask God for the desires of our hearts (Ps. 37:4). But let's want God more than anything else. Pray that your thoughts would be *His* thoughts; your heart, *His* heart; your will, *His* will. Then, when you pray in line with *His* desires for you, He will do what you ask in His perfect timing. "I will do whatever you ask in my name, so that the Father may be glorified in the Son. You may ask me for anything in my name, and I will do it" (John 14:13–14 NIV). Jesus is saying we can ask in His authority to advance His purposes for God's glory. **One purpose of prayer is to discover what is on God's heart so we can align our hearts to His.**

Prayer changes our hearts, but not always our circumstances. When our prayers align with God's will, He promises to hear us (1 John 5:14–15). His answer may be yes or not now. If any of our requests are out of His will, He will say no. Ask God to work in your heart to help you walk in His ways, even if the details do not make sense to you. In the garden of Gethsemane, Jesus prayed to escape the intense suffering He knew was only hours away. "My Father! If it is possible, let this cup of suffering be taken away from me. Yet I want your will to be done, not mine" (Matt. 26:39). Jesus wanted to escape suffering, but He wanted God's will *more*. He did not get the answer He requested, but He came out of that prayer time with a heart fully submitted to His Father's will and the courage to see that will accomplished. Prayer will not always change our circumstances, but it *will* help us to trust God *despite* our circumstances.

Pray with authority to take a stand against the devil's schemes. Prayer is not only a conversation with God but also a powerful weapon in spiritual warfare. As we learned on Days 26 and 27, both Scripture and prayer help us defeat the desires of the flesh and the attacks of the enemy. Jesus has always had authority over the enemy, and He gave us authority when He defeated Satan at the cross (Col. 2:15). **Now we need to claim Jesus's victory so we, too, can overcome the power of the enemy** (Luke 10:19). Rely on the strength of God and take action through prayer. As we discussed on Day 26, pray aloud with authority when temptation strikes: "I am a child of God, and in Christ I have victory over_____." Insert whatever sin or issue you're addressing. Remember the enemy cannot force us to sin. **We have authority through Jesus to resist the enemy and place ourselves under God's protection.**

Let's combine our knowledge of prayer with some practical guidelines that will help us pray, listen, and move forward in God's will:

1. **Pray in a group**—Effective group prayer (sometimes called corporate prayer) requires focus and humility. As we pray in agreement on the same concern, the Holy Spirit will guide us in a more specific way. Be genuine and transparent when prompted to pray. Do not be reluctant to contribute, concerned about others' opinions of you, or afraid of making a mistake. We are all learning from the Holy Spirit and each other. Even those who are fluent in prayer are still maturing in their faith. You may say something that brings encouragement or clarity to a prayer gathering.

Conversely, let's not dominate or pray a message for another participant to hear. Instead, humble yourself before the Lord (James 4:10). Praying with other believers brings us closer together and closer to God (Matt. 18:20). The early church modeled devotion to God and each other *as they worshiped and prayed together* (Acts 2:42–47).

2. **Pray alone**—Although we are never *spiritually* alone in prayer (Rom. 8), praying *physically* alone keeps our motives pure. We are free from the temptation to perform for others or worry about what other people think. Private prayer is most effective without distractions (no phone, no watch, no computer). Jesus says, "But when you pray, go into your room and shut the door and pray to your Father who is in secret. And your Father who sees in secret will reward you" (Matt. 6:6 ESV). Our secret prayers—the ones heard only by God—are especially precious to Him.

3. **Pray physically.** Use your body to help you express your feelings. A humble posture demonstrates a humble heart, so you might try kneeling before God (Ps. 95:6). You could also turn your face toward heaven (John 17:1), open your hands to receive (Ezra 9:5), or lie flat on the ground before God (Matt. 26:39). Come before God with the right heart attitude. He is God, and we are mortal. He provides everything, and we have nothing to offer except that which He gives us. Pray with all your strength.

4. **Pray out loud.** Speaking aloud may help you keep your focus. It will remind you that you are talking to a real person.

5. **Outline your prayer.** If you need to stay focused, take notes (in your journal, if possible). Write out your questions or praises. Concentrate on God, then write down what verses come to mind as you **listen for God's thoughts inside your thoughts**. Include these four elements as you pray: Adoration, Confession, Thanksgiving, and Supplication. (Remember the acronym ACTS.) Tomorrow, we will learn about this prayer outline from King Jehoshaphat's example.

James 5:16 says, "The earnest prayer of a righteous person has great power and produces wonderful results." God loves to talk with you, so spend some time talking with Him now. Then, *listen* for His answers. The results are life-changing.

DAY 36

Let the Bible Speak:
Matthew 6:1–18 (Optional: Psalm 86)

Let Your Mind Think:

1. How would you characterize your praying? To strengthen your times of prayer, look at prayers in the Bible. Many verses can be turned into prayers; verses that reflect on God's character and His promises can be paraphrased and spoken back to Him.

2. Are you a part of a prayer group? If not, is there a group of believers you could connect with for prayer?

3. What are you praying today? Consider creating a space for prayer in the corner of a room or in a closet. Post prayer prompts and Scriptures to help you pray intentionally. Devoting a space solely to prayer will help you prioritize prayer.

Let Your Soul Pray:
Father, I am amazed that You, the Creator of the universe, want to talk with me. Thank You! Grow me in prayer. Help me pray continually with a sincere heart. Make my heart and mind like Yours so I will be able to pray according to Your will . . . In Jesus's name, amen.

Let Your Heart Obey:
(What is God leading you to know, value, or do?)

Pray and Listen

Call to me and I will answer you and tell you great
and unsearchable things you do not know.
Jeremiah 33:3 (NIV)

Messengers ran to Jerusalem with a terrifying warning of an invading army approaching the city. "A great multitude is coming against you" (2 Chron. 20:2 ESV). An alliance of nations marched against King Jehoshaphat and the people of Judah. This unexpected news struck fear in the heart of the king. But rather than call in soldiers and draft battle plans, the wise king responded with faith. An order went out to the entire nation: EVERYONE FAST AND PRAY! The people stopped everything and immediately arrived from every town in Judah to the capital city to seek the Lord together. The king stood at the temple of the Lord, raised his voice to heaven, and led the prayer gathering.

God heard their prayers and miraculously rescued them: the alliance of nations coming against King Jehoshaphat turned *against each other*. The men of Judah never even picked up a weapon. Yet, they defeated an army so massive that it took them three days to gather all the possessions their enemies left behind.

We can learn a great deal from the prayer of King Jehoshaphat. His part in God's Story was to bring spiritual reformation to the southern kingdom, but he also modeled powerful prayer. When we look closely at his prayer at the national gathering, we find that it consists of four main elements: adoration, confession, thanksgiving, and supplication (ACTS).

1. **Adoration:** Jehoshaphat began by praying, "O Lord, God of our ancestors, you alone are the God who is in heaven. You are ruler of all the kingdoms of the earth. You are powerful and mighty; no one can stand against you!" (2 Chron. 20:6). When we start our prayers with worship, we remember who we are talking to—God Almighty. Picture yourself entering into God's throne room (Heb. 4:16) and express your love for Him. **Adoring God fuels our faith.** The problems we bring to Him start to shrink even before we talk about them when we consider them in light of God's power and majesty. Let's not wait until the battle is over to give Him praise. Take your time to honor your heavenly Father.

2. **Confession:** Jehoshaphat followed his worship with humility: "O our God, won't you stop them? We are powerless against this mighty army that is about to attack us. We do not know what to do, but we are looking to you for help" (2 Chron. 20:12). King Jehoshaphat acknowledged he was not strong enough or smart enough to face what was coming. But he kept his eyes on God. We can follow his example. After you praise God's perfection, **admit your own imperfection—not just obvious sins, but your weaknesses as well**. When you do, you root yourself in God's grace (Day 24), knowing "God opposes the proud but gives grace to the humble" (James 4:6).

3. **Thanksgiving:** Even though incredible danger advanced toward him, Jehoshaphat chose to be grateful for how God had cared for his people in the past:

> "O our God, did you not drive out those who lived in this land when your people Israel arrived? And did you not give this land forever to the descendants of your friend Abraham? Your people settled here and built this Temple to honor your name. They said, 'Whenever we are faced with any calamity such as war, plague, or famine, we can come to stand in your presence before this Temple where your name is honored. We can cry out to you to save us, and you will hear us and rescue us.' And now see what the armies of Ammon, Moab, and Mount Seir are

doing. . . . For they have come to throw us out of your land, which you gave us as an inheritance." (2 Chron. 20:7–11)

Gratitude helps us see the protective care of God. The more we remember His faithfulness, the more powerful our faith. And the more we look for God's hand on our lives, the more we see His hand in the details. We recognize every good gift is from Him, so we are not deceived (James 1:16–17). As the saying goes, gratitude makes what we have enough. King Jehoshaphat chose to remember God's faithfulness and gifts. He decided God would be enough. Let's give thanks, open our eyes to what God has already provided, and trust His future provision.

4. **Supplication:** Jehoshaphat asked God to rescue his people from their enemies because he knew he couldn't do it himself: "O our God, won't you stop them? We are powerless against this mighty army that is about to attack us. We do not know what to do, but we are looking to you for help" (2 Chron. 20:12).

As a child dependent on a parent to provide, we are dependent on our heavenly Father. God invites us to ask Him for what we need and delights to give us good gifts (Matt. 7:11). But if we do not turn to Him or trust Him, we are not inviting Him into the situation. "You do not have because you do not ask God" (James 4:2 NIV). **Place all your requests in His care, and let Him decide what is best.** What are your needs? Ask God to supply them. Pray for other people's, too. We should "always keep on praying for all the Lord's people" (Eph. 6:18 NIV). None of your requests are too big, and none are too small. Consider keeping a list of your supplications in your journal and update it weekly, recording when and how God answers your prayers. As you see God answer specific requests, your confidence in Him will grow. We'll learn more about praying for others on Day 41.

Including the elements of prayer (ACTS) will help us to keep focused. The enemy wants to disrupt our communication with God and will try to distract us. Resist his interruptions. If distracting thoughts are about ideas or tasks you need to complete, write them down, and leave them alone until after you've finished praying. If distracting thoughts are persistent, reject them in Jesus's name.

When we pray, whether alone or with a group, we need to remember to pause and *listen* to God. "He wakens me morning by morning, wakens my ear to listen like one being instructed" (Isa. 50:4 NIV). Take turns speaking and listening when you pray, just like you do in everyday conversations with people. Pray, "Speak, LORD, for Your servant is listening" (1 Sam. 3:9 NASB). God's voice is often like "the sound of a gentle whisper" (1 Kings 19:12), so quiet your heart to hear it. Be still and focus on Jesus. He says, "My sheep listen to my voice; I know them, and they follow me" (John 10:27).

After Jehoshaphat prayed, he listened for God. God answered Jehoshaphat, saying, "Do not be afraid! Don't be discouraged by this mighty army, for **the battle is not yours, but God's**. . . . You will not even need to fight. Take your positions; then stand still and watch the LORD's victory" (2 Chron. 20:15, 17, emphasis added). Amazing! No surprise, Jehoshaphat obeyed, and God's rescue came as promised. We can have the same confidence that He hears us: "The LORD is near to all who call on him, to all who call on him in truth. He fulfills the desires of those who fear him; he hears their cry and saves them. The LORD watches over all who love him" (Ps. 145:18–20 NIV).

We can plan to obey before we pray, knowing it's His battle, not ours, to win. And then we can follow His lead.

Let the Bible Speak:
2 Chronicles 20:1–23 (Optional: 2 Chronicles 6:1–11, 34–35)

Let Your Mind Think:
Practice writing out your prayers by using the following outline. Keep your prayers in a journal and record dates so that you can look back and see how God has answered you (a memorial stone–Day 17).

1. **A**doration (Worship God.)
2. **C**onfession (Confess your sins and your weakness.)
3. **T**hanksgiving (Give thanks for everything, even trials.)
4. **S**upplication (Make requests.)
5. *Listen* for God's responses, *write* down what He says, *ask* Him to confirm it, and *obey* by following His lead.

Let Your Soul Pray:
Father, teach me to pray. As I come to You, make me worshipful, humble, thankful, and confident in Your grace and power. Sharpen my awareness of Your voice. Teach me to listen. Help me study and meditate on Your Word so I can pray according to Your will and hear Your voice clearly . . . In Jesus's name, amen.

Let Your Heart Obey:
(*What is God leading you to know, value, or do?*)

Avoid Hindrances to Prayer

Then they will call to me but I will not answer;
they will look for me but will not find me,
since they hated knowledge and did not choose to fear the LORD.
Proverbs 1:28–29 NIV

We may not live long enough to learn from all our own mistakes. Sometimes it helps to learn from the mistakes of others. That may have been just what King Jehoshaphat was doing. Yesterday we saw how he prayerfully handled the multination invasion by humbly depending on God. Years before, another military threat required Jehoshaphat's father, King Asa, to respond. Rather than turn to God, he turned to another nation and paid them to fight their battle. Even though Asa had a history of experiencing God's delivering power, he had fallen to self-sufficiency and doubt. The prophet Hanani confronted King Asa:

> "For the eyes of the LORD range throughout the earth to strengthen those whose hearts are fully committed to him. You have done a foolish thing, and from now on you will be at war." (2 Chron. 16:9 NIV)

Because Asa's heart was not entirely loyal to the one true God, conflicts would mark the rest of his days. Like Jehoshaphat, we also can learn from King Asa to realize God is searching for those who are devoted to Him. He pursues believers who wholeheartedly seek

Him. When He finds our hearts committed to Him, God responds to our prayers and shows Himself strong on our behalf.

But sometimes when we pray, God does not respond. Our prayers feel like they fall flat on the ground. It's not that we need an amplifier or to speak more clearly. Sometimes God does not hear us because we have sin in our lives that blocks our prayers (Ps. 66:16–20; Isa. 5). Or, we're praying with the wrong motives. Yes, our own poor choices (*not* others' poor decisions) can hinder our prayers. Today, let's identify the major mistakes people can make when approaching God in prayer so we can avoid them. This list is not complete, but it contains the seven most likely reasons God does not answer our prayers.

1. **Unconfessed Sin:** Have you ever changed the topic when a conversation became uncomfortable for you? We do that with God too. When He reveals sin to us through the conviction of the Holy Spirit and we avoid confessing it, continuing to pray about other concerns, we create a hindrance. **God will not pay attention to our prayers until we confess the sin He has already revealed to us.** Why should we expect God to listen and respond to us when we do not listen and respond to Him? The psalmist writes, "If I had cherished sin in my heart, the Lord would not have listened" (Ps. 66:18 NIV). Our sin grieves God, and sin should grieve us, too (Eph. 4:30). That's why we need to confess sin as soon as God brings it to mind. He is faithful to forgive us (1 John 1:9) and restore our relationship with Him. Let Him restore you.

2. **Disobedience:** Along with confessing, we need to also repent by turning away from sin and toward God. When we are determined to go our own way and ignore God's instruction, our prayers are worthless to God. "If anyone turns a deaf ear to my instruction, even their prayers are detestable" (Prov. 28:9 NIV). There is a difference between someone who submits to the lordship of Jesus while sometimes struggling to obey and someone who prays to God for blessing while deliberately defying God. When we want God's blessings but reject God's ways, our prayers can be hindered, no matter how many other good things we do. "Does the LORD delight in burnt offerings

and sacrifices as much as in obeying the LORD? To obey is better than sacrifice, and to heed is better than the fat of rams" (1 Sam. 15:22 NIV). God knows our hearts and longs to forgive us, but we need to trust Him and follow Him.

3. **Selfishness:** Selfishness—indifference to others' needs—sabotages prayer. God wants us to take care of ourselves, but we need to also be sensitive to the needs of those around us. God's will shapes our prayers, and part of His will is for us to love and serve others: "Don't look out only for your own interests, but take an interest in others, too" (Phil. 2:4). God always sees our true motives. "When you ask, you don't get it because your motives are all wrong—you want only what will give you pleasure" (James 4:3). When our prayers are selfish, God may not answer them.

4. **Doubt:** When we pray with faith, we have confidence in who God is and what He has done. In contrast, when we pray *without* faith, we doubt His promises and abilities. **Asking God without believing God will help is evidence of doubt**. Are you praying in doubt or faith? "When you ask, you must believe and not doubt, because the one who doubts is like a wave of the sea, blown and tossed by the wind. That person should not expect to receive anything from the Lord" (James 1:6–7 NIV). It is normal to doubt God at times, and when this happens, we can ask God to strengthen our faith, praying like the man who cried out to Jesus, "I do believe; help my unbelief" (Mark 9:24 NASB). **Pray in faith, meaning faith in *God's goodness*, not faith that He will do everything we ask.** Our sincere desire for something does not force Him to grant our request. Remember: *God is good, no matter what happens.* When we believe that, we are confident in His answer to whatever we face. If we doubt that God is good, then we will doubt that His response will be good, whether it is a yes, no, or not now. **Ask with faith, and let *God* decide the outcome**, remembering that "he rewards those who sincerely seek him" (Heb. 11:6).

5. **Unforgiveness:** If we hold grudges, God may not listen to our prayers. Refusing to forgive others indicates that we do not

understand the immense cost of Jesus's sacrifice for us. But when we grow in God's grace and realize the extent of His forgiveness, we forgive others as we have been forgiven—even when people hurt us repeatedly. "Peter came to Jesus and asked, 'Lord, how many times shall I forgive my brother or sister who sins against me? Up to seven times?' Jesus answered, 'I tell you, not seven times, but seventy-seven times'" (Matt. 18:21–22 NIV). Forgiving others, even when—and especially when—it is complicated, gives God great glory and is evidence of our faith in Him. It is one of the most significant ways we as followers of Jesus demonstrate who we are in Christ. (Look at Day 10 and Day 25 for more on forgiveness.)

Let's be clear, forgiving others does not mean we should stay in abusive situations. You don't need to put yourself in any dangerous situation. As mentioned before, forgiveness is letting go of any anger or bitterness toward our abusers and allowing God's love and grace to heal you. It frees you so that you can experience God's forgiveness in your own life. **Even if they do not deserve it, forgive others because you were forgiven by God when you did not deserve it.** Ultimately, forgiveness frees you and frees your prayers.

6. **Offense:** Have you wronged or offended someone? Jesus says we need to make things right before we come to God in prayer. "So if you are presenting a sacrifice at the altar in the Temple and you suddenly remember that someone has something against you, leave your sacrifice there at the altar. Go and be reconciled to that person. Then come and offer your sacrifice to God" (Matt. 5:23–24). Sometimes we might not know what we've done wrong. The person acts differently or distances themselves. It's best to go to them and ask if we've done anything to them. Apologize. Ask forgiveness. Make it right. When Zacchaeus met Jesus, he repented from stealing. He made it right by giving half his possessions to the poor and paying back to people four times what he had taken from them (Luke 19:8). When we repent before God and make things right with others, we can do more than what is required. Sometimes the person we have wronged refuses to forgive, even after we've tried to make it right. We need to remember everyone processes pain differently, and they

may need more time. When this happens, pray and know **God is in charge of changing hearts, not us**. Leave the results with Him, knowing you did what He called you to do. Paul teaches, "If it is possible, as far as it depends on you, live at peace with everyone" (Rom. 12:18 NIV).

7. **Marital Conflict:** Strife in a marriage can also hinder prayer. The apostle Peter teaches, "You husbands must give honor to your wives. Treat your wife with understanding as you live together. She may be weaker than you are, but she is your equal partner in God's gift of new life. Treat her as you should so your prayers will not be hindered" (1 Pet. 3:7). Although Peter addresses this verse to husbands, wives, too, cannot create conflict in their marriages without consequences. If we create problems in our marriage, we will also disrupt our relationship with God. Do not worry about your spouse's attitudes and actions; just make sure that *your* attitudes and actions honor God.

If we learn from these mistakes, we can avoid making them ourselves. God takes sin seriously because He loves us. If He allowed us to have a vibrant prayer life with sin still blocking our relationship, He would be accepting attitudes and actions that violate His holy nature, and that hurts us. God loves us too much to do that.

So if you can relate to any of these prayer hindrances, know that God longs to forgive you. If you doubt, ask God to strengthen your faith. If you are carrying the baggage of unconfessed sin, disobedience, or selfishness, confess it to God. Then, move forward in repentance. If you are holding grudges, let them go. If you have offended someone or are in conflict with your spouse, make it right. Then your intimate friendship with the Lord will be restored. "The eyes of the LORD are on those who fear him, on those whose hope is in his unfailing love" (Ps. 33:18 NIV). God really does delight in hearing and answering your prayers.

DAY 38

Let the Bible Speak:
Isaiah 59 (Optional: Psalm 66)

Let Your Mind Think:

1. Are your prayers being hindered? After reading today's lesson, what do you think may be blocking your prayers?

2. When you pray, are you more motivated by God's will or by your own desires? Why do you think that's true?

3. Do you pray with faith or struggle with doubt? What could you do to enhance your faith?

Let Your Soul Pray:
Father, show me everything that hinders my prayers. Make me courageous in clearing out sin so I can enjoy clear communication with You. As soon as a hindrance creeps in, make me aware of it so I can deal with it immediately. Hear my prayers. Speak to me. Help me listen to You . . . In Jesus's name, amen.

Let Your Heart Obey:
(What is God leading you to know, value, or do?)

Fast in Prayer

Then when you call, the LORD will answer.
"Yes, I am here," he will quickly reply.
Isaiah 58:9

There are times in everyone's life when prayer alone will not do. The circumstances are too hard. The needs are too great. The decisions are too important. There are times when we need to hear from God, and we need to hear from Him immediately.

Consider Queen Esther and her part in God's Story. She risked her life to save the Jewish people from a horrible plot of genocide (Esther 4). The king's prime minister despised the Jews so much he devised a plan to destroy them throughout the empire. He set a date for their doom. Esther, a Jewish orphan who married the Persian king, needed to enter the king's court unannounced to beg the king for mercy for her people, but this was grounds for execution. The situation was dire. Mordecai, Esther's cousin and guardian, challenged her, "Who knows whether you have not come to the kingdom *for such a time as this*?" (Esther 4:14 ESV, emphasis added). Esther needed courage, and the Jews needed salvation. Everyone needed protection from evil. So they prayed and fasted for three days. Fueled by faith, Esther humbly entered the king's court, trusting God with the outcome. God graciously gave her favor with the king. Once again, God rescued His people when they turned to Him.[1]

---

1   Read the book of Esther to better understand God's providential care for His people.

Time and time again, we see in the Bible when it is appropriate to pray *and fast,* either individually or as a group. This kind of intense prayer is serious because the situation is serious. What sets biblical fasting apart from other fasts is the motive: seeking God's heart. Sometimes, to the point of tears. The Lord says, "Return to Me with all your heart, and with fasting, weeping and mourning" (Joel 2:12 NASB). Fasting is not merely removing food; it is pronounced prayer with repentance, intercession, or agony. Jesus also spoke of a time of sorrow when His disciples would fast. "But someday the groom [Jesus] will be taken away from them, and then they will fast" (Mark 2:20). But what is biblical fasting, and how can we do it in a way that pleases the Lord?

Fasting is an outward expression of an inward prayer. It is an act of self-denial by which we redirect our focus off self (our physical needs) to focus on God. Fasting is *not* a diet to lose weight, a punishment, or a requirement for salvation. In a fast, we are not bargaining with God; our self-deprivation does not earn us favor from Him. Instead, our prayerful fasting expresses our desperation for God to intervene in *His* way and our confidence that He will. There is power in fasting.

When we fast, we deny ourselves solid food to demonstrate our hunger for God. Physical deprivation heightens our awareness of the spiritual as our flesh submits to the Spirit. Rather than looking for food when we feel hungry, we allow those hunger pains to become prayer prompts that drive us to God. Our hunger or tiredness reminds us of our human weakness and the need for God's continuing grace. As we continue to pray and feed on His Word, the result is a more profound dependence on God and communion with Him. That is why some Christian traditions have forms of fasting as part of their regular practice. A good example is fasting during Lent (the forty days leading up to Easter Sunday) to prepare their hearts for celebrating the resurrection of Christ.

There are different kinds of fasts. Usually, fasting means abstaining from food and drinking only water for twenty-four hours, starting after an evening meal. (Remember King Jehoshaphat on Day 37? The people fasted in this way.) **Before you withhold food from your**

diet, consult with your doctor. A *water-only fast is not encouraged without medical supervision.* Another approach to fasting is drinking water, coffee/tea, and juice throughout the day, only breaking fast for an evening meal. You could also eliminate one meal per day or restrict your diet to vegetables, broth, juice, coffee/tea, and water for several days. These modified fasts allow you to have enough energy to function.

If you abstain from both food and water (called an "absolute fast"), your fast should be very short. It should never be undertaken without physical preparation, counsel, and supervision. If you are under eighteen years old, pregnant, or have a medical condition that prohibits a fast from food, you may decide to give up something else.[1] For instance, you could fast from technology (e.g., phone, computer, social media) or entertainment (e.g., television, movies, music).

God does not care as much about *what* we fast from as He does about *why* we fast. As we learned yesterday, motives matter to God.

Over the centuries, the Israelites became legalistic with fasting, and God exposed their hypocrisy. They acted like they wanted to glorify God, but in reality, they were only concerned with impressing others. They were proud of their religious rigor and thought God should be too. They wondered why God would not applaud their efforts, so He told them plainly: "I will tell you why! . . . It's because you are fasting to please yourselves. Even while you fast, you keep oppressing your workers. What good is fasting when you keep on fighting and quarreling? This kind of fasting will never get you anywhere with me" (Isa. 58:3–4). Their self-glorifying fast, as well as their unconfessed sin, angered God. Jesus warned, "When you fast, don't make it obvious, as the hypocrites do, for they try to look miserable and disheveled so people will admire them for their fasting. I tell you the truth, that is the only reward they will ever get" (Matt. 6:16). **God hates fasting for attention.**

---

1   The Bible does not speak of children fasting. Children are discouraged from fasting from food out of consideration for their metabolic and nutritional needs. If you have a history of medical problems or are pregnant or diabetic, you can still practice focused prayer in the spirit of fasting (while remaining on your prescribed diet) by considering giving up something other than food.

Our fasting should look very different from the fasting Jesus rebuked in Matthew 6. Instead, He instructs believers, "But when you fast, comb your hair and wash your face. Then no one will notice that you are fasting, except your Father, who knows what you do in private. And your Father, who sees everything, will reward you" (Matt. 6:17–18). Secrecy will keep your motives pure. When you fast with a group, others will know that you are fasting, but do not draw attention to yourself. **God loves discrete fasting.**

There are many biblical reasons[1] for fasting, but today we'll focus on two: fasting to solve a problem and fasting for spiritual revival. When the prophet Ezra returned from exile in Persia to Jerusalem, he had a problem. His part in God's Story was to reestablish God's law with other priests of the Lord, but enemies from surrounding areas opposed them. This was a serious threat, but the Israelites were too fearful and embarrassed to ask the king of Persia for help. Ezra reported, "I gave orders for all of us to fast and humble ourselves before our God" (Ezra 8:21). God responded, and Ezra continued, "So we fasted and earnestly prayed that our God would take care of us, and he heard our prayer" (Ezra 8:23). God approved Ezra's community fast, so we can look to it for guidance. Three points stand out:

1. **Ezra enlisted everyone affected by the problem to fast.** If a problem affects a group, the circle of fasting should be as large as possible. (A private problem requires a private fast.)[2]

2. **They fasted seriously and humbly.** They were desperate for God's solution, earnestly seeking Him for help. Be persistent in prayer as you fast.

---

1 God's Word gives us plenty of examples of fasting to follow. In the Old Testament, God's people repented and fasted for spiritual renewal (1 Sam. 7:1–8), for safety and problem-solving (Ezra 8:21–23), for mercy and favor (Neh. 1–2), for physical well-being (Dan. 1:12–20), and for protection from evil (Esther 4:16). In the New Testament, believers also fasted for personal devotion (Luke 2:37), for group (corporate) devotion (Acts 13:2), and for ministry preparation (Acts 14:23).
2 Elmer L. Towns, *Fasting for Spiritual Breakthrough: A Guide to Nine Biblical Fasts* (Ventura, CA: Regal Books, 1996), 46–47.

3. **They fasted *before* they tried to solve the problem.** Do not take action until you have prayed, fasted, and heard from God. It's critical that we *wait* for His response.

You may not be facing a life-threatening problem like Ezra, but fasting with prayer will help you as you seek wisdom for clearer decision-making.

God may call you to a fast for spiritual renewal—a fast for spiritual freedom, for an awakening, for a return to God in your marriage, in your community, in your nation, or even in your own life. The prophet Samuel called God's people to fast because they had been spiritually weak and wayward for years. The ark of the covenant, which symbolized God's presence, had been stolen because of the Israelites' sin. They felt like God had abandoned them, so Samuel called for a fast. Before he prayed for the people, he commanded them to get rid of all their false gods. They poured out water before the Lord in a ceremony, symbolizing cleansing and spiritual renewal. "They also went without food all day and confessed that they had sinned against the LORD" (1 Sam. 7:6). God responded by defeating their enemies and entrusting the ark to them once again. Samuel's fast gives us two points of guidance:

1. **As with Ezra, Samuel involved everyone in the fast.** The whole community wanted spiritual renewal, so the whole community fasted.

2. **They confessed and repented of their sins together.**[1] They took responsibility for the sin that had made them distant from God and spiritually famished. "We have sinned against the LORD" (1 Sam. 7:6 ESV, emphasis added). They not only confessed their sin but also repented by destroying their idols and returning to Him.

We can look at their part in God's Story and learn from their example. The discipline of fasting is not something to be treated

---

1   Ibid., 66–89.

lightly. Fasting is for situations that require serious attention. God invites us to fast and pray because it honors Him and benefits us by heightening our awareness of His presence in our situation. As you think about your life, maybe you can relate to Ezra's and Samuel's cries for God's intervention. If God is leading you to a fast, consider the questions below before you begin:

1. Identify the purpose of your fast. Why are you fasting?
2. Declare your faith in God's ability to intervene (Isa. 59:1).
3. Determine how you will fast (water and juice only, one meal per day, etc.). **Consult your doctor before withholding food from your diet.**
4. Decide when you will start the fast and when you will finish it.
5. Find a Bible promise to encourage you as you fast: "Then when you call, the LORD will answer. 'Yes, I am here,' he will quickly reply" (Isa. 58:9).

Fasting demonstrates to ourselves and to God that we are earnest about our relationship with Him. When you fast with your heart centered on God's will, expect answers from the One who loves you and longs to be found by you (Jer. 29:13). Draw closer to God and strengthen your faith as you humbly worship God through prayer and fasting.

Let the Bible Speak:
Isaiah 58 (Esther 4)

Let Your Mind Think:
1. Have you ever fasted in prayer? If so, do you feel it enhanced your prayer time? Explain.

2. Do you see any problems in your life or in your community that call for a fast?

3. Would you and your friends consider fasting for spiritual renewal? If so, talk and pray with one another about the possibility of fasting together.[1]

Let Your Soul Pray:
Father, help me develop in spiritual maturity, knowing how and when to fast. When I fast, help me not give in to self-pity or pride, but instead, help me give myself over to desperate, faith-filled prayer. May I always hunger for You above all else . . . In Jesus's name, amen.

Let Your Heart Obey:
(What is God leading you to know, value, or do?)

---

1   Visit allinmin.org for downloadable tools for a group fast.

Pray God's Word, Discover God's Will

If you abide in me, and my words abide in you, ask
whatever you wish, and it will be done for you.

John 15:7 ESV

No matter where in the world you live, you will find that people are creatures of habit. We wake up at the same time each morning. We prepare the same foods each day. We tend to sit in the same places at weekly church gatherings. But while the routines of daily life can be helpful, creating an environment of order and predictability, they can also be harmful to our habits of regular prayer. Mindlessly approaching God in the same way, with the same prayer, day after day, can cause our relationship with Him to feel stale and lifeless. Sometimes, we need to breathe life into our prayers, and we can do so with God-breathed Scripture.

Praying Scripture ignites communication with God. We see this practice modeled throughout the Bible as great believers—and our Lord Jesus Himself—prayed Scripture confidently. Scriptural prayers can help us keep our communication with God alive, effective, and focused on *Him* (not ourselves) and *His* glory (not our own). **In using His words, we seek to align our thinking with His and to pray in His will.** We trust the promise that He hears and answers prayers that align with His will (1 John 5:14–15). For this reason, the psalmist David said with confidence, "Take delight in the LORD, and he will give you the desires of your heart" (Psalm 37:4 NIV).

But some people misuse these Scriptures as if they are unique formulas to get what they want. *Delight in the Lord? Okay, I love You, Lord! I love to praise You, Lord! I'd love for You to answer all my prayers now, Lord.* That's not what is meant by those verses. To "delight in the LORD" is to desire Him, and He'll give you new desires—His desires. What does God want? His will is always

- for His glory (Rom. 11:36);
- to have a relationship with us (Matt. 23:37);
- to bring us to Himself through Christ (Rom. 5:1);
- for us to become like Christ (Rom. 8:29);
- for us to rejoice, give thanks, and pray continually (1 Thess. 5:16–18);
- for our holiness and sexual purity (1 Thess. 4:3);
- for all people to come to Him (2 Pet. 3:9);
- for truth to fill us (Col. 3:16);
- for our hearts more than our works (Hosea 6:6);
- for us to abide and enjoy abundant life (John 10:10; 15:1–17).

We know these things are God's will because His Word says so, and we can confidently pray that He will work to accomplish what He desires. However, when it comes to more specific, personal decisions—like where to move or find a job—we will not find detailed instructions in the Bible. That might sound discouraging at first. But as we continue rooting ourselves in God's Word, our minds are transformed. And we will become better at discerning His *unique* will for us and recognizing His hand in our particular concerns. The key is to replace worldly thinking with the mind of Christ: "Don't copy the behavior and customs of this world, but let God transform you into a new person by changing the way you think. Then you will learn to know God's will for you, which is good and pleasing and perfect" (Rom. 12:2).

Sometimes, even with our prayerful attempts to discern what God wants, we simply do not know what to pray anymore. When we don't know what to say, Scripture can give us the words. And we can also rely on the Holy Spirit to pray *for* us. God knows our every desire and need, even those that we do not yet recognize. We can trust Him to arrange circumstances and provide for us at just the right time, in just the right way, even when we don't have the right words:

> The Holy Spirit helps us in our weakness. For example, we don't know what God wants us to pray for. But the Holy Spirit prays for us with groanings that cannot be expressed in words. And the Father who knows all hearts knows what the Spirit is saying, for the Spirit pleads for us believers in harmony with God's own will. (Rom. 8:26–27)

With this help from the Holy Spirit, we can release our concerns to God, trusting Him to direct the outcome according to His will. We do not need to discern God's will *before* we pray. **Prayer leads us to discover God's will.** Through prayer, God changes your heart to line up with His will. Pray humbly for what you want, but pray with a heart surrendered to His purposes: "Yet not my will, but yours be done" (Luke 22:42 NIV). As God begins to show you His will, continue to trust Him by taking the next steps of obedience. The apostle Paul modeled this faithfully. Three times he asked God to remove "a thorn in [his] flesh, a messenger from Satan," and three times God denied his request (2 Cor. 12:7–10).

Nonetheless, Paul remained faithful to God because his desire was for God's will, above all. He learned through that experience that God's grace is enough to accomplish God's will. As a result, Paul "finished the race" and "remained faithful" to the very end (2 Tim. 4:7), and God was greatly glorified through his life.

When we lean on God and His Word in prayer, especially during hard times, we find more of His strength to live according to His plan. **Perhaps those difficult times are when we notice most how Scripture strengthens our prayers. Praying God's Word unleashes God's power to transform hearts and circumstances.** It is also "God-breathed and is useful for teaching, rebuking, correcting and training in righteousness, so that the servant of God may be thoroughly equipped for every good work" (2 Tim. 3:16–17 NIV). God's Word never fails; it speaks to us and equips us for His plans.

Knowing that God's Word always accomplishes its work, we can boldly claim His promises and trust that He will keep them.

There are more than seven thousand promises in Scripture, and most are conditional. Some promises are for particular people. And some promises require a particular action. When you read a promise, examine the original context carefully to see if it is conditional. Pay attention to whether *you* have to do something before *God* does something. When we weave conditional promises into prayer, we ask God to help us fulfill our responsibility. Then we call on Him to respond to our obedience as He promised. Here are some examples:

- "Submit yourselves, then, to God. Resist the devil, and he will flee from you. Come near to God and he will come near to you" (James 4:7–8 NIV).

  God, help me surrender to You and resist the enemy so he will leave me alone. Help me seek You. I come close to You in my heart right now. Please come close to me, Lord.

- "If we confess our sins, he is faithful and just to forgive us our sins and to cleanse us from all unrighteousness" (1 John 1:9 ESV).

  Father, thank You for Your faithfulness to forgive me. I confess I've _____. Please cleanse me from all unrighteousness and help me walk in Your Spirit for Your glory.

- "Seek the Kingdom of God above all else, and live righteously, and he will give you everything you need" (Matt. 6:33).

  Lord, help me prioritize Your purposes and live by Your principles over the things of this world. I know when I do, You will meet all my needs. I trust You.

Prayer stirs God's promises in our lives. **We might not know when or how God will fulfill the promise, but we know praying His promise helps us trust Him and live according to His will.** "For all the promises of God find their Yes in him. That is why it is through him that we utter our Amen to God for his glory" (2 Cor. 1:20 ESV). God loves us and wants us to pray, speak His Word in faith, claim His promises, and place our hope entirely on Him. "Remember your promise to me; it is my only hope" (Ps. 119:49).

Let the Bible Speak:
Matthew 6:9–13 (Optional: Romans 12:1–2)

Let Your Mind Think:
1. Knowing God's will helps us face problems and make decisions. What promise in Scripture are you resting on? Find one today that helps you in some way.

2. Have your heart's desires changed as you've grown in your friendship with God? Explain.

3. If you struggle in a particular area, find a verse or passage in Scripture now to help you overcome your problem. Write one down and memorize it (Day 34). Pray these words from Scripture regularly. God loves hearing His Word, and He loves hearing from you and how He can help you overcome.

Let Your Soul Pray:
Father, Your Word is powerful. Help me pray from Your Word so that I will pray according to Your will. Show me which promises You are fulfilling in my life, and help me memorize and pray them back to You. Give me the desires of Your heart . . . In Jesus's name, amen.

Let Your Heart Obey:
(What is God leading you to know, value, or do?)

DAY 41

Pray for Others—
The Great Reach
of Intercession

*I urge you, first of all, to pray for all people. Ask God to help
them; intercede on their behalf, and give thanks for them.*
1 Timothy 2:1

In the last moments before Jesus handed Himself over to be
crucified, He gave His disciples an immeasurable gift. He *prayed*
for them—and for *you*.[1]

Constant prayer characterized Jesus's relationship with His
disciples. He prayed before He chose them (Luke 6:12–16). He prayed
for them throughout His ministry. And His prayers for them and for
you did not stop when He ascended to heaven. **Today, right now,
Jesus continues to pray for you from His throne in heaven** (Rom.
8:34; Heb. 7:25). Jesus wraps those He loves in prayer, and so we—as
His ambassadors—do the same.

Who does God want us to pray for?

- Authorities (1 Tim. 2:1–2)
- Believers worldwide (Eph. 6:18)
- Sick people (James 5:14–15)

---

1 You can find this prayer—the longest prayer in the Bible outside of Psalms—in John 17.

- Fellow sinners (James 5:15–16)
- Enemies (Matt. 5:44; Luke 6:28)
- Harvest gatherers (Matt. 9:38)
- ALL people (1 Tim. 2:1)

Why is intercession (praying for others) so important? Praying for one another invites God into the relationship—it binds us together in love and unity. Intercession changes our hearts toward a person as we humble ourselves, "not looking to [our] own interests but [also] . . . to the interests of the others" (Phil. 2:4 NIV). We do not walk God's path alone. We have brothers and sisters who walk with us, and we are called to care for them and encourage them. **But it's hard for us to do anything of eternal significance for people *before* we pray for them. *After* we pray for them, every kind word and deed carries the power of God.** Consider these biblical examples of intercession:

- Abraham interceded for Lot, and God rescued him from the destruction of Sodom (Gen. 18).
- Moses interceded for a whole nation—the wayward Israelites—and God refrained from destroying them (Exod. 32–33; Ps. 106:23).
- Samuel interceded for God's people, and God forgave their sin and defeated their enemies (1 Sam. 7).
- Elijah interceded for the land, and God sent rain (1 Kings 18:41–46).
- Job interceded for the friends who had falsely accused him, and God forgave them (Job 42).
- Esther interceded for the Jews, and God delivered them from the Persians (Esther 4:15–17).
- The early church interceded for imprisoned Peter, and God opened the prison doors (Acts 12).
- Jesus interceded for us, and God rescued us from our sin (Isa. 53:12).

We have many examples of intercession in God's Word because it is so important to Him. Part of His will for us is to intercede for those He loves. So we need to ask Him to help us see others as *He* sees them. **God will give you wisdom and discernment about how to pray for needs brought to your attention.** If a friend is suffering because of persecution, He may guide you to pray for endurance or relief. If she is suffering because of bad choices, He may guide you to pray for *repentance* and deliverance. When God changes your heart to see others as He sees them, your prayers will change too. You might not pray, "*God, fix their problems,*" "*End their pain,*" "*Send them money.*" Instead, you might pray,

> *God, give them Your greatest blessings, even if receiving those great blessings requires pain. Bring relief as soon as possible, and provide great strength in the meantime. Deliver them from evil. Free them from sin and anything that hinders their relationship with You. Be glorified in their life. Give them endurance and enable them to experience You now more than ever. Give them Your joy and peace. Show me how I can help and encourage them.*

As we intercede for others, we need to remember that prayers said in faith and accompanied by action honor God and bless others. Do you feel like you do not have enough faith? If God gave you faith to come to Jesus, you already have enough faith to bring others to Jesus in prayer. Even faith as small as a mustard seed can move giant obstacles. "Truly I tell you, if you have faith as small as a mustard seed, you can say to this mountain, 'Move from here to there,' and it will move. Nothing will be impossible for you" (Matt. 17:20 NIV). God's response to our prayers is not related to the size of our faith. No matter how long you've been a believer or how much you've sinned in the past or how weak your prayer seems, your prayers can move mountains. We can pray big prayers over impossible situations with even tiny faith. *All things are possible* with our all-knowing, all-powerful, all-present God (Matt. 19:26; Mark 10:27).

Finally, **remember to pray with action**. "Devote yourselves to prayer with an alert mind and a thankful heart" (Col. 4:2). If you see a person or issue in need of prayer, pray right then. If we delay, we might become distracted. If someone invites you to pray for them, consider it a privilege, and keep their prayer requests confidential. When you intercede for others, God may show you how to help them.

- If you are praying for someone to find a job and you think of a helpful person who is hiring, connect your friend with the person hiring.
- If you are praying for a sick friend and realize you have nourishing food to share, bring food to your friend.
- If you are praying for someone to know Christ, look for an opportunity to share about Jesus.
- If you are married to an unbeliever, your prayers and godly actions will influence your spouse. The apostle Peter said about unbelieving husbands, "Even if some refuse to obey the Good News, your godly lives will speak to them without any words. They will be won over by observing your pure and reverent lives" (1 Pet. 3:1–2).

Prayer is not passive. Prayer is active. Do not delay in doing good (Prov. 3:28).

Our physical reach is limited, but our reach in prayer is limitless. We can advance the gospel globally through intercession and influence millions of people for the glory of God!

DAY 41

Let the Bible Speak:
John 17 (Optional: Colossians 1:9–12; 3; 4:2–6)

Let Your Mind Think:
Do you remember our new perspective as ambassadors of Christ (Days 17-19)? Today, let that calling guide your prayer as you pray from Colossians.

1. **Pray for the next generation (Col. 1:9–12).** Pray that they would know God, understand His will (v. 9), live fruitful lives (v. 10), experience God's power (v. 11), and joyfully give thanks to the Father (v. 12).

2. **Pray for your neighbors and the nations (Col. 4:2–6).** Pray for opportunities to share Christ (v. 3) and represent Him well with wise living and grace-filled words to share (vv. 5–6).

3. **Pray to give God glory (Col. 3).** Ask God to help you focus on Christ (v. 1) and help you to make His glory your highest goal (v. 3). Pray that your life will be clothed in compassion, kindness, humility, gentleness, and patience—holy and glorifying to Him as you freely love and forgive others (vv. 5–15).

Let Your Soul Pray:
Father, You say, "When they call on me, I will answer; I will be with them in trouble. I will rescue and honor them" (Ps. 91:15). May I never hesitate to call on You for myself and others . . . In Jesus's name, amen.

Let Your Heart Obey:
(What is God leading you to know, value, or do?)

Pray First. Pray Always. Pray Now.

Devote yourselves to prayer with an alert
mind and a thankful heart.
Colossians 4:2

One of the most significant, most profound, and most wonderful realities in all the universe is this: **God answers prayer**. Let us never get used to this amazing truth. Let us never take it for granted that God listens to our prayers and answers them. He answers our prayers because of who He is. Our response to His grace and goodness: May God's kingdom come and will be done in our lives, our marriages, our families, our churches, and our nations (Matt. 6:10). This week we have learned much about this special privilege we have with God:

- Prayer flows from and grows your relationship with God.
- Prayer is a conversation with God that sometimes changes your circumstances and *always* changes your heart.
- We need to watch for hindrances to prayer and resolve them immediately.
- We can fast or pray Scripture to strengthen our prayer life.
- We pray for others we know personally and, as God leads, for countless others.

Most importantly, the purpose of prayer is to know God's heart, and He often shows us His heart through His Word. That's why it

252 | YOUR TRUE STORY

is so important to study Scripture and memorize it. God's Word is His way of speaking to us. When we study and learn Scripture, the Holy Spirit will remind us of verses at just the right time (John 14:26). When He does this for you, pray about them.

God speaks in other ways too. "'In the last days,' God says, 'I will pour out my Spirit upon all people. Your sons and daughters will prophesy. Your young men will see visions, and your old men will dream dreams'" (Acts 2:17). Sometimes God speaks through circumstances, impressions, spontaneous flows of thought, dreams, visions, or others in the church. There are several biblical examples of this:

- **God spoke** to Abraham (Gen. 12:1), Hagar (Gen. 16:7–13), Moses (Exod. 3:5), all the prophets, Saul (Paul) (Acts 9:5), and John (Rev. 1:17–18).
- **God sent dreams** to Jacob (Gen. 28:12), Joseph (Jacob's son) (Gen. 37:5), Pharaoh (Gen. 41), Nebuchadnezzar (Dan. 2), Joseph (Mary's husband) (Matt. 1:20–21; 2:13), and the wise men (Matt. 2:12).
- **God gave visions** to Isaiah (Isa. 2:1), Jeremiah (Jer. 24:1), Ezekiel (Ezek. 1:1), Daniel (Dan. 10), Peter (Acts 10:9–16), Paul (Acts 16:9), John (Rev. 1), and many more.
- **God gave the church** to the people of Judea, Galilee, Samaria (Acts 9:31), Antioch (Acts 13), Jerusalem (Acts 15), and us.

How God speaks to us is not as important as how we *respond* to what we think He is saying. It is fascinating to know that God speaks to us in a variety of ways, but be careful. Mishearing God can lead to damage. **One thing is sure—when God speaks to us, He will never, ever contradict His Word.** Some have tried to predict the end times, believing they received special revelation, but God's Word says no one will know the day or hour Jesus will return (Matt. 24:36). Some leaders teach that *all* sickness is a result of unrepented sin. But the Bible teaches that all humanity suffers the consequences of sin, which includes sickness (Rom. 8:20–22).

When you believe you have heard from God, ask God to confirm the message. When you do, a pastor or a friend may unknowingly bring up a verse that applies to your situation. Or, in your devotional time with the Lord, you may be drawn to a verse that confirms what you heard. Mature believers and Bible-wise church leaders can also help you discern whether a message was from God. When you confirm that you have indeed heard from God, obey Him wholly and immediately. His Holy Spirit will empower you to follow His lead. Delayed or partial obedience is disobedience, and, as we learned earlier, disobedience can hinder our prayers.

As we continue our prayer journey with God, here are three suggestions to strengthen our times of prayer:

1. **Plan prayer.** We can feel free to share our hearts with God freely and spontaneously, but we also need to be intentional about *what* we pray—**include worship (adoration), confession, thanksgiving, and supplication** (Day 37). Otherwise, we might skip worship and spend all our time asking God for things, or we might get lost in confession and forget to give thanks. As suggested on Day 37, keep a list of prayer requests that you update weekly, and make notes describing when and how God answers those prayers. You might even set up a weekly prayer schedule for the "supplication" part of your prayer time to help you focus on specific people or concerns each day of the week. For example:

Sunday: Personal Concerns and the Week Ahead
Monday: Missionaries and Ministries (blessing and favor)
Tuesday: Teachers, Government Leaders, Military, and Police (wisdom and protection)
Wednesday: Family Members (prayer requests)
Thursday: Friends (prayer requests)
Friday: Neighbors and Nations (for revival, spiritual awakening, and peace for Jerusalem [Ps. 122:6–9])
Saturday: Pastors (to rest well and preach with God's power)

If your worship community offers them—whether from your local church or accessible online—you might also consider using prayer outlines, prayer guides, or prayer calendars.

2. **Prioritize prayer.** Jesus often withdrew to a private place to start His day in prayer, and He communicated with His Father throughout the day. He watched His Father. He did what He saw His Father doing (John 5:19). He listened to His Father's words and said what He heard His Father saying (John 12:49). Jesus's disciples witnessed firsthand His reliance on prayer. When they became leaders in the early church, they delegated other tasks to devote themselves to prayer and teaching God's Word (Acts 6:4). The Holy Spirit moved mightily in response to their prayers (Acts 1:14–2:4). He can do the same for us.

3. **Picture praying in God's throne room.** Praying is not only an action but a location. "Let us then with confidence draw near to the throne of grace, that we may receive mercy and find grace to help in time of need" (Heb. 4:16 ESV). When we pray, we draw near to the throne of God. The writer of Hebrews reminds us that Jesus is our Great High Priest (Heb. 2:17; 4:14) and urges us to draw near in confidence to God's throne. Thinking about prayer this way changes how we approach God with our prayers. You may choose to kneel or bow your head to ready yourself physically for this encounter.

God's throne is unlike any throne on earth. He is seated on grace. He gives us grace. His grace is sufficient to meet our needs at the right time. Because Jesus is our Great High Priest, we can draw near to the throne of grace. The Lord says, "My grace is sufficient for you, for my power is made perfect in weakness" (2 Cor. 12:9 NIV). We are called to endure, and we have grace to keep us through our journey—our true story with God and His purpose for us. What a beautiful and glorious picture we can remember when we approach God in prayer!

Friend, you are invited to enjoy an ongoing conversation with God from the moment you wake up and throughout the day. Believe the One to whom you pray is "gracious and compassionate, slow to anger and rich in love" (Ps. 145:8 NIV). He is our good Father, and He delights to hear the prayers of His children (Prov. 15:8).

Let the Bible Speak:
Luke 18:1–14 (Optional: Hebrews 4:14–16)

Let Your Mind Think:
1. How does knowing you are approaching God's throne of grace change the way you approach prayer?

2. Answer Week 6 Discussion Questions.

Let Your Soul Pray:
Father, thank You for inviting me to Your throne of grace. Guide me as I pray. What a blessing that You want to hear from me, that You want me to pour out my heart to You. Please help me know Your heart as I begin this continual conversation with You. Please provide Your mercy and grace in my time of need . . . In Jesus's name, amen.

Let Your Heart Obey:
(What is God leading you to know, value, or do?)

WEEK 6 DISCUSSION QUESTIONS:

Review this week's lessons and answer the questions below.
Share your answers with your friends when you gather this week.

1. What helps you focus when you pray? Praying out loud? Kneeling? Journaling? Outlining prayers? Something else?

2. We discussed four main elements (ACTS) of prayer: adoration, confession, thanksgiving, and supplication. Which of these comes most easily to you? Which would you like to develop more? The Lord's Prayer is a great example that includes these main parts. If you do not know the Lord's Prayer, turn to Matthew 6:9–13 and read it now.

3. When has God used prayer to change your heart without changing your circumstances? What is the biggest answer to prayer you can remember?

4. Are there any hindrances to prayer in your life? What action will you take today to overcome these hindrances? Ask someone to hold you accountable for making any change God is calling you to make.

5. Share prayer needs and practice intercession by praying for each other. Let the others know if and when God answered those prayers.

WEEK SEVEN

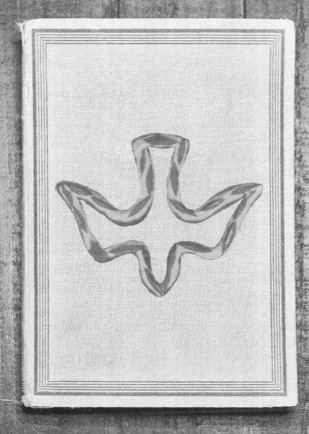

THE HOLY SPIRIT—LIVING YOUR STORY IN GOD'S STRENGTH

Know the Power
of God in You

I will ask the Father, and he will give you another
advocate to help you and be with you forever—the
Spirit of truth. The world cannot accept him, because
it neither sees him nor knows him. But you know
him, for he lives with you and will be in you.

John 14:16–17 NIV

We have saved the most incredible gift for our last week together.
You heard about Him throughout this journey because it is impossible not to talk about Him. But now, let's officially meet the One
who enables you to know God, abide in Jesus, and fulfill your part in
God's Story. Now it is time to know the Holy Spirit and discover how
to enjoy His presence.

The reality is many believers around the world understand the
Holy Spirit exists but do not know how to interact with Him. They
may regularly attend church, study the Bible, and volunteer in ministry. Yet, something seems missing in their relationship with God.
They may wonder why they lack joy or experience little victory over
sin or feel restless and frustrated. They do not realize it is not something in life they are missing but someone. No one has taught them
how to have a daily, life-giving relationship with God through the
Holy Spirit, based on the finished work of Jesus. God never intended
for His children to feel this way. That is why when Jesus went to
heaven, He left us three things:

1. His Body: The Church (Col. 1:18)

The church is the family of God, not a building.[1] The Bible calls this gathering of believers the body of Christ (Day 12). Just as different parts of the body serve different functions but make up one person, we as believers make up the body of Christ. We encourage and support one another. **The Holy Spirit gives us special abilities–spiritual gifts–to work well together as a faith family** (1 Cor. 12). Because we all do not have the same gifts, we bless one another in different ways, but always with the purpose of helping one another to the glory of God. The Holy Spirit and the church work together in Scripture.

2. His Mind: The Word of God (1 Cor. 2:16)

Jesus Christ is the Word become flesh (John 1:14). When Jesus (God's Word in *human* form) returned to heaven, the Scriptures (God's Word in *written* form) remained with us. Through God's Word, we know God's mind–His will and thoughts–and we renew our minds (Rom. 12:1–2). **Through the Holy Spirit, the mind of Jesus Christ is given and understood.** "These are the things God has revealed to us by his Spirit, . . . 'Who has known the mind of the Lord so as to instruct him?' But we have the mind of Christ" (1 Cor. 2:10, 16 NIV). The Holy Spirit and the gospel go together in Scripture.[2]

3. God's Spirit: The Holy Spirit (Rom. 8)

Jesus also left us the Holy Spirit, the Helper, the Spirit of Truth. The Holy Spirit is not separate from God but *is* God (2 Cor. 3:17). When we turn from our sin and place our trust in Jesus alone for salvation, God forgives us of our sins and *renews us* through the Holy Spirit (Titus 3:5 NIV). **The Holy Spirit fills us, comforts us, teaches us, prays for us, and empowers us.** In Jesus's last words to His disciples, He focused on this gift of the Holy Spirit (John 14:15–27; Acts 1:8). The Holy Spirit and the born-again believer always are one in Scripture.[3]

Yes, it is the Holy Spirit who is working in and through the

---

1   Read Day 12 on "How to Find a Good Church."

2   J. D. Greear, *Jesus, Continued . . . : Why the Spirit Inside You Is Better than Jesus Beside You* (Grand Rapids, MI: Zondervan, 2014), 21.

3   Jesus used the term "born again" when talking with a religious leader about salvation (John 3:3–8).

church, revealing the mind of Christ, and helping us to live the life of faith. Our ability to fulfill God's purpose rests on our relationship with God through the Holy Spirit. We need to learn about Him, and we need to lean on Him as He points us to Jesus (John 15:26). Now for the introductions.

Who is the Holy Spirit? The Bible describes the Holy Spirit as fully God. Along with God the Father and God the Son (Jesus), God the Spirit is the third person of the Trinity. One God in three persons—together, yet distinct. We see the Trinity present at creation (Gen. 1:2, 26), active in Jesus's baptism (Matt. 3:16–17), declared in the Great Commission (Matt. 28:19), referenced in New Testament letters (2 Cor. 13:14), and woven throughout Scripture. Since the Holy Spirit is God, He is equal in every way with God the Father and God the Son.

Like the Father and the Son, the Spirit is also a *person*, not a vague power. The Holy Spirit is not an impersonal force but a person with His own mind, emotions, and will. He actively relates to us, communicates with us, and helps us. He is "the eternal Spirit" (Heb. 9:14) who will be with us *forever* (John 14:16).

When Jesus's time on earth was ending, He told His disciples, "It is for your good that I am going away" (John 16:7 NIV). For our good? Think about that statement. How could it possibly be good for Jesus to leave? Jesus went on to explain, "Unless I go away, the Advocate will not come to you; but if I go, I will send him to you" (John 16:7 NIV). Only after Jesus left would the Advocate, the Holy Spirit, come to them. **Jesus knew that God the Spirit living *inside* them was better than God the Son living *beside* them.** Unimaginable, but true.

The Holy Spirit is given to all believers. Right now, the Holy Spirit resides inside you. You are now God's temple.[1] As walking holy places, we have the Holy Spirit working in us and through us to bring the light and love of Jesus to the world. We are not just saved *from* our sins; we are also saved *for* God's purposes and empowered by God's Holy Spirit. We can do nothing of lasting value or for God's glory on our own. "'Not by might nor by power, but by my Spirit,' says the Lord Almighty" (Zech. 4:6 NIV).

---

1   1 Cor. 3:9, 16–17; 6:17–19.

To fulfill our part in God's Story, we need the Holy Spirit in every area of our lives as our

- Resident Teacher–revealing and reminding us of the truth in God's Word (John 14:26).
- Forever Helper–leading and helping us at all times (John 14:16).
- Missions Director–empowering us as Jesus's witnesses to the world (Acts 1:8).
- Prayer Intercessor–praying for us when we do not know what to pray (Rom. 8:26).
- Sin Breaker–freeing us from sin (Rom. 8:2, 12–13).
- Truth Revealer–guiding us into all truth (John 16:13).
- Gift Giver–equipping us with spiritual gifts (Rom. 12:3–8; 1 Cor. 12).
- Fruit Producer–harvesting spiritual fruit in our lives (Gal. 5:22–23).
- Salvation Sealer–pledging our eternal state as God's children (Eph. 1:13–14).

That's why Jesus talked about Him *again* after His resurrection. Moments before He returned to heaven, Jesus promised His disciples:

> You will receive power when the Holy Spirit comes upon you. And you will be my witnesses, telling people about me everywhere–in Jerusalem, throughout Judea, in Samaria, and to the ends of the earth. (Acts 1:8)

Through the power of the Holy Spirit, they would represent Jesus locally (Jerusalem), in the surrounding region (Judea), in places some people avoid (Samaria), and in the rest of the world. Of all the advice and encouragement Jesus could have offered to His disciples, His last words were about the Holy Spirit. Jesus's life depended on the Holy Spirit–from His birth and baptism to His anointing, life direction, and death.[1] Ultimately, Jesus was raised from the dead by the Spirit (Rom. 8:11). If Jesus depended on the Holy Spirit during

---

1 Luke 1:35; Luke 3:22; Luke 4:18; Luke 4:1; Heb. 9:14.

His time on earth, how can we live any differently? Ask yourself the following questions:

- Do I need discernment to understand Scripture? (John 14:26; 1 Cor. 2:13–14)
- Would I like to be reminded of God's Word at the right time? (John 14:26)
- Do I want to be empowered to fulfill God's purposes? (Acts 1:8)
- Am I willing to be led by the Holy Spirit? (Rom. 8:14; Gal. 5:18)
- Do I need help sometimes when I pray? (Rom. 8:26–27)
- Would I like to be free from the grip of sin? (Rom. 8:2, 12–13)
- Do I desire to obey God's Word? (Ezek. 36:27)
- Am I seeking to grow in godliness? (2 Cor. 3:18; 2 Thess. 2:13)
- Do I need wise answers when I am questioned about God? (Luke 12:12)

If you answered yes to any of the above questions, you are ready for the Holy Spirit to do more of His work through you. And He is ready to work with you, too. The more you allow the Holy Spirit full access to your life, the more awareness you will have of God's abiding and loving presence. The result is a deeper love for Jesus—exactly why the Holy Spirit came. As Jesus came to earth to exalt and reveal God the Father (Matt. 11:27), the Holy Spirit came to earth to exalt and glorify Jesus (John 16:13–14).

"In the last days, God says, I will pour out my Spirit on all people. . . . And everyone who calls on the name of the Lord will be saved." (Acts 2:17, 21 NIV)

In the Old Testament, many people ignored God the Father. In the New Testament, many people ignored God the Son. Today, let us not make the mistake of neglecting God the Spirit. Instead, let's strengthen our bond with God through the Holy Spirit by inviting Him to work in and through us. He will do it. Tomorrow you will find out how. It is going to be a great final week together.

Let the Bible Speak:

John 14:15–27 (Optional: Acts 1–4. As time permits this week, **read the New Testament book of Acts**, often called "Acts of the Holy Spirit," to better understand the Holy Spirit and how He works in believers' lives.)

Let Your Mind Think:

1. Who is the Holy Spirit? Reread some of the Bible verses above and describe Him in your own words.

2. In what ways can He affect your life?

3. We are so used to people working with us or for us. What does it mean for the Holy Spirit to work *through* us?

Let Your Soul Pray:

Father, thank You for the wonderful gift of Your Holy Spirit. I want a deep, life-giving relationship with You, through the Holy Spirit, based on the finished work of Jesus. Help me to delight in Your Spirit as I walk in Your ways. Apart from You, I can do nothing. Remind me to open the gift of Your Spirit each day, living by Your grace, for Your glory . . . In Jesus's name, amen.

Let Your Heart Obey:

(What is God leading you to know, value, or do?)

Be Filled with the Spirit–Surrender

Be filled with the Spirit.
Ephesians 5:18 NIV

What would you do if Jesus came to visit you in person? You'd probably welcome Him, serve Him your finest food, and present the best part of your life to Him. What if He told you that He was going to live with you *forever*? Everything would change. You might relax and let Him into every part of your life. Every day you would live in the reality of Jesus's presence, His love for you, and His ability to solve any problem. Life would be so different.

That is exactly how life can be now. The Holy Spirit is with us, and not just with us, but *in* us. Once we ask Jesus to be our Lord, the Holy Spirit is always ready to help us and guide us–in every area of our lives. No, not everything will go our way or in our timing, but we have no reason to worry because we know we can rest in His care. How do we know?

God gives us the Holy Spirit when we believe in Jesus.[1] Not just for a moment, but for all time. Jesus promises the Holy Spirit will live in us *forever* (John 14:15–17). But the Holy Spirit living *in* us at the point of our salvation is different from the Holy Spirit *filling* us. We do not decide to have the Holy Spirit living in us when we

---

1   John 7:37–39; Rom. 8:9; 1 Cor. 12:13; Gal. 3:2; Eph. 1:13–14. There is much discussion on this topic, but believers worldwide agree God wants to work in and through His children. Please keep reading for more.

place our faith in Jesus—that is an automatic, unconditional blessing (Eph. 1:13). We *do* choose to yield ourselves to the Holy Spirit for Him to work in and through us—that is a conditional blessing (Eph. 5:18).

We see this relationship in the book of Acts. The Holy Spirit demonstrated His power in believers who were "filled with the Holy Spirit." Notice these verses specifically refer to the filling of the Holy Spirit:

- "Then Peter, filled with the Holy Spirit, said to them: 'Rulers and elders of the people!'" (Acts 4:8 NIV).
- "After they prayed, the place where they were meeting was shaken. And they were all filled with the Holy Spirit and spoke the word of God boldly" (Acts 4:31 NIV).
- "Brothers and sisters, choose seven men from among you who are known to be full of the Spirit and wisdom. We will turn this responsibility over to them" (Acts 6:3 NIV).
- "They chose Stephen, a man full of faith and of the Holy Spirit" (Acts 6:5 NIV).
- "But Stephen, full of the Holy Spirit, looked up to heaven and saw the glory of God, and Jesus standing at the right hand of God" (Acts 7:55 NIV).
- "[Barnabas] was a good man, full of the Holy Spirit and faith, and a great number of people were brought to the Lord" (Acts 11:24 NIV).
- "Then Saul, who was also called Paul, filled with the Holy Spirit, looked straight at Elymas and said, 'You are a child of the devil and an enemy of everything that is right!'" (Acts 13:9–10 NIV).

A glimpse of heaven? Powerful preaching? Bold leadership? Yes, all of these believers, known for their faith and power in the Lord, were *filled* with the Holy Spirit. God empowered them, equipped them, and unified them to launch Jesus's message from Jerusalem to the ends of the earth. Here's the truth: God desires to fill us today with that same Holy Spirit power (Eph. 1:19). How does He do it?

Let's take a closer look at Ephesians 5:18. The original Greek word for "fill" in this passage is both a command and a present-tense verb, an ongoing reality. By examining the original language, we learn that *God alone* does the filling, not us. God also *commands* us to be filled, repeatedly, which means that it is an ongoing process, similar to our need to abide in Jesus continually (Week 4).

Maybe you're wondering, "How can I get more of the Holy Spirit?" **We do not need to *get* more of the Holy Spirit; we need to *give* the Holy Spirit more of us.** "God gives the Spirit without limit" (John 3:34 NIV). The Spirit of God will fill whatever space you make available to Him. Sometimes, we allow other things to fill us instead of the Holy Spirit. A sin-filled life cannot be filled with the Spirit any more than a bucket full of dirt can be filled with fresh water. The greatest obstacle to a relationship with the Spirit is a refusal to cooperate with Him. Believers can be indifferent and unconcerned about becoming effective or victorious followers of Christ and wonder why they lack joy or feel defeated. If we do not make room for the Holy Spirit, we will be frustrated and shallow in our faith. Remember, we were never designed to live as Christ-followers in *our* strength.

Do you want to make room for the Holy Spirit? First, take inventory of what's in your heart right now. *Prayerfully* and honestly answer the questions below. When you are finished, look at those areas where you are filling yourself with something other than God's Holy Spirit.

1. Love—Do I give my time and attention to others, including those I find difficult or different from me?
2. Joy—Do I rejoice when others succeed, or do I find it hard to celebrate with them?
3. Peace—Do I pursue peace with others, asking for forgiveness when necessary?
4. Patience—Am I controlled by truth or by my emotions and circumstances?
5. Kindness—Am I consistent in kindness, or am I critical or irritable with others?
6. Goodness—Do I bear others' burdens, or am I secretly pleased when others fail?

7. Faithfulness—Am I faithful, committed in my thoughts and actions, to my friendships (or, if married, to my spouse)?
8. Gentleness—Am I gentle with others, or do I respond harshly?
9. Self-Control—Am I creating good habits, or am I addicted to something that hurts me or others?
10. Gratitude—Am I consistently grateful, or do I complain often?
11. Humility—Do I humble myself to serve others, or do I think certain tasks are below me?
12. Generosity—Do I share Jesus with others when prompted by the Holy Spirit?
13. Obedience—Do I obey God or delay obedience?
14. Contentment—Am I satisfied with what God has provided, or do I desire what others have?
15. Forgiveness—Have I extended forgiveness to those who have hurt me or withheld it from them?
16. Encouragement—Do I try to encourage people or try to impress them?
17. Godliness—Am I teachable and willing to learn, or do I become defensive when corrected and resist biblical accountability?
18. Confidence—Am I confident in who I am in Christ or self-focused?
19. Noble—Do I shut down gossip, or do I enjoy or condone gossip by remaining silent when it is spoken in my presence?
20. Biblical Community—Am I faithful to my church, or is a biblical community not a priority?
21. Holiness—Do I pursue holiness in what I say, do, watch, listen to, or read?

Although these questions may be tough, self-examination is necessary (2 Cor. 13:5). Celebrate areas where God's work of transformation is taking place in your life. Acknowledge and repent of the sins that this list revealed to you. "Repent, then, and turn to God, so that your sins may be wiped out, that times of refreshing may come from the Lord" (Acts 3:19 NIV). Repentance is hard, ongoing work, not a one-time event, but God is *already* on your side. **The Holy Spirit is our Helper, and our heavenly Father is eager to forgive.** "Who is a God like you, who pardons sin and forgives the transgression of the remnant of his inheritance? You do not stay angry forever but delight to show mercy" (Mic. 7:18 NIV). **When we genuinely ask for forgiveness, God says, "Done!" We can rest in God's grace and the freedom of redemption**. There is now "no condemnation for those who belong to Christ Jesus. . . . The life-giving Spirit has freed you from the power of sin that leads to death" (Rom. 8:1–2).

A word of caution: Changing directions to follow the Holy Spirit instead of our old sin patterns will require intentionality and perseverance. In Matthew 12:43–45, Jesus teaches that a house swept clean but left *unoccupied* is like cleaning up our life by removing bad influences, but then *not* allowing the Holy Spirit to fill up the new space we've created. It is like giving an invitation to the enemy to move back in with even more demonic influence, leaving us worse than we were before. Practically, this means we replace bad habits and sinful addictions with new, godly thought patterns and practices *through the Holy Spirit's power*. A recovering alcoholic, filled with the Holy Spirit, finds a healthy way to relax or socialize. This way, they are not led into temptation (James 1:13–18). Spirit-filled thinking helps to create the right behaviors and to crowd out the enemy. Pray to keep your "house" filled with the Spirit.

This critical next step on your faith journey can transform your true story from ordinary to extraordinary. Are you ready to yield your life to the Holy Spirit? You do not need to overcome all sin before this can happen. The Holy Spirit will help you.

1. **Confess your sins to God.** Start with a clean sweep of the wrong you have done, the good you have failed to do, and the things you have kept from God. Humble yourself.

2. **Repent.** "Turn away from evil and do good" (Ps. 34:14 ESV). Surrender all you are and all you have to God. The Holy Spirit often nudges us when we do what He forbids ("grieve" Him [Eph. 4:30–31 ESV]) or fail to do what he commands ("quench" Him [1 Thess. 5:16–19 ESV]). Pay attention to His promptings, obey Him immediately, and deal with sin quickly.

3. **Ask the Holy Spirit to fill you, and believe that He will.** God loves to fill us with the Holy Spirit: "If you then, though you are evil, know how to give good gifts to your children, how much more will your Father in heaven give the Holy Spirit to those who ask him!" (Luke 11:13 NIV). And He commands that we be filled by Him: "Be filled with the Holy Spirit" (Eph. 5:18). Have faith in this promise, trusting that He will fill you.

4. **Fulfill the mission of God as you fill yourself with the Word of God.** "Let the word of Christ dwell in you richly" (Col. 3:16 ESV). The Holy Spirit reveals God's will in God's Word. **When we pursue God's mission, we position ourselves for the Holy Spirit to fill us and flow through us to bless others.** Check to see how you are positioned. You will find great spiritual resources and power available when you do what the Holy Spirit prompts you to do according to God's Word. Pray when He leads you to pray. Share Jesus when He tells you to share.

You may not feel the Holy Spirit flow in and through you, but know He is at work in spectacular and straightforward ways. You will find greater effectiveness, faith, power, and love while you live out your true story. As we learned last week, if we ask anything according to God's will, He will hear us and give us what we ask for (1 John 5:14–15). God's will is for the Holy Spirit to fill you—repeatedly (Eph. 5:18). You will experience an unspeakable joy and closeness to Jesus as the **Holy Spirit fills you and makes Jesus more real to you**. Friend, be filled with the Holy Spirit.

DAY 44

Let the Bible Speak:
Romans 6 and 8:1–17 (Optional: Acts 5–8)

Let Your Mind Think:

1. How do repentance and obedience position us to be filled with the Holy Spirit? What attitude do you need to fully yield to the Holy Spirit in all things?

2. What did the checklist tell you about what currently fills you?

3. How can you make more room for the Holy Spirit in your life? If the Spirit is in you, what else is true of you now (Rom. 8:10)?

4. Take a moment to confess your attitudes and sins, and repent. Ask God to fill you with His Spirit, and believe that He will.

Let Your Soul Pray:
Lord, fill me with Your Holy Spirit. I want Jesus to be more real to me. I do not want to grieve Your Spirit by sinning, nor do I want to quench Your Spirit by ignoring what You tell me to do. I confess I've filled myself with lesser things. Forgive me. Show me how to change. Guide and direct my thoughts, words, actions, and emotions so they may be pleasing to You . . . In Jesus's name, amen.

Let Your Heart Obey:
(What is God leading you to know, value, or do?)

DAY
45

Be Purified for Resurrection Life— Sanctification

May God himself, the God of peace, sanctify you through and through. May your whole spirit, soul and body be kept blameless at the coming of our Lord Jesus Christ.

1 Thessalonians 5:23 NIV

God did not save us just to make us better people. He saved us to rescue us from the penalty of our sins and reestablish our relationship with Him—for His glory. We become better people *through that relationship*: "If anyone is in Christ, he is a new creation. The old has passed away; behold, the new has come" (2 Cor. 5:17 ESV). New! **God saves us *through* Jesus and then, through the power of the Holy Spirit, transforms us to *be like* Jesus.**

Yes, this change process—called **sanctification**—remains with us for the rest of our faith journey. Becoming a believer is only the beginning of our journey of sanctification. The process of living differently and becoming like Jesus requires both time and help from God. The *Holy* Spirit is responsible for making us *holy*—re-creating us to be like the One whose image we were always intended to bear (Gen. 1:27).

> **Sanctification:**
> Being made holy. The original Greek word, *hagiazo*, means "separate," "set apart," or "making holy." "Growing in every way more and more like Christ" (Eph. 4:15).

In the days ahead, we'll learn how the Holy Spirit matures us through serving, sharing Jesus, and even through suffering. Today, let's learn how we cooperate with Him.

Sanctification requires obedience (1 Pet. 1:2). After God's Word tells us what to do, the Holy Spirit helps us discern our response (Rom. 8). When we meditate on God's Word, we renew our minds, and our thoughts start changing (Rom. 12:1–2). We begin to think more about what is "excellent and worthy of praise" (Phil. 4:8). Our thoughts shape our words and actions so we say what is "good and helpful" (Eph. 4:29) and we "do what is right" (1 John 2:29).

But sanctification is not about following rules. Sanctification is about following Jesus. God is more interested in who we're becoming than how we behave. **If we are becoming like Christ, we will act more like Him and find more satisfaction in Him alone.** Christlike behavior grows out of a Christlike heart, not out of the religious legalism we learned about on Day 25. Jesus condemned the Pharisees because their behavior looked clean on the outside, but their hearts were dirty on the inside:

> "Hypocrites! For you are so careful to clean the outside of the cup and the dish, but inside you are filthy—full of greed and self-indulgence! . . . Outwardly you look like righteous people, but inwardly your hearts are filled with hypocrisy and lawlessness." (Matt. 23:25, 28)

We are to focus not on outward behavior but on a *heart* that is growing more and more like Christ (Eph. 4:15). It's not about rules; it's about a *relationship*. To understand this process better, let's consider one of Jesus's illustrations. Multiple times in Scripture, Jesus compares people to wheat. By examining how wheat grows, we learn more about our growth in Christ.

1. **We cannot force spiritual maturity, so we need to have faith in the Holy Spirit to grow us.** A grain of wheat does not force itself to grow. It does not think, "I need to sprout. Now I need to grow a stem, and after that, I've got to force out some grain." The apostle Paul became frustrated with believers who trusted Christ to rescue

them from sin but did not trust Christ for spiritual growth. The Galatians were obsessed with following rules and spreading false teachings that salvation came with *extra* rules. Paul asked them, "How foolish can you be? After starting your new lives in the Spirit, why are you now trying to become perfect by your own human effort?" (Gal. 3:3). We need to welcome the Holy Spirit to do His work in us. To be filled with Him (Day 44). We can see the growth He produces over time:

> "The Kingdom of God is like a farmer who scatters seed on the ground. Night and day, while he's asleep or awake, the seed sprouts and grows, but he does not understand how it happens. The earth produces the crops on its own. First a leaf blade pushes through, then the heads of wheat are formed, and finally the grain ripens." (Mark 4:26–28)

2. **We cooperate with the Holy Spirit by cultivating favorable conditions for growth.** Even the healthiest grains will not grow without good soil, water, and sunlight. Wheat grains that were found tucked away in ancient jars for thousands of years might seem beyond the age of viability, but as soon as archaeologists discovered them and planted them in good soil, they grew just like you'd expect any good grain to grow. The same principle applies to us. If you want to grow in Christ, you need three things:

- Good Soil: Is your heart good soil? Are you trusting and obeying God through His Word (Day 30)?
- Fresh Water: Are you growing deep roots in God's Word so you can soak up the living water of the Holy Spirit (Day 24)? Are you abiding in Him?
- Sunlight: Are you walking in the light of Jesus? Do you ask God to expose your sin so He can heal you (Day 26)?

Notice that the environment you create is more about your heart than your circumstances. Even if you live in a place hostile to Jesus's followers or experience struggles, you can cultivate healthy conditions for spiritual growth within your heart and mind.

3. **Spiritual growth happens in community.** If planted alone, a wheat stem will not survive. It cannot support its height, and before it reaches maturity, it will fall over, limp or broken entirely. But when planted in a field with millions of other wheat seeds, that single stalk of wheat will stand tall as storms pass overhead. Even in fierce winds, the stems support one another and sway as a unit in graceful harmony. The same is true for us. **We cannot grow alone.** If you do not have a faith family, ask God to help you. Look for a church where God's Word is taught and lived faithfully (see Day 12, "How to Find a Good Church"). If you live where churches are scarce, meet regularly with at least one or two friends who follow Jesus (see Day 17, "Weekly Gatherings"). The Holy Spirit will use your faith family to encourage you and help you grow in spiritual maturity.

4. **Spiritual growth happens when we die to our old ways.** How does wheat grow and multiply? Jesus teaches, "I tell you the truth, unless a kernel of wheat is planted in the soil and dies, it remains alone. But its death will produce many new kernels" (John 12:24). For generations of wheat to continue to multiply, individual grains must fall to the ground and die. The seed coat splits, and its stored food is used to fuel the new life of the now-growing plant. As it matures, it is capable of producing many more grains than the single grain it came from.

As followers of Christ, we also go through the process of dying in several ways:

- We first die to **sin** when we place our faith in Christ. We are "crucified with Christ" and "dead to sin" (Gal. 2:20; Rom. 6:11 NIV).
- As we follow Jesus, we continue dying each day to our **old ways**. "Whoever wants to be my disciple must deny themselves and take up their cross daily and follow me" (Luke 9:23 NIV).
- We die daily to our **worldly desires** as we resist temptation and put sin to death through the power of the Holy Spirit (Rom. 8:13; Col. 3:5).

- We die daily to our **selfishness** as we meet others' needs and bless them at our own expense (Phil. 2:4).

This process of dying may seem frightening, but as believers, **we can *embrace* death because it leads to resurrection.** Jesus teaches, "For whoever would save his life will lose it, but whoever loses his life for my sake will save it" (Luke 9:24 ESV). **Sanctification is the process of dying to sin and self so the life of Christ can fill us more and more.** When the Spirit calls you to die to yourself in some way, remember He is eager to fill that space with the life of God.

Jesus felt so strongly about our sanctification that moments before His arrest, He prayed for us, "They are not of the world, just as I am not of the world. Sanctify them in the truth; your word is truth" (John 17:16–17 ESV). Jesus knew that the world and our old sin natures would fight against the Holy Spirit's work in us. He also knew God's Word could overcome that opposition. That is why the *daily* practice of time spent focusing on our relationship with God through His Word is so important. Through God's Word, the Holy Spirit shows us what needs to change and gives us the grace to make those changes (Gal. 5:16–17). Little by little, the Holy Spirit grows us in holiness. He transforms our thinking (Rom. 12:2) and kills the roots of sin in our lives. **Try this the next time you are struggling to obey:**

1. Ask for the Holy Spirit's help (Luke 11:13).
2. Allow Him to open your eyes and your heart to discover what is hindering you (Ps. 19:8). Look to God's Word for answers.
3. Wait on God. Repent if prompted. Pray with authority (Day 36)! As you do, He will break any layers of unbelief or hardness of heart. You will find satisfaction in Jesus Christ. You will eventually turn away from everything else to gain more of Him (Phil. 3:8).

Here's an example of how this works: Let's say you struggle with the sin of gossip. You are tempted to talk badly about another person to a friend, but then you remember to pray. You ask God to help you keep a tight rein on your tongue (James 1:26). The Spirit exposes where you have been spiritually blind (Ps. 119:18). As He opens your eyes, you begin to see that other person with more compassion, more like He sees them. You also clearly see gossip for the evil that it is. You choose not to talk about that friend. That one transformational step of obedience grows your heart and changes your behavior. Now, your joy in the Lord satisfies your heart so that your prior behavior—a desire to gossip—becomes less appealing.

Remember to be patient with yourself. Sanctification takes time, but gradually you will see real improvements in your character and your habits. You will become more loving, compassionate, and patient as you abide in Christ and obey God's Word. Complaining will give way to thanksgiving. Flashes of anger will become less frequent and spontaneous praise more frequent. Your value and identity will be found in Christ alone. Bible study and prayer will become a delightful part of your daily rhythm. You will begin to see things from God's point of view and want His will above all else.

When we see positive changes, we can be encouraged that the Spirit is transforming us day by day. "And we all, with unveiled face, beholding the glory of the Lord, are being transformed into the same image from one degree of glory to another. For this comes from the Lord who is the Spirit" (2 Cor. 3:18 ESV). We are being changed in the only way that really matters—from the inside out to reflect God's glory!

Let the Bible Speak:
Ephesians 4:1–16 (Optional: Acts 9–12)

Let Your Mind Think:
1. Like wheat, we grow in community. Why is community so important for followers of Jesus?

2. If you are not connected to a church or do not have a close faith family, what can you do to connect with other believers?

3. How does dying daily to yourself improve you? How does it improve relationships with others, including your faith family?

Let Your Soul Pray:
Father, grow me through sanctification. Make me more like Jesus each day. Strengthen my faith family so we can grow together. Help us die to ourselves daily so Your Holy Spirit will fill us more and more . . . In Jesus's name, amen.

Let Your Heart Obey:
(*What is God leading you to know, value, or do?*)

Grow in the Spirit—Serve

Whoever wants to be a leader among you must be your servant,
and whoever wants to be first among you must become your
slave. For even the Son of Man came not to be served but
to serve others and to give his life as a ransom for many.
Matthew 20:26–28

God does not need our service. God invites us to serve because *He loves us.* As you serve with Him, you get to know Him better. You experience His love as it flows through you to others, which is life-giving *and* life-changing. Yes, serving God by serving others is another way the Holy Spirit sanctifies us. As we understand how to become the hands and feet of Jesus, we serve with a "get to serve" not a "have to serve" attitude. Sometimes, though, we may resist serving. We may feel called to serve but struggle with the details—what we should be doing, where or when we should be doing it, or even who to help. We're not alone. Moses also struggled with these details.

Moses is one of the greatest leaders in all of Jewish history and one of the few Spirit-led believers recorded in the Old Testament. Yet, he almost missed his part in God's Story. We learned a little about Moses's story in Week 3. Remember, God called Moses to lead His people out of Egyptian slavery and then to establish God's law among them. When God called Moses to serve, he said, "Send anyone else." Moses's refusal angered God (Exod. 4:13–14). God had appeared to Moses in the form of a burning bush, and God could have easily consumed Moses in flames. But He didn't. He was patient with Moses, and He is patient with us as well (1 Tim. 1:16).

Notice how God used the details of Moses's life.[1] Through unusual circumstances, Moses was a Hebrew boy who was raised in the Egyptian king's palace as a grandson to Pharaoh. Here are some ways his background helped him fulfill God's calling on his life:

- He was given an education, which helped when God inspired him to write the first five books of the Bible.
- He was groomed to stand before kings, which helped when God called him to speak to the new pharaoh.
- He was taught leadership and organizational skills, which helped when God called him to lead the nation of Israel.
- When he fled to Midian (before his calling to lead the Hebrew people), he learned patience and also how to navigate the wilderness, which helped during his forty years of wilderness wandering.

We may not all be called to lead like Moses, but we are *all* called to serve. How might you be called to serve? Start by looking at your biography. Where do you live? What languages do you speak? What skills and talents do you have? What trials have you experienced? As you answer questions like these, pray and ask the Spirit to help you identify pieces of your story that God might want to use in His service.

As you ask God how you might serve Him, also consider what you *like* to do.[2]

1. In the past, when have you experienced the most joy and fruitfulness in serving God?
2. When have you felt God working in and through you most?
3. Based on those answers, how can you make the greatest impact for the kingdom of God?

---

1   Jill Briscoe, *Here Am I, Lord . . . Send Somebody Else: How God Uses Ordinary People to Do Extraordinary Things* (Nashville: W Publishing, 2004).
2   Glenn Reese (Pastor, Chets Creek Church in Jacksonville, FL), in discussion with the author, August 10, 2010.

If you are just getting started, look for the greatest needs in your church or community. Consider how your passions and skills might meet some of those needs. Do you love to pray? Can you cook or sing? Coach sports or direct plays? Do you have hobbies that might minister to the needs of others (e.g., knitting blankets for the local homeless shelter)? Are you good at teaching others or organizing gatherings? Are you adept at starting businesses or handling finances? Even being a good listener is a much needed and valuable skill. *Everyone* has something to offer. You may not know what to do ahead of time, but **God will reveal your gifts to you *as you serve***. Give yourself permission to try things and learn along the way; it takes time to find your fit, and it doesn't need to happen right away. Trust God to reveal your next step, and then faithfully move forward. Before long, you will see the greater plan unfold, and you will experience the blessing of serving. Jesus loves to bless *you* as He blesses others *through* you. That is why He said, "It is more blessed to give than to receive" (Acts 20:35).

Part of that blessing comes in the form of spiritual growth: **the Holy Spirit grows *us* as we serve God by serving *others***. The Holy Spirit is also called the Spirit of Jesus (Phil. 1:19), and just as Jesus humbled Himself to become a servant to all, the Spirit of Jesus will also make you a servant as you grow in His image. In Christ, we "serve in the new way of the Spirit," empowered by God, not ourselves (Rom. 7:6 NIV). **The Spirit motivates us with *love*, not duty, to work for *God's glory*, not our own.** As we "serve God by his Spirit," we need to rely on the strength of Christ and "put no confidence in the flesh" (Phil. 3:3 NIV). **We find true joy when we do what God designed us to do in His power, for His glory.** And remember, God will never ask you to serve in some way and then not give you the grace and power to do it (Josh. 1:9; 2 Cor. 12:9).

Only you have *your* unique part in God's Story. Let's learn how to serve *well*. The apostle Paul teaches us ways to serve:

1. **Serve sacrificially.** Serving others *only when it is convenient* for us is nearly impossible. Rarely do we schedule volunteering when our calendars reveal free time. We need to be intentional to serve,

and it requires a sacrifice of our time or resources—or both. When we serve, we make ourselves a "living sacrifice" (Rom. 12:1 NIV), which is a beautiful offering to the Lord. We put others' needs ahead of our own as Jesus did. Jesus sacrificed His comfort long before He sacrificed His life on the cross. When exhausted by ministry demands, He set His individual needs aside to teach and feed people around Him—often numbering in the thousands (Mark 6). When you sacrifice in little or big ways—your comfort, rest, and time—"your faithful service is an offering to God" (Phil. 2:17).

2. **Serve humbly.** Sometimes we are tempted to serve to impress others. We miss the point of exalting Jesus, not ourselves, as we meet the needs of others. Jesus said, "Beware of practicing your righteousness before other people in order to be seen by them, for then you will have no reward from your Father who is in heaven" (Matt. 6:1 ESV). Humbling ourselves by serving others without looking for attention is part of our journey away from selfishness. When we serve in true humility, we think of others' needs as much as our own (Rom. 12:10). Paul repeatedly wrote the early churches stressing the importance of serving humbly. "Do nothing out of selfish ambition or vain conceit. Rather, in humility value others above yourselves, not looking to your own interests but each of you to the interests of others" (Phil. 2:3–4 NIV). He instructed them to serve everyone regardless of financial position or status (Rom. 12:16).

Jesus, the King of kings, perfectly modeled serving with humility. He "did not consider equality with God something to be used to his own advantage; rather, he made himself nothing by taking the very nature of a servant" (Phil. 2:6–7 NIV). **The One all should serve became the servant of all!** Jesus shared this paradox with His disciples: "Anyone who wants to be first must be the very last, and the servant of all" (Mark 9:35 NIV). Humble yourself, and *God* will lift you up (James 4:10). **Your value is not based on what you do or what others say; your value comes from who you are in Christ.**

3. **Serve lovingly.** Have you ever been given a gift out of obligation? Or, maybe someone helped you with a project but did so with

resentment? It's not a good feeling. You might prefer the person to keep the gift or not help at all. When we serve without love, it's like giving God a gift in this same way. Any act of service—no matter how exceptional—is worthless if done without love (1 Cor. 13:3). On Day 6, we learned that we will be rewarded by how well we *loved*, not by the good deeds we did. How does love serve?

- Love serves generously, practicing hospitality (Rom. 12:13).
- Love serves actively, meeting real needs (1 John 3:18).
- Love serves compassionately, showing genuine sympathy (Rom. 12:15).
- Love serves peacefully, living in harmony with others regardless of social status (Rom. 12:16, 18).
- Love serves gracefully, actively blessing its enemies (Rom. 12:14, 17, 19–20).

4. **Serve in the Spirit.** When believers place our faith in Jesus for salvation, the Holy Spirit gives us special gifts—spiritual gifts.[1] Men and women in every season of life *work together* to fulfill God's mission.[2] Every person has an essential role in serving as God's image-bearer. **The Holy Spirit produces *fruit* of the Spirit in you as you use the *gifts* of the Spirit for God's glory.** Watch how the Holy Spirit grows you and your gifts when you use them. As we learned, the church is called a body because each part, though different, is essential to the functioning of the whole. Just as different parts of the body work together, different believers need to come together by using their gifts to build up the body of Christ to the glory of God (Eph. 4:12). When we serve our brothers and sisters, we honor Christ's sacrifice for the church (Eph. 5:25) and become more like the community God had in mind at creation—a community of unity, love, and creativity.

---

1 For lists of specific spiritual gifts found in the Bible, read Romans 12:3–8, 1 Corinthians 12:8–11, and Ephesians 4:10–12.

2 Due to lack of training, women worldwide often have unclear expectations on how they can serve the church or advance the gospel. Review Acts and the New Testament letters for examples of men and women working together on teams. Women, in every season of life, are given spiritual gifts to fulfill their essential roles in the community, church, and home.

We are designed to serve our own families too. God cares deeply about our service to our faith family, but service to them does not excuse us from our responsibilities to our natural families. We cannot serve others well in the church if our families are in turmoil at home. That is why one of the requirements for leadership in the church is a well-managed family (Titus 1:6–7). "If anyone does not know how to manage his own family, how can he take care of God's church?" (1 Tim. 3:5 NIV). Jesus admonished religious leaders for condoning people's decision to give resources to a religious community instead of providing for their parents' needs (Mark 7:11). Paul preached the same: "Anyone who does not provide for their relatives, and especially for their own household, has denied the faith and is worse than an unbeliever" (1 Tim. 5:8 NIV). God does not want us to choose between serving our faith family and our immediate family. He wants us to serve *both*. But He also does not call you to serve without His grace for each step of the way.

Serving is another opportunity for the Holy Spirit to grow you—re-create you—to become more like Christ, the servant Savior. By serving you'll discover new gifts God has given you, and you'll learn how to rely more on Him. You'll deepen relationships and start new ones as you look *to serve* rather than *be served*. Best of all, your friendship with God grows as you serve together and live out your part in His Story.

DAY 46

Let the Bible Speak:
1 Corinthians 12–13 (Optional: Acts 13–16)

Let Your Mind Think:
These questions from today's reading may help uncover gifts and passions for serving:

1. When have you experienced the most joy and fruitfulness in serving God?

2. When have you felt God working in and through you most?

3. Based on those answers, how can you make the greatest impact for the kingdom of God?

Let Your Soul Pray:
Father, I give You my life to do whatever You want me to do, to go wherever You want me to go, and to say whatever You want me to say. Help me use the spiritual gifts given to me for Your glory. Make me like Jesus, the servant of all. Thank You for Your sacrificial, humble, and loving service to us, Lord . . . In Jesus's name, amen.

Let Your Heart Obey:
(What is God leading you to know, value, or do?)

DAY
47

Grow in the Spirit—Share

"I have been given all authority in heaven and on earth. Therefore, go and make disciples of all the nations, baptizing them in the name of the Father and the Son and the Holy Spirit. Teach these new disciples to obey all the commands I have given you. And be sure of this: I am with you always, even to the end of the age."
Matthew 28:18–20

Picture a world where God decided *not* to involve us in sharing the good news of Jesus with others. Instead, He rescues people without any believers' involvement. What would that world look like? Let's imagine that in this strange world you go to a church where everyone became a follower of Jesus without any human intervention. You find your seat, and the music begins. But the songs are all different in this strange world. "Amazing Grace" and other songs based on New Testament teachings do not exist because the New Testament was not written.

In our world, the New Testament was written by disciples commissioned to make more disciples. But if there were no commissioning people to make disciples, there would be no reason to write about God's mission.

In such a world, our purpose—our entire existence—would change for the worse. Our joy in sharing Jesus and His teachings with others would disappear. We would miss the thrill of seeing someone go from spiritual death to spiritual life. Our privilege of being God's tool to transform a human soul would be lost. Our attitudes, actions, and callings would be very different. If God had not invited us to be a part of His work of salvation, our lives would lack so much joy, hope, and purpose.

Praise God that is *not* our world! **For God so loved the world that He gave us the ministry of reconciliation** (2 Cor. 5:18–20). This priceless gift is for our good. We draw close to God as we *work with Him* to make disciples. Yes, God can and does rescue people without involving others, but it is a privilege that God chooses to spread the good news *through us* (2 Cor. 2:14). We are given this gift to share Jesus with others so they can be forgiven, made new, and reconciled to God's forever family. We have eternity-changing medicine to give to people who are dying spiritually. We cannot keep the gift of God's grace to ourselves. Jesus already did the hardest part. All we need to do is share His story. And when we do, there is *no greater feeling* than when God works through us to rescue those heading down the wrong path. When they turn from their sins and say yes to Jesus, their eternity changes right before our eyes!

Surprisingly, some churches and believers operate as if they exist in the strange world we only imagined. They are uninvolved; sharing the good news of Jesus with others (called evangelism) is not a priority. Instead, they tuck away Jesus's Great Commission, hiding it away like they would hide spending money in a drawer. They may lack joy, growth, hope, unity, or purpose. They may wonder why they are not growing personally or corporately. They are unaware that they are not doing what God designed them to do. Because the truth is that **not sharing the gospel is a violation of God's command**.

Thankfully, Jesus's mission is *always* to seek and save the lost (Luke 19:10). Through the Holy Spirit, these churches and believers *can* change. The Holy Spirit can create healthy faith families where those new to the faith are mentored by mature believers. Are you in need of a fresh start? God can help you return to the main reasons why you exist:

Love God,

Love everyone, and

Make disciples!

Disciple-making starts with Jesus—His good news and His Great Commission. When Jesus entrusted His disciples with His message,

He gave specific instructions found in Matthew 28:18–20. Now it's our turn. God has entrusted the gospel to us, so let's examine this passage and be disciple-makers for this generation.

1. Jesus was **"given all authority"**—To make disciples, we need to be disciples. Earlier in Matthew, Jesus said, "Whoever wants to be my disciple must deny themselves and take up their cross and follow me" (Matt. 16:24 NIV). Have we denied ourselves to follow Jesus and submit to His authority?

2. **"Therefore, go"**—Given Jesus's authority, are we willing to go and share?

3. **"make disciples"**—This command means to make followers, believers who learn more and more about Him. Will we share the love of Jesus, model the life of Jesus, and teach the Word of Jesus?

4. **"all the nations"**—Every soul matters to God. Are we willing to share Jesus with everyone?

5. **"baptizing them"**—Baptism is the outward sign of an inward change, and believers' first step of obedience. Are we baptized? Will we lead others to be baptized?

6. **"Teach these new disciples to obey all the commands"**—We are instructed to obey, not just know, Jesus's teachings. Will we teach *and obey* Jesus's message?

7. **"I am with you always"**—Do we believe Jesus is with us always? Will we trust Him?

God chose you to be His ambassador.
Jesus promises to be with you.
The Holy Spirit empowers you to fulfill this command (Acts 1:8).
You can do it.

Jesus says, "As the Father has sent me, I am sending you" (John 20:21 NIV). **When you take steps of obedience, God equips you with everything you need to do His will.** When you are sharing, the Holy Spirit gives you strength *and* words.[1] In the process, the Holy Spirit grows your faith–sanctifies you–through disciple-making.

How do we make disciples? Let's consider Jesus's prayer request: "The harvest is plentiful, but the workers are few. Ask the Lord of the harvest, therefore, to send out workers into his harvest field" (Luke 10:2 NIV). Jesus used the symbolic meaning of harvest to explain how people are ready to be gathered into God's family. Like a field ready for harvest, people are ripe for the gospel. We ask God, the Lord of the harvest (Matt. 9:38), for harvest workers and go with Him when He sends us. Disciple-making often follows a four-part harvest process:[2]

1. **Sow** seeds of the gospel with <u>prayer</u>. As Jesus requested, start with prayer. When we pray, we cast life-giving seeds of the gospel. We go to the fields, the places where people are far from God (across the street or across the world).

2. **Water** those seeds with God's Story–<u>the gospel</u>. When we share God's Story and our story as His witnesses, the gospel seeds are nourished in people's lives.

3. **Grow** those sprouted seeds with the light of God's Word. As new believers learn from you, help them to <u>pray and study the Bible</u> for themselves so they can grow strong.

4. **Harvest** the fields by gathering believers to form the church. As believers, we are bundled together for encouragement, discipleship, and community. We train <u>new laborers</u> to be sent into <u>new fields </u>to sow and water gospel seeds in others' lives. This commissioning starts the disciple-making process once again.

---

1   Matt. 10:19; Luke 12:12; Acts 1:8; 2 Cor. 5:20.
2   Church planting movements worldwide follow a similar process called 4 Fields Training.

Now, let's take the tools we've learned through this faith journey and see how they fit in the four-part disciple-making process:

1. **Sow** seeds of the gospel with <u>prayer</u>.
   a. Create a **relationship map** of those in your life far from God (Appendix). Pray for and plan opportunities to share Jesus's love.
   b. Pray for others, pray with authority, pray and fast for spiritual awakening (Week 6).

2. **Water** those seeds with God's Story—the gospel.
   a. Share God's Story blending in the **Gospel Bread** ingredients (Day 18).
   b. Start spiritual conversations using the **Listen, Learn, Love, Lord** approach (Day 18).
   c. Share your story using "**Sharing Your Story**" as a guide (Day 18).

3. **Grow** those sprouted seeds in a small weekly gathering for training and support.
   a. Gather three to five new believers together using the "**Weekly Gatherings**" format (Day 17).
   b. Train believers to obey Jesus's teachings (Weeks 3–7).
   c. Use a Bible reading plan to **study the Bible together** (Day 33).

4. **Harvest** the fields by gathering believers to form the church and unleashing them to become disciple-makers.
   a. Gather together as a faith family for worship, the Lord's Supper, serving, and training (Days 12 and 43).
   b. Teach believers how to use their spiritual gifts to serve Jesus and others (Day 46).
   c. Encourage believers to go together to new fields using the **Listen, Learn, Love, Lord** tool (Appendix). Review weekly for prayer and accountability (see Luke 10:1–11).

How do you know if the disciple-making approach is effective? The evidence is in changed lives. You can always improve on the process or tools listed above, but know God alone is the one who grows His harvest of people (1 Cor. 3:6–7). We may not be able to disciple everyone, but we can disciple one person. Then, encourage that person to disciple another and take on a new learner. Even if you are a new believer, you can still make disciples.

Think about what would happen if you discipled one person every year. Then, the next year that person started discipling one person each year. Then everyone who had been discipled continued discipling one new person each year. In thirty years, if this disciple-making cycle continued, more than one billion people would come to faith in Christ! Think about that. God could change your family, your town, and your nation through you!

Let the Bible Speak:
Luke 10:1–11; Romans 10:9–17 (Optional: Acts 17–20)

Let Your Mind Think:
1. Do you know anyone who needs or wants to be discipled? Ask the Holy Spirit to lead you to two or three new believers to form a Weekly Gathering for making disciples.

2. Examine Luke 10:1–11 and find all the dos and don'ts Jesus instructed the disciples before He sent them to work the harvest. Which ones make an impression on you?

3. Complete or review the **Listen, Learn, Love, Lord** tool in the appendix and review it regularly with your group (1 Pet. 3:15).

Let Your Soul Pray:
Father, thank You for entrusting me with Your ministry of reconciliation. Create opportunities for me to introduce people to Christ. Help me share the love of Jesus, model the life of Jesus, and teach the Word of Jesus to all those You place in my life. I want to be a disciple who makes disciples through Your power for Your glory alone . . . In Jesus's name, amen.

Let Your Heart Obey:
(*What is God leading you to know, value, or do?*)

Grow in the Spirit—Suffer

Consider it pure joy, my brothers and sisters, whenever you face
trials of many kinds, because you know that the testing of your
faith produces perseverance. Let perseverance finish its work so
that you may be mature and complete, not lacking anything.

James 1:2–4 NIV

You and I may be tempted to think that if we live a good life, we
will receive material blessings and the world will be drawn to Jesus.
It could be possible that the whole world might follow Jesus if He
made our problems disappear and our wealth grow, but then we
might no longer have Christianity. Instead, we'd probably have terrible idolatry—people coming to Christ for what He *gives*, not who
He *is*. Our testimony is often most potent when it seems that all we
have is suffering but we can still say, "Jesus is enough."

To fully embrace that truth requires faith and, sometimes, the
experience of God holding us, helping us, and changing us through
trials. It's how we *respond* to those hardships that defines our character and determines whether we grow or we crumble. We can
choose anger or joy, clenched-fisted control or open-handed surrender. **Our response to trials reveals the type of relationship we
have with Jesus.** As the Holy Spirit matures us through serving and
sharing, He also matures us through suffering.

> Suffering produces perseverance; perseverance, character; and character, hope. And hope does not put us to shame, because God's love has
> been poured out into our hearts through the Holy Spirit. (Rom. 5:3–5 NIV)

Did you notice God pours love into our hearts through the Holy Spirit? This love carries us through suffering. It is also a love that flows through us to others. Suffering not only grows us in Christlike character but also draws others to Him. Nothing is more powerful than watching someone suffer with dignity and joy when they have the hope of Christ.

Let's acknowledge that some suffering is the result of sin; our poor choices have consequences. But for today, let's focus on the suffering that is the work of the enemy. Jesus said, "The thief comes only to steal and kill and destroy; I have come that they may have life, and have it to the full" (John 10:10 NIV). Suffering on its own *is* evil and *is* used by Satan to steal, kill, and destroy, but **Jesus wages war on suffering. He works to stop it or relieve it, and in either case, He *always* uses it for good.**

Remember Joseph (Day 15)? He was sold into slavery and wrongly imprisoned. He still told his brothers, "You intended to harm me, but God intended it for good to accomplish what is now being done, *the saving of many lives*" (Gen. 50:20 NIV, emphasis added). Salvation came to many as a result of Joseph's suffering many severe trials. No matter how painful your suffering, know that "in *all things* God works for *the good of those who love him,* who have been called according to his purpose" (Rom. 8:28 NIV, emphasis added). *All things*—the good, the bad, and everything in between—are used by God *for the good of those who love Him.* That means **sometimes our greatest good is *not* our immediate comfort**. Verse 29 explains: "For those God foreknew he also predestined to be *conformed to the image of his Son*" (NIV, emphasis added). When we read those two verses together, we can confidently conclude that our greatest good is becoming like Christ. Jesus warns us:

> "If the world hates you, remember that it hated me first. The world would love you as one of its own if you belonged to it, but you are no longer part of the world. I chose you to come out of the world, so it hates you. Do you remember what I told you? 'A slave is not greater than the master.' Since they persecuted me, naturally they will persecute you." (John 15:18–20)

We are to expect hostility and discrimination toward believers for their faith in Christ.[1] Countries with governments who view Jesus as a threat to their power, or where religion is connected to cultural identity, terribly mistreat Christians. These governments often deny believers fundamental human freedoms. We should not be surprised then when we are persecuted or asked to pray for the persecuted church. "Everyone who wants to live a godly life in Christ Jesus will be persecuted" (2 Tim. 3:12 NIV).

So now that we know to expect it, how do we live victoriously while suffering persecution? We endure persecution by abiding in Christ, our sympathetic Savior who suffered persecution *for* us and still suffers *with* us. When Jesus confronted Saul (later known as the apostle Paul) for persecuting believers, He asked, "Saul, Saul, why are you persecuting me?" (Acts 9:4 ESV). Jesus did not identify Himself as "Jesus, the Lord of those you are persecuting." No, He said, "I am Jesus, *whom you are persecuting*" (Acts 9:5 ESV, emphasis added). Jesus takes the persecution of believers personally. When we abide in Him and He in us, He does not just watch us endure persecution; He endures it with us. **Intimacy with Christ is one of the greatest blessings of persecution**. As we experience persecution, we can embrace Jesus and know we are blessed.[2]

Until the day we are in His presence, and all tears are wiped away (Rev. 21:4), we need a plan to respond to suffering and persecution. Let's look to God's Word:

1. **Cry out to God.** David declared, "In my distress I called to the LORD; I cried to my God for help. From his temple he heard my voice; my cry came before him, into his ears" (Ps. 18:6 NIV). David also said, "O LORD, I am calling to you. Please hurry! Listen when I cry to you for help" (Ps. 141:1). Even Jesus cried out to God from Gethsemane. God can handle your anger, your tears. Rely on Him to help you. Paul wrote that he experienced overwhelming suffering, to the point of death. He also wrote that in those moments, he cried out to God, who rescued Him (2 Cor. 1:8–9). Depend on God. He will take care of

---

1   Acts 14:22; 1 Pet. 4:12.
2   Matt. 5:11–12; 2 Cor. 4:15–18; 1 Pet. 4:14, 16.

you. He will give you what you need and show you where you to go (Matt. 10:16–23).

2. **Take life one day at a time.** Jesus warns that we should not get ahead of ourselves worrying about the future when each day has enough trouble of its own (Matt. 6:34). Right before He says that, He also gives the key to living free from worry: "Seek first his kingdom and his righteousness, and all these things will be given to you as well" (Matt. 6:33 NIV). By seeking God's kingdom *first*, we can look at life through a kingdom perspective and set our priorities there instead of on this complicated world. When we develop a kingdom perspective, we focus less on what is missing. We also focus more on what God *is* doing and how He *is* providing for our needs. As our perspectives change, we may see a higher purpose in trials: they can produce the perseverance we need when times are tough, and God may gain glory because His power works best in our weakness (2 Cor. 12:9).

3. **Stand firm.** Friend, "stand firm in the faith; be courageous; be strong" (1 Cor. 16:13 NIV). The only way we can successfully stand firm in faith is by choosing to abide in Jesus and to receive His strength (John 15). We can pray to ask God to change our circumstances, give us wisdom, and be everything we need in our difficulties. We can pray and say, "Lord, You are my strength. You are my refuge. You are my deliverer in whom will I trust" (see Ps. 18:2). Trusting God and releasing every worry to Him helps us to stand firm. We can remind ourselves of the many examples of God's faithfulness, revealed in His Word and our own lives (memorial stones). "Stand firm. Let nothing move you. Always give yourselves fully to the work of the Lord, because you know that your labor in the Lord is not in vain" (1 Cor. 15:58 NIV).

4. **Receive and share God's comfort.** God uses His Word to minister to the deepest parts of our souls. The book of Psalms is full of beautiful examples of how God draws near to those who are hurting and brokenhearted (Ps. 34:18). He also uses *us* to draw near to each

other, to offer tangible, practical support to one another—a timely visit, a warm meal, an encouraging hug of empathy. As we receive comfort from Him and other believers, we are strengthened and empowered to be a blessing to others.

> He comforts us in all our troubles so that we can comfort others. When they are troubled, we will be able to give them the same comfort God has given us. For the more we suffer for Christ, the more God will shower us with his comfort through Christ. (2 Cor. 1:4–5)

Our painful experiences help us empathize with others who suffer. When we need help, let's not be afraid to be vulnerable and *receive* it. As we've been learning throughout this journey, Jesus designed us to be one body, working together and supporting one another (1 Cor. 12:12–27). When we comfort others with the comfort we have received, our comfort multiplies, and the glory is God's.

5. **Love your enemies.** We forgive as we have been forgiven. Jesus forgave His executioners even as He hung bleeding on a cross. He taught, "You have heard that it was said, 'Love your neighbor and hate your enemy.' But I tell you, love your enemies and pray for those who persecute you" (Matt. 5:43–44 NIV). Remember that we were once enemies of God, and He still loved us (Rom. 5:8). He wants to rescue our persecutors as much as He wants to rescue us. We are all made in His image. **Will you be a channel of God's love to them?**

Just before his death, Stephen asked God to forgive his persecutors, including Saul, who persecuted believers and approved of Stephen's execution (Acts 7–8). In a short time, God answered Stephen's prayer by rescuing Saul, also known as Paul. A man who had done so much evil to believers was transformed by the love of Christ and made an apostle (Acts 8–9; 13). Paul suffered much persecution for his faith and eventually led one of *his* persecutors—a jailer—to Christ (Acts 16). Friend, release any bitterness and thoughts of revenge and pray for those who persecute you. God has a plan for them and wants to rescue them with the same long arm of love He used to rescue you (Isa. 59:1).

While we await our heavenly home, remember that Jesus is worth all the trials we might endure on earth because we follow Him. We can trust Him when He says: "In this world you will have trouble. But take heart! I have overcome the world" (John 16:33 NIV).

Life is short, and suffering is temporary, but Jesus is with you *always* (Matt. 28:20). Keep running your race—*persevere*—for the glory of God (Heb. 12:1–3). "And the God of all grace, who called you to his eternal glory in Christ, after you have suffered a little while, will himself restore you and make you strong, firm and steadfast" (1 Pet. 5:10 NIV). The Holy Spirit will strengthen you to endure suffering on earth until you receive your reward in heaven. In the meantime, the Spirit is growing you in Christlikeness, re-creating you, and restoring you as God's image-bearer. That is *always* good.

DAY 48

Let the Bible Speak:
Hebrews 11:1–12:3 (Optional: Acts 21–24)

Let Your Mind Think:
1. Read Hebrews 11:32–40. What helped these faithful people persevere despite the circumstances? How do you think they were strengthened?

2. Persecution takes many forms. It can be a loss of a job. It can be neighbors who shy away from you because of your faith. Or, as we've seen in the Bible and current events, it can be harsh treatment and even death. Describe a time when you have been persecuted for following Jesus. How did you respond? What kept you focused on Jesus instead of the circumstances?

3. When have you seen God use evil for good in your life?

Let Your Soul Pray:
Father, I thank You that Christ carries my burdens and empathizes with my suffering. Strengthen me to endure suffering for Your glory. Help me to rely on You, to receive and share Your comfort, to love my enemies, and to stand firm. You are worth it . . . In Jesus's name, amen.

Let Your Heart Obey:
(*What is God leading you to know, value, or do?*)

Wake, Watch, Work—Jesus Christ Is Coming

Be on guard! Be alert! You do not know when that time will come.
Mark 13:33 NIV

Let's start today with the best news ever: **Jesus is coming back for us**. One of the most magnificent promises we look forward to as believers is His return. The suffering and persecution we might be experiencing now are not forever. God's Story, including your true story, has a marvelous ending. Jesus told His disciples the night before His crucifixion, "When everything is ready, I will come and get you, so that you will always be with me where I am" (John 14:3). This promise gives us hope and encourages us to live in such a way that we will be ready to meet Him.

According to God's Word, we are living in the last days. The apostle Paul wrote, "The hour has already come for you to wake up from your slumber, because our salvation is nearer now than when we first believed" (Rom. 13:11 NIV). No one knows the exact day when Christ will return (Mark 13:32), but we *do* know that our time here is limited. Even if you live one hundred years, that is only a short breath compared to eternity. What should we do with the time we have left? "The end of all things is near. Therefore be alert and of sober mind so that you may pray" (1 Pet. 4:7 NIV). Stay alert by reflecting on God's Word and praying.

If we remain spiritually alert, we will recognize false teachings about Jesus. Jesus warns that in the last days, we will see an increase in false teachers; they will claim to speak for Christ even though they are His enemies. They will distort God's Word and deceive many:

- "People will not put up with sound doctrine. Instead, to suit their own desires, they will gather around them a great number of teachers to say what their itching ears want to hear. They will turn their ears away from the truth and turn aside to myths" (2 Tim. 4:3–4 NIV).

- "Watch out for false prophets. They come to you in sheep's clothing, but inwardly they are ferocious wolves" (Matt. 7:15 NIV).

> ### Do all religions lead to God?
> No. It is true that all people will face the one true God when they die—whether they worshiped Him or denied Him. (See Day 6.) But not all people go to heaven to live in a perfect, loving relationship with God. When we stand before God, only those forgiven of sin, standing firm in faith, and clothed in the righteousness of Jesus Christ will enter. Those standing in the righteousness of their own works and religions will not.

- "For such people are false apostles, deceitful workers, masquerading as apostles of Christ. And no wonder, for Satan himself masquerades as an angel of light. It is not surprising, then, if his servants also masquerade as servants of righteousness. Their end will be what their actions deserve" (2 Cor. 11:13–15 NIV).

The only way to recognize and reject false teaching is by comparing it to what is true. **We can guard against false teaching by studying God's Word.** We can be like the Bereans, who tested all of Paul's words against Scripture to confirm their truth (Acts 17:11). The Bible reveals many signs of deception that we will see in the last days. It tells us, specifically, what to reject:

1. **Reject any teaching that devalues Jesus and His cross.** "If someone claims to be a prophet and does not acknowledge the truth about Jesus, that person is not from God. Such a person has the spirit of the Antichrist, which you heard is coming into the world

and indeed is already here" (1 John 4:3). The word *antichrist* means "against Christ." Teaching influenced by the spirit of the Antichrist distorts the truth about the person and work of Christ. **Jesus Christ is God and the only source of salvation.** "Salvation is found in no one else, for there is no other name under heaven given to mankind by which we must be saved" (Acts 4:12 NIV). **Remember, if there were any other way to be saved, then Jesus would *not* have had to die on the cross.** Some people falsely teach that we must add our works to Jesus's work on the cross to be saved. Let's remember Jesus's last words spoken from the cross: "It is finished," meaning our sin, our debt, has been paid in full (John 19:30, emphasis added). We obey God from the overflow of our love for Him, not to earn salvation. Any teaching that *denies* Jesus is God, Jesus is the only way, or Jesus's work on the cross is sufficient is false. Jesus alone is supreme:

> The Son is the image of the invisible God . . . all things have been created through him and for him. He is before all things, and in him all things hold together. And he is the head of the body, the church; he is the beginning and the firstborn from among the dead, so that in everything he might have the supremacy. (Col. 1:15–18 NIV)

2. **Reject any teaching that glorifies humans or human leaders.** Jesus gave detailed signs of the end times (Matt. 24). He warned that false teachers would glorify themselves and perform wonders to deceive people (Matt. 24:24). We are *all* born sinners (Psalm 51:5), utterly dependent on God (John 15:5; Acts 17:25). Beware of any teaching that turns human leaders, even godly ones, into other saviors. Paul corrected believers who were tempted in this way:

> You are still worldly. . . . For when one says, "I follow Paul," and another, "I follow Apollos," are you not mere human beings? What, after all, is Apollos? And what is Paul? Only servants, through whom you came to believe—as the Lord has assigned to each his task. I planted the seed, Apollos watered it, but God has been making it grow. So neither the one who plants nor the one who waters is anything, but only God, who makes things grow. (1 Cor. 3:3–7 NIV)

We are to not only avoid glorifying leaders but also run from leaders who glorify themselves. If they are not leading as a servant, the example that Jesus modeled for everyone, then they are not leading in a way that pleases God. And God will humble them (Matt. 23:12).

3. **Reject any teaching that promises worldly comfort, riches, and health.** False teaching exists that leads believers to *use God* rather than *trust God*. They often state that through positive speech or financial donations, believers can achieve excessive financial blessings and complete physical well-being here and now. This false teaching focuses on the gift rather than the Giver, the here and now versus eternity. This teaching causes great confusion.

Does God want to heal you? Yes, and He does both spiritually and physically. "He will wipe every tear from their eyes, and there will be no more death or sorrow or crying or pain" (Rev. 21:4). We can ask Him for physical healing and believe that He will heal. But *we need to trust His timing*, whether healing happens in this lifetime or in eternity. Unless Jesus comes back, all of us alive today will die from physical causes. But, ultimately, we are healed in heaven.

Does God want to provide for your needs? Yes, the Bible offers many examples of how God provides for us. Like any good father, God wants us to ask Him to meet our needs. "Give us today the food we need" (Matt. 6:11). God knows what is best for us, but again *we trust His timing* and His ways to meet our needs. Remember Psalm 23 (Day 22), "The Lord is my shepherd; I have all that I need" (v. 1).

When prayers for healing or provision seem unanswered, false teachers often point to the believer's lack of faith or financial giving as the problem. They fail to point to Jesus and His teaching as our example and our direction. Jesus said to store up *heavenly* treasure and warned against focusing on earthly pleasure.[1] If we are healed, and our needs are met, we glorify God! If not, we trust God is working for our good (Day 48). Continue to pray and abide in Jesus.

---

1   Matt. 6:19–24; Luke 12:33–34; 18:24; 1 Tim. 6:9; 1 John 2:15–17.

4. **Reject any teaching that demands obedience to strict rules not found in God's Word.** Some believers require adherence to nonbiblical traditions to prove they are saved. They often believe church traditions are equal to or greater than the authority of the Bible. As we learned on Day 31, only the Bible is the inspired Word of God (2 Tim. 3:16). Jesus rebuked people for adding their own rules to God's commands (Matt. 23:4; Mark 7:1–23). Paul warned against focusing on outward performance rather than inward heart change:

> You have died with Christ, and he has set you free . . . So why do you keep on following the rules of the world, such as, "Don't handle! Don't taste! Don't touch!"? Such rules are mere human teachings about things that deteriorate as we use them. These rules may seem wise because they require strong devotion, pious self-denial, and severe bodily discipline. But they provide no help in conquering a person's evil desires. (Col. 2:20–23)

Following extra rules does not make us holier; following *Jesus* does. "It is for freedom that Christ has set us free. Stand firm, then, and do not let yourselves be burdened again by a yoke of slavery" (Gal. 5:1 NIV). No more slavery to legalistic activity that brings honor to people, not God. We are now "slaves of Christ, doing the will of God from the heart" (Eph. 6:6 NASB).

5. **Reject any teaching that excuses sin.** Any teaching that permits intentional, ongoing sin mocks Jesus's sacrifice for sin. Such false teachers "mouth empty, boastful words and, by appealing to the lustful desires of the flesh, they entice people . . . [and] promise them freedom, while they themselves are slaves of depravity–for 'people are slaves to whatever has mastered them'" (2 Pet. 2:18–19 NIV). Jesus did not free us from sin so that we could go on sinning. "Shall we go on sinning so that grace may increase? By no means! We are those who have died to sin; how can we live in it any longer?" (Rom. 6:1–2 NIV). Salvation is not just a one-time event, saving us from hell, but a lifetime of transformation as new creatures in Christ, freed from the bondages of sin. We do not live as we once did before Jesus saved

us. The book of Hebrews warns us against living a careless Christian life. "How shall we escape if we neglect such a great salvation?" (Heb. 2:3 ESV). We are changed by Jesus, and that change affects every aspect of our life. "You, my brothers and sisters, were called to be free. But do not use your freedom to indulge the flesh; rather, serve one another humbly in love" (Gal. 5:13 NIV).

Friend, be encouraged. God has appointed humble leaders worldwide who acknowledge Jesus as Lord, who teach according to Scripture, and who encourage righteous behavior. **The Holy Spirit—the Spirit of Truth—will guide us and protect us from false teaching.** He will help us to share God's truth with others and do so *with love*. When the time is right, Jesus will come again. Be alert, watch for false teaching, and serve Jesus diligently until He returns or calls you home to heaven. Your faithfulness will be rewarded when you hear the most precious words of our Lord and King: "Well done, good and faithful servant" (Matt. 25:23 ESV).

Let the Bible Speak:
Matthew 24; 2 Peter 2:1–3 (Optional: Acts 25–28)

Let Your Mind Think:
1. Review the list detailing how you can reject false teachers. What on this list sticks out to you? How can you prepare yourself to reject false teachers?

2. Why do you think some false teachers are so popular in today's cultures? Why do you think it's challenging for people to simply believe the gospel message and trust Jesus?

3. What will help you recognize true teaching from God's Word as opposed to false teaching from those who might ask, like the serpent in Genesis 3:1, "Did God really say . . . ?"

Let Your Soul Pray:
Father, wake me up. Anchor me in Your Word so I will not be deceived by false teaching. Help me point others to truth and do so with love. When I grow weary, strengthen me with Your grace for Your glory. When You return, may You find me faithful, so I might hear Your precious words, "Well done" . . . In Jesus's name, amen.

Let Your Heart Obey:
(*What is God leading you to know, value, or do?*)

DAY

50

Celebrate Your True Story

Then celebrate the Festival of Harvest to honor the LORD
your God. Bring him a voluntary offering in proportion
to the blessings you have received from him. This is
a time to celebrate before the LORD your God.
Deuteronomy 16:10–11

Let's go back in time to the days just after Jesus rose from the dead. Back to the city where it all happened.

Fifty days after the first Passover/Easter weekend, festivities, food, and foreigners filled Jerusalem. For hundreds of years, the Jews celebrated the Festival of Weeks (or Harvest) fifty days after Passover (Lev. 23:9–20). Each day counting up to Day 50 heightened their anticipation for this thanksgiving harvest holiday. Flowers decorated homes. Special loaves of bread rested on each family's table. People carried their new grain offering through the streets. Bulls and goats, lambs and rams herded through the crowds. A procession of Jewish pilgrims from distant lands marched up to Jerusalem. Where were all these people—young and old, rich and poor, native and foreign—headed? They were headed to the temple for a sacred assembly.

Rather than joining the joyful celebration, Jesus's followers—men and women—gathered together hidden away empty-handed (Acts 1:12-14). What offering did they have for the holy gathering? Just weeks before—after mourning the loss of their Friend, their Leader, their King—their hearts burst with gladness when they saw Jesus alive again. They ate, laughed, cried, and talked with the resurrected

Jesus. Pure joy. But after forty days, He left again. This time, Jesus ascended straight to heaven right before their eyes. He told them to wait for a powerful gift—the Holy Spirit (Acts 1:4–8). But waiting is hard. They stared at each other, empty and unsure, as a parade of people passed outside their door. Unlike the rest of Jerusalem, they had no gift to give God today.

Their Day 50 holy day was unique in another way. More than fifteen hundred years before, the escaping Israelites arrived at Mount Sinai, where Moses met with God. Fifty days after the first Passover in Egypt, God gave Moses the Ten Commandments. These laws were not just rules showing how life worked best but a gift to us all because they revealed our sin (Rom. 7:7) *and our need for a Rescuer.*

Day 50 held so much significance—gifts *from* God and gifts *for* God—but much had changed for the disciples when this Day 50 came:

- The disciples knew the Rescuer—the promised gift—had come. *The Law and the Prophets had been fulfilled.*
- The disciples were witnesses to God's Story, but *they were too uncertain to tell it.*
- The disciples knew to wait. *They did not know the times, dates, or details.*

Finally, the waiting came to an end, and it was more than worth it. On that glorious Sunday, the Holy Spirit came to the entire house where they hid, *just as Jesus had promised.*

> Suddenly a sound like the blowing of a violent wind came from heaven and filled the whole house where they were sitting. They saw what seemed to be tongues of fire that separated and came to rest on each of them. All of them were filled with the Holy Spirit and began to speak in other tongues as the Spirit enabled them. (Acts 2:2–4 NIV)

The disciples burst out of the room. A crowd from all over began to listen as the disciples spoke, and they were amazed: "We hear them declaring the wonders of God in our own tongues!" (Acts 2:11

NIV). They could not keep the Holy Spirit to themselves because the Holy Spirit cannot be tucked away in a room or one part of our lives or on one day of the week. He *filled* the disciples and flowed through them to reach the world. Fifty days after Passover/Good Friday, when Jesus gave us *His all*—the Holy Spirit poured out *on all* (Acts 2:17). Men and women. Old and young. No one was left out. No tribe or nation or group unwelcome. Jesus, and now the Holy Spirit, came for all. The apostle Peter boldly spoke to the crowd and quoted the prophet Joel:

> "In the last days," God says, "I will pour out my Spirit upon all people. Your sons and daughters will prophesy. Your young men will see visions, and your old men will dream dreams. In those days I will pour out my Spirit even on my servants—men and women alike—and they will prophesy. . . . Everyone who calls on the name of the LORD will be saved." (Acts 2:17–18, 21)

Forever known as Pentecost, this Day 50 marked the birth of the church. As the disciples proclaimed the gospel in different languages, people divinely gathered from the nations responded—a crop of three thousand souls were saved on that harvest holiday (Acts 2:41). Those new believers would change the world as they returned to their homelands and shared God's True Story. All because the Holy Spirit's birthday gift empowered believers to share the new birth gift of Jesus (John 3:3). We know this to be true:

- All believers have **spiritual gifts** to share God's True Story.
- All believers **work together** to advance God's True Story.
- All believers in **all seasons of life** have an important role in God's True Story.
- All believers are **changed** by God's True Story and **bring change** to the world!

A beautiful exchange happened: Instead of God's law written on stone, the law would be written on hearts (Jer. 31:31–33). Rather than giving a harvest offering to God, Jesus—the Lord of the harvest—gave the Holy Spirit. Pentecost provided a new celebration for the new church. Just as those disciples fulfilled their part in God's Story, it's your turn to do the same.

Today is *your* Day 50!

On the kingdom calendar, your time has come. God has appointed this time and place for you to know Him and know your part in God's Story (Acts 17:26–27). Just as Pentecost provided a new revelation to the apostles, this study has provided a new revelation for you. As the Holy Spirit fills you to conform you more and more to God's image, you can break free from anything that holds you back from being all that He has called you to be. **You can delight in the One who is good, lovely, wise, pure, beautiful, heroic, and true.**

It's time to celebrate! It's time to thank God for what He's done in and through you these past seven weeks! Let's take a moment to remember all that He's done for you through each week.

Week One: God's Story

You are a part of God's Story. You know how everything started (creation), how everything broke (sin), how everything could be rescued (Jesus), and how everything will end (re-creation).

Week Two: Your Story

You are a chosen, forgiven, worshiping, adopted, embraced, and holy child of God. Your new life has meaning and purpose. You are so loved by God.

Week Three: Your Divine Purpose

You understand what God created you to do *with* Him. Your purpose affects heaven and glorifies God as you love Him, love others, and make disciples.

Week Four: Your Abiding Friendship

You are called God's friend. You know His plans and abide in Jesus. You rest in and receive all you need from the True Vine, your sufficient Source. You know how to resist temptation, and God bears fruit through you.

Week Five: Your Life-Changing Bible Study

You know God inspired the writing of the Bible, and you've taken a tour through it. You know how to study it, memorize it, and victoriously battle the enemy with it.

Week Six: Your Powerful Prayer Life

You know God loves to talk with you and align your heart to His. You know how to fast and pray, remove hindrances, pray for others, and unlock supernatural peace.

Week Seven: Your Spiritual Counselor

You learned how to be filled with the Holy Spirit to free you from sin's grip, grow you in godliness, help you make disciples, protect you from false teaching, and comfort you in suffering.

You did it! You didn't give up. You may not feel like celebrating, but you should. With God, you navigated hard and holy steps on this faith journey to discover your true story. Just like the disciples on Pentecost, you changed. Now you are called to bring change to the world.

On Day 1, you wrote down what your story has been so far with God. Take a few minutes to write down how your story has unfolded along this 50-day faith journey. Compare the two. How have you grown in your relationship with God?

Look back at your faith journey and know this path is what God had in mind all along. God has chosen you and placed you exactly where you are "for such a time as this" (Esther 4:14 ESV). God is weaving together your story—and it's beautiful. Your new chapter begins now.

Friend, as this 50-day faith journey comes to an end, I want to thank you for answering God's call to discover *Your True Story*. It's been an honor to walk with you. I pray God's blessings on your life so that your love would grow with knowledge and you'd walk in righteousness for God's glory (Phil. 1:9–11). One day, when we're all together in heaven, I will cheer you on as our King Jesus presents you blameless:

> To him who is able to keep you from stumbling and to present you before his glorious presence without fault and with great joy—to the only God our Savior be glory, majesty, power and authority, through Jesus Christ our Lord, before all ages, now and forevermore! Amen. (Jude vv. 24–25 NIV)

DAY 50

Let the Bible Speak:

Ephesians 3:14–21 (Optional: Book of Ruth—Customarily read on Shavuot [Pentecost], this short story offers hope and redemption and reveals God's rescue plan with a harvest theme.)

Let Your Mind Think:

1. As you think about your life in Christ, describe your personal celebration. What makes you the most thankful about your 50-day journey?

2. Answer Week 7 Discussion Questions.

Let Your Soul Pray:

Father, thank You for You. Thank You for sending Your Son, Jesus, and for pouring out Your Spirit to the world. Thank You for writing me into Your True Story. Help me to abide in Jesus and be filled with the Spirit for Your glory alone. "My future is in your hands" (Ps. 31:15) . . . In Jesus's name, amen.

Let Your Heart Obey:

(What is God leading you to know, value, or do?)

Let's Stay Friends:

Please go online to www.yourtruestorybook.com to let us know you completed this Bible study. We want to celebrate and provide you with videos, downloads, and more. **You'll receive a certificate of achievement and our prayers**. Thank you.

WEEK 7 DISCUSSION QUESTIONS:

**Review this week's lessons and answer the questions below.
Share your answers with your friends when you gather this week.**

1. Jesus told His disciples it was good for Him to leave them and return to heaven because in His absence He would send the Holy Spirit. Why is the Holy Spirit so valuable? How does the Holy Spirit help believers?

2. How can the Holy Spirit grow us through serving? Share an example of this if you have one. What attitude should we have as we serve? Is there anyone you find difficult to serve? How can you show him or her God's love this week?

3. Read Romans 8:28–29. How might God bring good out of our hardship? How might this encourage you to persevere through suffering?

4. Have you encountered false teaching, and how did you know it was false? How can you stay motivated as you live out your story with God?

5. **Repetition is key to learning. Ask God who to invite to go through this study again.** Is there a new believer or someone seeking God whom you could disciple using this tool?

Acknowledgments

Books are written in community, and *Your True Story* is no exception. By God's grace and many prayers, believers from diverse Christian traditions contributed to this faith journey.

Before writing one word, our ministry prayer team trailblazed the path with their powerful prayers. I love you, Christy Price, Missy Blanton, Hilary Windsor, Linda Reppert, Diane Engelhardt, Paddy Creveling, Cynthia Webb, Jenny Krishnarao, Riann Boyd, and Melanie Gauthier.

I'm immeasurably grateful to Mary Ann Wilmer for her hard work and heart to help launch this project well. Many thanks to Dr. Archie England, Danita Brooks, Kim Driggers, Tara Krishnarao, and Wayne Hastings & Co., who helped us finish well.

Many thanks to the All In Ministries International team and supporters for testing the materials, especially the early review by Glenn Reese, Kelley Hastings, Christy Price, Erin Crider, and Amy Tiede. Special thanks to Chets Creek Church for your encouragement and help.

To my family, I'm grateful for your unwavering love and support. (Mom, thank you for everything.) My sons, nieces, and nephews were my inspiration. I pass this faith journey to you, like a baton, to run your Hebrews 12:1–3 race. Never give up. Jesus is worthy of it all.

To my best friend, Brett, your "co-called" approach to our marriage made this faith journey possible in more ways than one. It's the honor of my life to be your wife. I love you so much.

More than anything, I'm eternally grateful to God—our Author—for writing our true stories. May God receive all the glory from the fruit of this work.

Not to us, LORD, not to us but to your name be the glory,
because of your love and faithfulness.
Psalm 115:1 NIV

WEEKLY GATHERINGS OUTLINE

To grow authentic relationships in the context of disciple-making, consider using the below approach for your weekly small groups.* Divide your time into the following three parts, and invite the Holy Spirit to take over:

1   PAST

Care:

- What are you grateful for this week?
- What is a concern?

Pray/Worship:

One person prays and invites God to lead this time together.

Accountability:

Review goals set from the prior week to *lovingly* hold each other accountable.

Mission:

Review the group's mission/vision (e.g., "Enjoy God and exalt Him" or "Be a disciple who makes disciples").

2   PRESENT

Lesson:

Read a passage of Scripture *twice* in different translations, if available.

Ask:

- What do you learn about God?
- What do you learn about people?
- What does God want you to know, value, or do?

(On occasion, consider using this time to learn a disciple-making training tool, like how to share your testimony or how to share the gospel. Be sure to practice these tools within your group before moving on.)

3   FUTURE

Set Goals:

Invite everyone to pray silently, asking God how we should respond.

Answer:

- How can you act on what you learned?
- Who will you train with this passage?
- With whom will you share the gospel?

Record & Share Goals:

Each person records their goals in their journal/phone. Share goals with the group.

Commission:

One person closes in prayer.

*Adapted from #NoPlaceLeft 3/3rds approach.

Appendix

Tools to Share Your Faith

Steps to Sharing God's Story Using 3 Circles

1. **Draw left circle with a heart**—explain God's love and design for our lives.
2. **Draw right circle and sin arrow**—explain how we all choose to go our own way rather than trusting God. That's called sin and creates brokenness in relationships, starting with our relationship with God.
3. **Draw three arrows** from brokenness circle in direction away from God. Explain that each arrow represents ways people try to fix their brokenness—with accomplishments, possessions, religion, trying to be good, or addictions. Only a relationship with God can restore them.
4. **Draw bottom circle**—explain how God sent His only Son, Jesus **(draw downward arrow),** to take our punishment for sin by dying on a cross **(draw cross)**. Jesus rose from the dead **(draw up arrow)**, defeating death and proving to the world He is God, our Savior.
5. **Draw arrow from brokenness to Jesus**—explain how when we turn from our ways (repent) and follow Jesus as our Leader **(draw crown above circle)**, our relationship with God is restored **(draw arrow back to God)**.

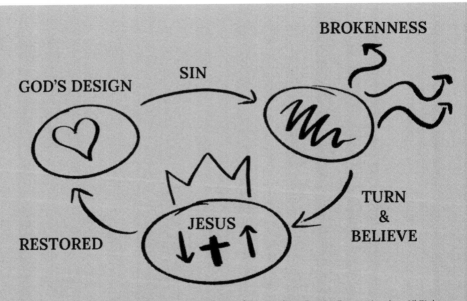

Learn

Learn their story and what they believe. Listen for a connection to **share your God story**.

- Do you have any spiritual beliefs?
- Do you believe in God?
- Who do you think Jesus is?
- Has anyone shared the gospel with you before?

Create and practice sharing your God story in 15–20 seconds. Here is a suggested approach:

"There was a time in my life when I was...

_____

(Insert two words/phrases that describe your life before Jesus.)

"Then I was forgiven by Jesus and chose to follow Him."

"My life changed. Now, I...

_____

(Insert two words/phrases that describe your life after you met Jesus.)

Ask: "Do you have a story like that?"

Listen

Create a **relationship map** of people you know who are far from God.

1. Pray for discernment from the Holy Spirit and write your name in the center circle.
2. Fill in connecting circles of people you know who are far from God. Add circles as needed.
3. Add circles to their circles of people they know who are also far from God (spouse/coworker).
4. Begin praying for those you know and those they may reach. In John 17:20, Jesus prayed for those who would believe through others. Let's pray like that, too.

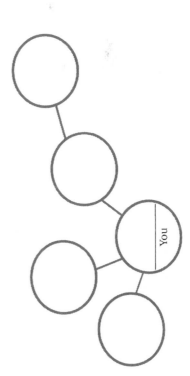

You

Love

Share God's Story and include the four Gospel Bread ingredients:
Love, Sin, Jesus, Repentance & Faith.

Practice drawing the 3 Circles God Story:

Ask: Is there anything keeping you from receiving God's forgiveness & following Jesus as your life Leader?

Share the elements of prayer: Believe, Forgive, Help.

Lord

Your commitment to Jesus.

As a new person in Christ, I _____, am Jesus's ambassador and He has authority over all of my life (2 Cor. 5:17–21).

Abiding in Jesus, I will obey His command to make disciples knowing He is with me always and the Holy Spirit will help me (John 15; Matt 28:18–20; Acts 1:8).

- I will pray for the people on my relationship map

  _____
  (Insert times / days when you will pray, e.g., mornings or on Mondays.)

- I will share God's Story with someone on my relationship map

  _____
  (Insert frequency of how often you will share, e.g., once a week or month.)

- I will disciple an existing believer to be a disciple-maker

  _____
  (Insert frequency and method of discipleship, e.g., weekly phone calls.)

_____
(Signature and date)

Cut and fold this paper and keep it in your Bible. Review regularly in your weekly gatherings. Download this tool at allitmin.org.

Bibliography

Alcorn, Randy C. *Heaven Study Guide*. Carol Stream, IL: Tyndale House Publishers, 2006.

Barry, J. D., and L. Wentz. *The Lexham Bible Dictionary*. Bellingham, WA: Lexham Press, 2016.

Blue, Ron, and Karen Guess. *Never Enough? 3 Keys to Financial Contentment*. Nashville, TN: B & H Publishing Group, 2017.

Briscoe, Jill. *Here Am I, Lord—Send Somebody Else: How God Uses Ordinary People to Do Extraordinary Things*. Nashville: W Pub. Group, 2004.

Chan, Francis, and Lisa Chan. *You and Me Forever: Marriage in Light of Eternity*. Singapore: Imprint Edition, 2015.

Danker, Frederick W. *Lexical Evolution & Linguistic Hazard: An Introduction to A Greek-English Lexicon of the New Testament and Other Early Christian Literature*, Third Edition (BDAG), Edited by Frederick William Danker, Based on Walter Bauer's *Griechish-Deutsches Wörterbuch Zu Den Schriften Des Neuen Testaments Und Der frühchristlichen Literatur*, Sixth Edition, Ed. Kurt Aland and Barbara Aland, with Viktor Reichmann and on Previous English Editions by W.F. Arndt, F.W. Gingrich, and F.W. Danker. Chicago: University of Chicago Press, 2000.

Elwell, Walter A. *Evangelical Dictionary of Biblical Theology*. Grand Rapids, MI: Baker Books, 2001.

Gangel, Kenneth O., and Max E. Anders. *John*. Nashville, TN: Holman Reference, 2000.

Geisler, Norman L. *Systematic Theology: In One Volume*. Minneapolis: Bethany House Publishers, 2011.

Greear, J. D. *Jesus, Continued . . . : Why the Spirit Inside You Is Better than Jesus Beside You*. Grand Rapids, MI: Zondervan, 2014.

Grudem, Wayne. *Systematic Theology: An Introduction to Biblical Doctrine*. Leicester: Inter-Varsity, 2007.

Habermas, Gary R. *The Historical Jesus: Ancient Evidence for the Life of Christ*. Joplin, MO: College Press, 1996.

Hauer, Cheryl. "God's Invitations." Bridges for Peace, November 21, 2017. https://www.bridgesforpeace.com/letter/gods-invitations/.

Hendricks, Howard G., and William Hendricks. *Living by the Book: The Art and Science of Reading the Bible*. Chicago: Moody Press, 2007.

Holladay, William Lee., and Ludwig Hugo Koehler. *A Concise Hebrew and Aramaic Lexicon of the Old Testament*. Grand Rapids, MI: W.B. Eerdmans Pub. Co., 1993.

Hughes, R. Kent. *John: That You May Believe.* Wheaton, IL: Crossway Books, 1999.

Jones, Ian F. *The Counsel of Heaven on Earth: Foundations for Biblical Christian Counseling.* Nashville, TN: Broadman & Holman Publishers, 2006.

Keller, Timothy. *Walking with God through Pain and Suffering.* London: Hodder & Stoughton, 2015.

Kitchen, K. A. *On the Reliability of the Old Testament.* Grand Rapids, MI: William B. Eerdmans, 2006.

Kroll, Woodrow Michael. *Facing Your Final Job Review: The Judgment Seat of Christ, Salvation, and Eternal Rewards.* Wheaton, IL: Crossway Books, 2008.

MacDonald, James. Walk in the Word Radio, AM 550, Jacksonville, FL, 2009.

Miller, Mike, and Michael Sharp. "Worship Leadership" Intensive Class Notes: Three Stages of Worship, New Orleans: New Orleans Baptist Theological Seminary, May 2014.

"Mitzvot." ReligionFacts, June 22, 2017. http://www.religionfacts.com/mitzvot.

NoPlaceLeft International Coalition. https://noplaceleft.net.

Pratt, Zane. "Making Disciples in Another Culture." Breakout, Send Conference, Orlando, FL, July 26, 2017.

Towns, Elmer L. *Fasting for Spiritual BreakThrough: A Guide to Nine Biblical Fasts.* Ventura, CA: Regal Books, 1996.

Tripp, Paul. "Why Do I Need the Bible?" Paul Tripp Ministries, Inc., May 13, 2019. https://www.paultripp.com/app-read-bible-study/posts/001-why-do-i-need-the-bible.

Vine's Complete Expository Dictionary of Old and New Testament Words. Nashville: T. Nelson, 1984.

Wallace, J. Warner. *Cold-Case Christianity: a Homicide Detective Investigates the Claims of the Gospels.* Colorado Springs, CO: David C Cook, 2013.

Whelchel, Hugh. "The Four-Chapter Gospel: The Grand Metanarrative Told by the Bible." Institute for Faith, Work & Economics, February 14, 2012. https://tifwe.org/the-four-chapter-gospel-the-grand-metanarrative-told-by-the-bible/.

Whitacre, Rodney A. *John.* Downers Grove, IL: Inter-Varsity Press, n.d.

Wilbur, Hervey. *The Assembly's Shorter Catechism, with the Scripture Proofs in Reference: with an Appendix on the Systematick Attention of the Young to Scriptural Knowledge.* Newburyport: Printed by Wm. B. Allen & Co., 1816.

Our Gift to You

You did it! We want to celebrate and provide you with videos, downloads, and more. You'll receive a certificate of achievement and our prayers. Please go online to **YourTrueStoryBook.com** to let us know you completed this journey.

Let's Be Friends

We've walked together for 50 days and do not want to say goodbye.

Stay connected and share your true story here:

Facebook— www.facebook.com/allinmin
Instagram—@allinministriesinternational
YouTube— All In Ministries International
LinkedIn— All In Ministries International

Your True Story is for all people everywhere.

ALL IN MINISTRIES
INTERNATIONAL

All In Ministries International equips women to be disciple makers of Jesus.

Share Your Faith • Reach Under-Resourced Women • Equip Leaders

Three ways we can serve together:

Be a Disciple Maker

You can reach women in your community or across the world to be disciples of Jesus. Our free online resources will help you.

Be a Trainer

Use our training course to facilitate disciple making gatherings locally and globally. Be a part of a worldwide network of volunteer trainers.

Be a Missions Partner

Invite us to work alongside your ministry. While your team serves, we facilitate women's discipleship training.

All In Ministries International Incorporated is a 501c3 nonprofit organization.

To learn more, visit allinmin.org.
Change the World One Woman at a Time